Human Resource Management for MBA and Business Masters

Third e

Iain Henderson

The Chartered Institute of Personnel and Development is the leading publisher of books and reports for personnel and training professionals, students, and all those concerned with the effective management and development of people at work. For details of all our titles, please contact the publishing department:
tel: 020 8612 6204
email: publish@cipd.co.uk
The catalogue of all CIPD titles can be viewed on the CIPD website:
www.cipd.co.uk/bookstore

Human Resource Management for MBA and Business Masters

Third edition

Iain Henderson

Chartered Institute of Personnel and Development

Published by the Chartered Institute of Personnel and Development
151 The Broadway, London SW19 1JQ

This edition first published 2017

Designed and typeset by Exeter Premedia Services, India
Printed in Great Britain by CPI Group (UK) Ltd, Croydon, CR0 4YY

British Library Cataloguing in Publication Data
A catalogue of this publication is available from the British Library

ISBN 9781843984429
eBook ISBN 9781843984597

Chartered Institute of Personnel and Development

151 The Broadway, London SW19 1JQ
Tel: 020 8612 6200
Email: cipd@cipd.co.uk
Website: www.cipd.co.uk
Incorporated by Royal Charter.
Registered Charity No. 1079797

Dedication

To Morag, once more.

Contents

List of figures and tables

Acknowledgements

My wife, Morag, again uncomplainingly provided the support required to produce a book of this nature.

As with the earlier editions I am very grateful for the kind and patient support I received from the editors and other members of staff at CIPD Publishing.

I should like to thank Mike Beer and Bert Spector for their kind permission to use their 'Harvard Model of HRM' in Fig 1.1; Blackwell Publishing for their permission to base Fig 1.2 on material first published in the *Journal of Management Studies*; the European Foundation for the Improvement of Living and Working Conditions for permission to use the case studies 'Training Academy' in Chapter 3, 'Turbulent Times in Air Transport' in Chapter 4 and 'Kvadrat' in Chapter 5; and *Socialist Worker* for permission to use material from their article 'Teamworking: Workers' Liberation or Management by Stress?' in Chapter 5. I should also like to thank the Chartered Institute for Personnel and Development for permission to use the materials from their various publications, including *People Management*, which are cited in the text.

Preface to the third edition

This third edition, entitled *Human Resource Management for MBA and Business Masters Students,* follows the first and second editions of *Human Resource Management for MBA Students.* Like those editions, this one aims to present the essence of the subject in accessible terms, grounded wherever possible in empirical evidence, but, as the revised title indicates, it is aimed at a wider student audience: MBA students as before, but also students who are studying for other business or management Masters degrees which include HRM modules as part of their programmes.

I am grateful to reviewers, both of the earlier editions and of draft versions of the present one, for their always constructive comments. I have tried to respond to these appropriately wherever possible.

There have been some significant developments in the management of human resources in the five years since the second edition was published, many of which will continue to affect managerial policies and practices for the foreseeable future. Most notably perhaps are the new forms of employment that have arisen. Frequently utilising social media, these have given rise to the so-called 'gig economy' which may alter fundamentally the employment relationship for many people. The text has been comprehensively revised to reflect these and other changes. The reader is introduced to the new professional framework for HR professionals which the CIPD has developed, and more emphasis has been given to the international aspects of HRM.

Walkthrough of textbook features and online resources

CHAPTER INTRODUCTIONS

Each chapter opens with an introduction outlining the purpose and content of the chapter.

LEARNING OUTCOMES

On completion of this chapter you should:

- have a good appreciation of what the human resource management (HRM) function in contemporary organisations comprises
- have some appreciation of the development of HRM
- have an appreciation of the practical application of HRM
- understand the relationship between HRM and strategy

LEARNING OUTCOMES

At the beginning of each chapter a bulleted set of key learning outcomes summarises what you expect to learn from the chapter, helping you to track your progress.

? REFLECTIVE ACTIVITY 1.2

In terms of the perspectives examined above, how would you describe:

- your personal perspective?
- the managerial culture of your own organisation?

REFLECTIVE ACTIVITY

In each chapter, a number of questions and activities will get you to reflect on what you have just read and encourage you to explore important concepts and issues in greater depth.

HRM IN ACTION: GOOGLE'S FOUR RULES OF RECRUITMENT

CASE STUDY 2.1

Yvonne Agyei, the tech giant's international HR head, on its unexpectedly process-driven hiring methods – and the search for 'Googleyness'

The popular perception of Google's recruitment process is a fun-filled mix of gimmicky games, endless interviews and mind-bending conundrums. But according to the Silicon Valley start-up's international HR head, there's a lot more humdrum science to it than you might expect.

request further interviews if it feels questions haven't been relevant or probing enough. Google became notorious for averaging around nine interviews per hire, but Agyei said it was now deploying a 'rule of four' to streamline its processes: 'You must make a decision within four interviews – you ought to have enough information on anyone by then.'

But what is Google actually looking for, and how does it know when it's found it? Agyei outlined four key attributes every employee should have:

CASE STUDY: HRM IN ACTION

A range of case studies from different countries illustrate how key ideas and theories are operating in practice around the globe, with accompanying questions or activities.

◉ HRM DILEMMA 2.1

If we raise the bar, we reject more candidates who could do the job.

Two kinds of decision error may occur in every selection process, however constituted:

i   'false positives' or erroneous acceptances, where applicants are selected but prove to be inadequate, and

HRM DILEMMA

In each chapter, a number of questions and activities will get you to reflect on what you have just read and encourage you to explore important concepts and issues in greater depth.

KEY ISSUES IN RESOURCING

In this chapter we have been concerned with 'employee flow' through the organisation; in particular, with how the organisation obtains the human resources it needs and how it manages the exit of employees. We first discussed some basic underlying principles involved in recruitment and selection, and two important findings soon emerged. First, recruitment and selection should be seen as stages in a wider process of managing the human resource flow. This is because decisions made at the recruitment or selection stages will inevitably impact on later activities, such as need for training and level of job performance. Second, organisations should recruit using a model based on initially identifying the criteria for job success and then systematically seeking applicants with the necessary qualities to achieve that success. We noted that in the twenty-first century capability and attitude were often more important than the possession of particular knowledge or skills at the time of recruitment. A competency framework is often useful in recruitment and selection. Some of the most commonly used selection techniques were examined. We introduced the concept of talent management, which in a sense bridges recruitment and selection and employee development.

KEY ISSUES

In each chapter, a number of questions and activities will get you to reflect on what you have just read and encourage you to explore important concepts and issues in greater depth.

EXPLORE FURTHER

Armstrong, M. (2014) *Armstrong's Handbook of Human Resource Management Practice*. 13th edition. London: Kogan Page.

- Chapter 1, 'The essence of human resource management'; and Chapter 2, 'Strategic HRM'.
- These chapters provide brief overviews of their topics, useful for quick reference and starting exam revision.

Boxall, P. and Purcell, J. (2006) *Strategy and Human Resource Management*. Basingstoke: Palgrave Macmillan.

- Chapter 1, 'Human resource management and business performance' – this is a scholarly introduction to HRM which makes explicit linkage to business performance.

Boxall, P., Purcell, J. and Wright, P. (eds) (2007) *The Oxford Handbook of Human Resource Management*. Oxford: Oxford University Press.

EXPLORE FURTHER

Explore Further boxes contain suggestions for further reading and useful websites, encouraging you to delve further into areas of particular interest.

ONLINE RESOURCES FOR TUTORS

- Lecturer's guide – Including guidance on the questions and activities within the text.
- PowerPoint slides – design your programme around these ready-made lectures.
- Additional case studies – these can be used as a classroom activity, for personal reflection and individual learning, or as the basis for assignments.
- Exam style questions – a series of questions for each chapter to test your understanding of the text.

ONLINE RESOURCES FOR STUDENTS

- Additional case studies – these can be used for personal reflection and individual learning, or as the basis for assignments.
- Exam style questions – a series of questions for each chapter to test your understanding of the text.
- Annotated web links – access a wealth of useful sources of information in order to develop your understanding of the issues in the text.

Human resource management

INTRODUCTION

Good managers are not only effective in their use of economic and technical resources, but when they manage people they remember that these particular resources are special, and are ultimately the most important assets of the organisation. Indeed, they are the only real source of continuing competitive advantage and the best managers never forget that these assets are human beings.

LEARNING OUTCOMES

On completion of this chapter you should:

- have a good appreciation of what the human resource management (HRM) function in contemporary organisations comprises
- have some appreciation of the development of HRM
- have an appreciation of the practical application of HRM
- understand the relationship between HRM and strategy
- appreciate 'best-practice' and 'best-fit' models of HRM and strategy
- recognise some of the key themes of HRM in the twenty-first century
- understand the importance of new forms of employment for HRM.

The precise meaning of the term 'human resource management' (HRM) is often a source of particular confusion to non-specialists. Older terms for the 'people management' function of an organisation such as 'personnel management' or 'personnel administration' are still sometimes used and it is often assumed that 'HRM' is just a fancy new title for the same thing.

One of the main objectives of this first chapter is to show this is not the case.

An additional source of confusion is that the term HRM is used in two senses: (1) to mean various 'people management' activities such as hiring, firing, rewarding, and so on, and (2) a particular approach to the whole question of managing people. The first sense (1) might be described as 'operational' and the second (2) as 'strategic'. These senses are not always clearly distinguished in discussions and debates on HRM.

Of course in practice operational and strategic approaches are necessarily connected in that particular operational HRM policies and practices are determined by decisions taken at the strategic level, but nonetheless it is an important distinction to make and we should always be clear about whether we mean the operational or strategic sense, or both, when we say HRM.

We will try to clarify these meanings and definitions in this text.

We can say that, broadly, the 'people management' function within an organisation may be described as:

> All the management decisions and actions that directly affect or influence people *as members of the organisation rather than as specific job-holders*;

and that HRM is currently the principal model or paradigm for the people management function.

HRM is not directly concerned with executive or line management of individuals and their jobs. Management of specific tasks and responsibilities is the concern of the employee's immediate supervisor or manager – that is, the person to whom their performance is accountable (sometimes this might be the person's team). So HRM managers do not have line authority over employees (other than over their own staff in HRM sections or departments).

The term 'human resource management' was being used by Peter Drucker and others in North America as early as the 1950s without any special meaning, and usually simply as another label for 'personnel management' or 'personnel administration'. It was viewed as a bundle of operational techniques, not a distinct managerial discipline or function. By the 1980s, however, HRM in the strategic sense had come to mean a 'radically different philosophy and approach to the management of people at work' (Storey 1989, pp4–5) with an emphasis on performance, workers' commitment, and rewards based on individual or team contribution.

One of the main characteristics of HRM is the devolution of many operational aspects of 'people management' from specialists directly to line managers. HRM itself has been called 'the discovery of personnel management by chief executives'. Line managers are thus frequently confronted with HRM operational decisions and activities in their day-to-day business in a way that was not the case previously.

This process has been accelerated by other developments which add to the burden of the line manager while increasing the effectiveness of the organisation as a whole. Outsourcing of large areas of the traditional personnel management department's routine functions has happened on a massive scale in the last three decades. Outsourcing of non-core functions, allowing the organisation to concentrate on its core competencies, has been one of the single most important recent organisational factors in both business and the public sector. It is extremely unlikely that this will be set in reverse in the foreseeable future.

In the case of HR services, the 'dis-integrating' effects of outsourcing have been amplified by such related developments as 'e-HR', in which the use of new technologies allows the provision of 'self-service' HR to employees and managers, and 'HR business partnering', in which large organisations disperse 'HR partners' to constituent businesses (Caldwell and Storey 2007).

New forms of employment – particularly those such as 'crowdworking' which exploit information and communications technology (ICT), including social media – are accelerating the divide in organisations between a core of high-value, permanent employees and others who enjoy significantly poorer employment rights and protection. Indeed, in some of these new working relationships the status of the worker can be that of a self-employed contractor rather than an employee as such.

Some of these developments are outlined later in this chapter and a fuller account is given in Chapter 9.

These developments in HRM, in outsourcing and in new forms of employment have not removed the need for HR specialists, but these people are just that – technical experts who act as internal consultants and to whom line managers can refer as required. This means that it will be more important than ever for line managers to communicate effectively with HR specialists and be able to weigh up their advice in an intelligent and knowledgeable manner – and to do that they have to speak the language and understand the concepts of the expert.

> **?** **REFLECTIVE ACTIVITY 1.1**
>
> Write down what you think human resource managers are actually supposed to do.

REFLECTIVE ACTIVITY 1.1 ANSWER GUIDANCE

See section 1.1.

1.1 WHAT DO HR MANAGERS ACTUALLY DO?

Torrington *et al* (2014) – an authoritative text widely used in teaching managers who are studying for the professional exams of the Chartered Institute of Personnel and Development (CIPD) – describe the role of HR management as comprising specific objectives under four headings: staffing, performance, change management and administration.

- *Staffing objectives* are firstly concerned with 'getting the right people in the right jobs at the right times' – that is, the recruitment and selection of staff – but increasingly these days also advising on subcontracting and outsourcing of staff. Staffing also concerns managing the release of employees from the organisation by resignation, retirement, dismissal or redundancy.
- *Performance objectives*: people managers have a part to play in assisting the organisation to motivate its employees and ensure that they perform well. Training and development, reward and performance management systems are all important here. Grievance and disciplinary procedures are also necessary, as are welfare support and employee involvement initiatives.
- *Change management objectives* include employee relations/involvement, the recruitment and development of people with the necessary leadership and change management skills, and the construction of reward systems to underpin the change.
- *Administrative objectives* include: the maintenance of accurate employee data on, for example, recruitment, contracts and conditions of service, performance, attendance and training; ensuring organisational compliance with legal requirements, for example in employment law and employee relations; and health and safety.

General managers are increasingly involved directly in all of the first three types of objectives. Administrative objectives tend to remain the preserve of dedicated HR support staff.

The above closely reflects the arguments in David Ulrich's highly influential *Harvard Business Review* article of 1998, 'A new mandate for human resources', which helped to shape HRM in the twenty-first century. After acknowledging that some commentators had been calling for the 'abolition of HR' on the grounds of serious doubts about its contribution to organisational performance, Ulrich agreed that: 'there is good reason for HR's beleaguered reputation. It is often ineffective, incompetent and costly' (Ulrich 1998, p124).

His solution was for HR to be 'reconfigured' to focus on outcomes rather than on traditional processes such as staffing or compensation: 'HR should not be defined by what it does but by what it delivers – results that enrich the organisation's value to customers, investors and employees.'

His recommendations were that:

- First, HR should become a 'partner' with senior and line managers in strategy execution.

- Second, it should become an 'expert' in the way work is organised and executed, delivering administrative efficiency to ensure that costs are reduced while quality is maintained.
- Third, it should become a 'champion for employees', vigorously representing their concerns to senior managers and at the same time working to increase employees' contribution – 'that is, employees' commitment to the organisation and their ability to deliver results'.
- Finally, HR should become an 'agent of continuous transformation', shaping processes and a culture that together improve an organisation's capacity for change.

Ulrich and Brockbank (2005) increased the number of roles to five, with distinct responsibilities for 'human capital developer' and 'leader', as follows:

- *strategic partner* – aligning HR with business strategy as before but with new emphasis on transformation and cultural change
- *functional expert* – both for those operational policies and practices that are the direct responsibility of HR and wider aspects for which HR has indirect responsibility, such as communication
- *employee advocate* – corresponding to the earlier employee champion
- *human capital developer* – with emphasis on coaching behaviours and attitudes
- *leader* – primarily of the HR function, but also contributing to the leadership function of the organisation as a whole.

The structure of the present text reflects Ulrich and Brockbank's roles as follows:

The *strategic partner* role is examined under the topic of strategic human resource management in this chapter (section 1.8); that of *functional expert* in Chapter 2; *employee advocate* in Chapter 4; *human capital developer* in Chapter 3; and *leader* in Chapter 9.

Ulrich's, and later Ulrich and Brockbank's, view of the HR role has set the agenda for people management in the twenty-first century as being essentially about its contribution to organisational performance.

Linda Holbeche, the then Director of Research and Policy for the UK professional body for HR managers, the CIPD, wrote that 'building organisational capability is HR's heartland', and she added that HR managers 'can help make capitalism human' (Holbeche 2007, pp10–11).

These two statements more or less sum it all up.

1.2 CIPD 'PROFESSION FOR THE FUTURE'

With the mission of 'championing better work and better working lives', the CIPD has developed a new professional framework for HR professionals in the UK.

The CIPD recognised that more flexible and innovative ways of working were evolving in the twenty-first century. These are driven by continuing globalisation and changes in technology, workforce demographics and by new expectations of both employees and employers. Concerned that 'best practices' are often quickly made obsolete by these changes, the CIPD now recommends that professionals follow a set of principles which are reflected in a framework of professional standards ('best practice' in the context of HRM is defined in section 1.10). This framework is intended to:

- develop a fit-for-purpose body of professional knowledge
- benchmark organisational HR standards against professional standards
- support judgements of ethical and professional practice
- support the acknowledgement of professional membership designations.

The framework is shown in Table 1.1, which articulates five key standards.

Table 1.1 CIPD five key standards

Standard	Statement
Knowledge and skills	Draws together people expertise, knowledge and skills with business and commercial acumen to practise professionally
Social and ethical responsibility	Champions ethical and fair practice
Situational judgement	Applies a combination of professional principles, knowledge and practised judgement to make informed decisions
Professional development	Commits to continually acquire professional knowledge and expertise
Behaviours	Exercises professional behaviours in a range of contexts

The standards imply a number of themes for HR professionals:

- a greater awareness and understanding of the nature and speed of change in the world of work and its impact on the employment relationship
- greater emphasis on situational judgement, moving away from simply benchmarking best practices to focusing of the principles that underlie HR practices
- a greater emphasis on ethical practice, which should consider the impact, both short and long term, of HR policies and practices on all stakeholder groups
- an openness to a broader knowledge base drawn from the disciplines of the social sciences and humanities (**cipd.co.uk/pff**).

1.3 THE EVOLUTION OF HRM

But what exactly does this rather self-important-sounding phrase 'human resource management' actually mean? To many people it is seen as just a fancy or pretentious re-labelling of what used to be called 'personnel management'. But to many managers and management theorists it is vital to the survival and success of organisations in the twenty-first century. Why they think so really derives from one single, simple idea: that people – their skills, knowledge and creativity – are *the* key resource for economic and organisational success in what Peter Drucker (1993) called 'the knowledge-based economy'.

Another way of putting this is to say that 'people are an asset not a cost' (Beer *et al* 1984).

By the 1970s a settled idea of people management in large organisations had evolved in developed free market economies, and this was typically termed 'personnel management' (PM), or sometimes 'personnel administration' (PA). It reflected the predominantly Taylorist organisation of work, which had developed to exploit the technology available for the mass production of industrial goods. It acknowledged and incorporated the institutions of collective industrial relations, recognising the role and power of trade unions.

The extraordinary economic (if not human) success of Taylorist industrial practices ensured that this became the standard model for all large organisations, even those in service industries and in the public sector, and PM techniques used in industry – for example in recruitment and selection – were usually assumed to be best management practice.

A revolution in people management occurred in the 1980s that overturned the established paradigm of personnel management in favour of 'human resource management' (HRM). If today, 30 years later, one surveys the academic and professional management literature on people management, whether aimed at specialists or at general managers, one would think the revolution had been total. Normative models of HRM and examples of HRM 'best practice' abound, with little or no apparent trace of traditional personnel management.

However, if in fact we look at the empirical evidence, we are forced to conclude that indeed there has been a revolution, but that it is not complete in terms of either organisational culture or management practice. Few, if any, new operational techniques of people management have been developed within HRM: it is often the scope and manner of their use, and the intent behind their employment – in a word, the strategy, or at least strategic intent – that is different. For example, psychometric testing and personality profiling have been available for decades, but in personnel management- these were used only for executive and other highly paid appointments. Many firms now routinely apply such techniques to all appointments (at least core ones), the intention being not to predict whether one high-cost appointment will be successful in a particular role but rather to ensure that all employees can accept a strong common culture.

People management, as a distinct concern of management which was separate from the day-to-day supervision of employees, originated in the UK in the nineteenth century amidst the factory conditions of the first Industrial Revolution. The unrestricted capitalism of the initial industrialisation of the UK was restrained, to an extent, by the Factory Acts of the 1840s, which compelled factory owners to consider the well-being of their workforces, at least to some degree. Enlightened capitalists such as Rowntree and Cadbury, who were often motivated by religious convictions, appointed 'welfare officers' to monitor and improve the conditions and lives of workers. Their actions would often seem intrusive and paternalistic today – for example, they discouraged drinking out of work hours as well as during. Caring for the welfare of employees was thus the first true 'people management' role in the sense of organisational responsibility beyond that of specific job performance.

With the rise of industrial trade unionism in the twentieth century, another role evolved in people management – that of negotiating and communicating with the collective representatives of the workforce (the workplace 'shop stewards' and the full-time paid trade union officials) on behalf of the organisation.

The rise of 'scientific management' and the organisation of industrial work along Taylorist lines also led to increased interest in more rigorous selection of personnel administered by management, instead of the haphazard traditional methods which often relied on the foremen or 'gangmasters' to pick men and women for work. It also led to management taking an interest in organising and providing skills training.

Following the Second World War, social science – particularly as employed in the Human Relations School – started to exert a direct influence on work in the areas of job design, attempting to ameliorate the worst side effects of scientific management while still achieving its productive and economic benefits. Although such developments might not affect people management directly, they shaped the culture in which it was operating and evolving. The conscious application of social science also encouraged the use of more sophisticated techniques in recruitment and selection, which did have an impact on people management policies and practice.

By the 1970s a fairly consistent set of activities and roles had developed for people management, which in most large organisations was perceived as a specialist management function, usually termed personnel management and comprising the areas of recruitment and selection, pay and conditions of service, employee welfare, industrial relations, training and development, and employee exit (retrenchment, redundancy or retirement). Most day-to-day people management, especially in the area of employee relations, was handled by personnel specialists and not by line managers. In the UK the professional status of personnel managers was supported by the formation of the Institute of Personnel Management (IPM), which was later to evolve and become the present-day CIPD.

Of course personnel management was not without its critics. Peter Drucker (1955) thought that 'personnel administration', as he called it, was just a set of unrelated, albeit individually important, activities. The Drucker critique can be read now as an early plea for people management to be returned to line managers, as later advocated by HRM models. The ambiguity of traditional personnel management was noted with apparent conflict between the welfare role expected by employees and the efficiency and cost control increasingly demanded of it by management (see Legge 1995). Radical critics disliked it on principle (see below).

The approach to people management which is now usually termed 'HRM' originated in manufacturing industry in the USA during the late 1970s and early 1980s and represented a significant break with the personnel management paradigm. A number of factors led to this new management thinking, principally loss of faith in the traditional approach to mass production, the example of Japanese work organisation and manufacturing processes, and the realisation of the impact of new technology on work practices (Gallie et al 1998).

The remarkable success of Japanese manufacturers in the 1970s and 1980s in capturing Western markets for sophisticated products, such as electronics and cars, brought to a head long-standing concerns about traditional Taylorist/Fordist models of work organisation. These models were characterised by low- or semi-skilled work, close supervision, pay being linked to quantity of output, and – at least in mass production industries – assembly-line technologies in which the pace of work was controlled by machine. Academic studies had shown concern about some of the human effects of Taylorism and Fordism for decades, and this led to the rise of the Human Relations School, but by the 1980s it was recognised by business and managers as well that the costs of such systems were becoming unacceptable in terms of low levels of job involvement and weak commitment to the employing organisation. There was an increasing willingness on the part of employees to disrupt production to achieve higher financial or other rewards despite the damage such action could have on the long-term health of the organisation. Crucially, it had also become recognised that these traditional systems of work organisation were intrinsically unable to produce the quality output now required to compete in a global marketplace (Beer et al 1984, pviii).

The perceived superiority of the Japanese model was confirmed for many Western managers and academics by an influential MIT study in the 1980s which concluded that Fordist methods would inevitably be replaced in the car industry by the 'lean production' model of work organisation typified by Toyota's work methods. This approach to work organisation was seen to combine the best features of both craft production and mass production (Kenney and Florida 1993) and to achieve very high levels of employee commitment with resulting benefits in quality and flexibility.

Technology also played a part in shifting managerial concern towards human resources. Managers had become aware that the rapid development of new technologies in competitive markets meant that organisations faced continual technological change, which in turn implied the need for continuous learning by employees. Employers would have to be able to assess individual employees' training needs and provide the necessary investment in changing and upgrading skills.

All this implied the development of a much closer relationship between managers and employees, and therefore also changes in the work of managers as well as that of workers. In particular, it meant that the traditional approach of managing people – 'personnel management' or 'personnel administration', which had evolved to help manage Taylorist/Fordist organisations more effectively – was no longer viable. In an increasingly competitive global economy, with advancing technology and better-educated workforces, it was not enough to manage people reactively or passively. In the industries that mattered, competitive advantage now ultimately came not from capital investment but from human resources, and these had to be managed proactively and strategically if an organisation was to be successful.

The collectivised employment relationship, in which trade unions represented the workforce and bargained with employers on its behalf for wages and conditions of employment (often on an industry-wide basis), had come to be seen as a hindrance to the adoption of the new technologies and work practices which were necessary to compete with the Japanese. In fact, most Japanese workers in the major exporting industries were unionised, but the Japanese trade unions did not share the pluralist culture of their counterparts in the West (see section 1.4).

Initially, the new human resource policies were linked to non-unionised and greenfield sites. Typically, these were in large-scale manufacturing, where the Taylorist/Fordist pattern of work organisation had been most dominant, but the new approach soon exerted influence in all sorts of organisations and in every part of the economy, including services and the public sector.

Theoretical and academic models of HRM signalled from the outset the importance of strategy in normative models of HRM. HRM was regarded as superior to personnel management or personnel administration partly because it was supposed to be 'strategic' in two senses: (1) the function itself was conceived of in strategic rather than reactive ways; and (2) the HRM strategy would be intimately linked to, and consciously supportive of, overall business and corporate strategies.

1.4 PERSPECTIVES IN THE MANAGEMENT OF PEOPLE

Managerial perceptions of how people view relationships within their organisations are important in our analysis of human resource management. Our 'frame of reference' will influence how we expect people to behave, how we think they *ought* to behave, and how we react to the behaviour of others. We are concerned here with three major perspectives: the 'pluralist', the 'unitarist' and the 'radical' or 'critical' (Fox 1966).

1.4.1 THE PLURALIST PERSPECTIVE

The pluralist perspective reflected the culture of the typical Western industrial workplace from the Second World War until the 1980s. It rests on the assumption that society consists of various groups which will each have their own interests and beliefs. It is naive to pretend that the interests of workers and managers/owners can be fully reconciled, and so institutions such as trade unions and arrangements such as collective bargaining are needed to achieve workable compromises between these differing interests. In the pluralist view, conflict at work is seen as inevitable, because management and workers will not have identical interests, but conflict is not in itself 'wrong'. The issue is not to try to eliminate it, which would be impossible, but rather how it should be handled. In cases where conflicts seem to be insoluble at the workplace or industry level, third-party intervention – often through state agencies (for example, the Advisory, Conciliation and Arbitration Service (Acas), in the UK) – can provide solutions.

1.4.2 THE UNITARIST PERSPECTIVE

From the unitarist perspective, a work organisation has a purpose (or set of purposes) common to all members of it – owners, managers and workers. So there should be no real conflict of interest between these groups. Everyone has the same ultimate interest in high levels of efficiency which will generate high profits and add to shareholder value – and allow the payment of high wages. It is a win/win situation for all concerned. Managers and those they manage are really all members of the same 'team'. Management has special leadership responsibilities and should pursue policies which allow the organisation to achieve its goals and satisfy shareholders (and other stakeholders), but which are also fair to employees. On this view, conflict within the organisation between management and the workforce is perceived as being the result of some sort of failure; it is not regarded as necessary or inevitable – in principle, at least, it could be eliminated. From this perspective trade unions are often seen as competing for the loyalty of the employees, and collective bargaining may be regarded as unnecessary.

The unitarist perspective in its purest form was traditionally found in private, typically family-owned employers, but HRM is usually associated with unitarism (sometimes termed 'neo-unitarism' to distinguish it from the earlier, more paternalistic, family-firm version).

1.4.3 THE RADICAL/CRITICAL PERSPECTIVE

Quite different from both pluralism and unitarism, the radical/critical perspective derived originally from the Marxist view of society and industrial capitalism. In essence, this saw all work as inevitably being exploitative of workers. Conflict between management and labour was unavoidable as part of wider class conflict in society. Management always, and inevitably, represented the interests of capital. There may be few unreconstructed Marxists in the twenty-first century, but shades of post-Marxist thought persist, and there are cultural and social radicals of various types who reject the mainstream, free-market culture in which most organisations now operate. To such radicals, as to nineteenth- and twentieth-century Marxists, work organisations reflect the inherently unfair or oppressive structures of society (for example, to radical feminists they reflect the patriarchal nature of society) and help to buttress these same structures.

Postmodern intellectuals often share this view (see McKinlay and Starkey 1998), and many writers on HRM and management within the Critical Management School hold a radical perspective in this sense (see, for example, Legge 1995, Thompson and McHugh 2002).

From the radical perspective even 'enlightened' management practices and philosophies such as the Human Relations School, or employee 'empowerment', or profit-sharing are really either hopelessly naive and doomed attempts to overcome the inevitable exploitative nature of capitalism/existing society, or are conscious and cynical strategies to fool the employees. Even pluralistic industrial relations structures can be seen in this light.

?   REFLECTIVE ACTIVITY 1.2

In terms of the perspectives examined above, how would you describe:

- your personal perspective?
- the managerial culture of your own organisation?

1.5 THE THEORY OF HUMAN RESOURCE MANAGEMENT

We noted above the practical considerations such as quality, competition and technology which led to questioning the traditional forms of people management. Management theorists were as concerned as practising managers and governments were about the evident failure of the Taylorist/Fordist approach and produced a number of academic models of HRM.

The theoretical heritage of HRM includes the managerial writings of Peter Drucker, the Human Relations School, human capital theory, and organisational development. Interest in HRM proceeded alongside other developments in economics, business strategy and organisational change. Many of these ideas revolved around the notion of the resource-based theory of the firm (Barney 1991) and core competencies (Prahalad and Hamel 1990), which argued that sustained competitive advantage ultimately derives from a firm's internal resources provided that these (1) can add value, (2) are unique or rare, (3) are difficult for competitors to imitate, and (4) are non-substitutable. Of course, human resources fit such a list of criteria well (Storey 2001).

The term 'human capital' originated in the study of economics to mean the stock of skills that the labour force possesses and can be traced back to Adam Smith's *Wealth of Nations*. The concept also implies that there can be investments in people such as education, training and improvement to health which increase an individual's productivity. This human capital is an asset to the individual, increasing their market value as an employee, as well as to the organisation and indeed the wider society.

The CIPD defines human capital as 'people at work and their collective knowledge, skills abilities and capacities to develop and innovate' (CIPD 2016e).

We can easily see that the idea of human capital must be of central interest to HRM. As we said in the introduction to this chapter, we think that ultimately people are the only source of sustainable competitive advantage. So human capital is an aspect of many HR strategic and operational activities, including the composition of the workforce, recruitment and retention, performance management, learning and development, and talent management.

One of the challenges in managing human capital is measuring it. This leads to the topic of HR analytics, which is discussed in Chapter 9.

A British Standard (BS76000) has been a developed to provide a common framework for organisations to assess their human capital. The CIPD Human Capital blog can be found at: **cipd.co.uk/community/blogs/b/human_capital_blog**

One of the first, and most important, intellectual proponents of HRM was the Harvard Business School (HBS). The faculty and alumni of the school agreed in the early 1980s that a new course in HRM was required to equip general managers to deal with the changes that were occurring both in society and in the competitive environment in which business had to operate. Accordingly, in 1981, HBS introduced a course in HRM in its core MBA curriculum, the first new required course since Managerial Economics 20 years before (Beer *et al* 1984, pix). The primary intention of Beer *et al* was to develop a framework for general managers to understand and apply HRM in their organisations.

The 'Harvard model' linked choices on HR policies to stakeholder interests, situational factors and short- and long-term consequences. Of course, there have been significant developments in management practice and theory since the 1980s when the Harvard model was first conceived – for example, in areas such as knowledge management, talent management, ethics and corporate governance, the details of which often transcend the limits of the Harvard model. Technological advances also have had an obvious major impact on work, including HRM (for example the use of social media for recruitment, teleworking, the use of virtual teams). Nonetheless, the model proved to be remarkably durable because it was the first real attempt to provide a comprehensive 'map of the HRM territory' which reflected the 'emerging view that people are an asset and not a cost' (Beer *et al* 1984, p292) and that the HR function should be involved in all strategic and business decisions.

The Harvard model is illustrated in Figure 1.1.

Figure 1.1 The Harvard model

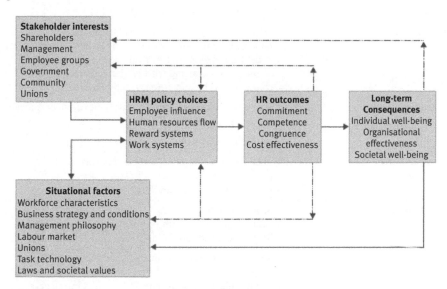

Source: Beer *et al* (1984, p16: 'Map of the HRM territory')

Two main variants of HRM were identified early in academic discussions of HRM: 'hard' HRM, with an emphasis on the strategic, quantitative aspects of managing human resources as an economic factor in production, and 'soft' HRM, rooted in the Human Relations School and emphasising communication, motivation and leadership (Storey 1989). All models of HRM are concerned with strategic issues, but 'hard' models typically have a stronger focus on ensuring that the HRM strategy 'fits' and is driven by the overall corporate strategy. This is a matter of degree, however, since all HRM models stress the importance of taking a strategic view of the human resource.

Critical and postmodernist interest has always been high in academic treatments of HRM, especially in the UK – for example Legge (1995). As might be expected, such commentators tended to be hostile to the HRM model and were, and are, often opposed to its adoption, fearing that it represents continuing or even enhanced exploitation of ordinary employees. But even non-radical critics have pointed out that the specific practices associated with HRM are actually rather varied in nature, even in the theoretical models, and some have questioned whether they really can be regarded as making up a coherent approach to the management of people. For example, performance-related payment systems on the one hand seem to represent an individualisation of the employment relationship, whereas the promotion of team involvement – for example quality circles and total quality management (TQM) – represent the opposite (Gallie *et al* 1998, pp6–7).

1.6 SUMMING UP THEORETICAL HRM

We can consider the key characteristics of HRM and how these contrast with earlier approaches to people management (Table 1.2).

Strategic nature: traditionally, personnel management or personnel administration usually worked on a short timescale – 'fire-fighting' (that is, dealing with immediate problems such as local industrial relations issues, or urgent staff shortages) rather than taking a long-term, strategic view of people management issues. Manpower planning might have been an exception to this general rule and, occasionally, management development.

Table 1.2 Ideal characteristics of human resource management

Characteristics	Human resource management (HRM)
Strategic nature	• Dealing with day-to-day issues, but also proactive in nature and integrated with other management functions • A deliberately long-term, strategic view of human resources, contrasting with earlier approaches characterised by an ad hoc, reactive mindset
Psychological contract	• Based on seeking willing commitment of the employee rather than compliance
Job design	• Typically team-based, not Taylorist/Fordist
Organisational structure	• Flexible with core of key employees surrounded by peripheral shells • High degree of outsourcing
Remuneration	• Market-based • Individual and/or team performance • 'Pay for contribution' rather than 'pay by position'
Recruitment	• Sophisticated recruitment for all employees, not just senior staff • Strong internal labour market for core employees; greater reliance on external labour market for non-core
Training/development	• A learning and development philosophy transcending job-related training; an ongoing developmental role for all core employees including non-management; strong emphasis on management and leadership development • a learning organisation culture
Employee relations perspective	• Unitarist and individualistic with high trust; as opposed to pluralist, collectivist and low trust
Organisation of the function	• Largely integrated into line management for day-to-day HR issues • Specialist HR group to advise and create HR policy
Welfare role	• No explicit welfare role
Criteria for success of the function	• Control of HR costs, but also maximum utilisation of human resources over the long term; rather than a simple focus on minimising labour costs

Source: adapted and developed from Guest (1987)

Note the implications for this longer-term perspective for all HR issues, and the necessity for an articulated strategy for HRM, which should not only be coherent in itself but should be informed by, and support, the business strategy of the organisation.

The psychological contract: this is not to be confused with the legal contract of employment, or any written statement of terms and conditions of employment. As the term implies, it exists purely in the mind of the employee and their managers, and so is unwritten and never clearly articulated. It has been described by Armstrong (2014, p419) as: 'the psychological contract is a set of unwritten expectations that exist between individual employees and their employers.'

There will always be some sort of psychological contract between the employee and the organisation, but David Guest concluded that: 'a positive psychological contract is worth taking seriously because it is strongly linked to higher commitment to the organisation, higher employee satisfaction and better employee relations' (Guest 1996).

Earlier models of people management assumed that the basis of the psychological contract was compliance – the employee would do as they were told and the employer in turn expected this. Management should be able to determine exactly what is required of the employee and enforce at least minimal compliance. The HRM model, on the other hand, assumes that the employee shows positive, willing commitment. Because more is expected from employees, management cannot always specify exactly what is required, and so employees must use their own judgement and initiative to a much greater extent than in the past. They must also extend and upgrade their skills and knowledge bases.

Job design: the search for greater commitment in the HRM approach implies that employees should be allowed and encouraged to use self-control in matters of work and organisational discipline, rather than be driven by a system of compliance and direction imposed upon them by management. Teamworking and similar initiatives should be common under HRM.

Organisational structure: reflecting the higher-commitment working associated with HRM, we would expect to find less hierarchical and more flexible organisational structures, with the team as the 'organisational building block' and with fewer management levels. Organisations following an HRM approach will typically be flexible with a core of key employees surrounded by peripheral shells of other workers, rather than the traditional hierarchical, pyramid-shaped bureaucratic structure. Note that the core employees are not all senior executives – the core is defined as comprising those members of the organisation who possess the skills, knowledge and competence necessary for the organisation's success. Core workers will possess considerable market attractiveness and will consequently enjoy better remuneration and terms of employment than others. In return, they will be expected to provide high levels of performance and flexibility in working, and accept the need for continuous learning and re-skilling to support incessant technological and process improvement. The peripheral shells of employees act as buffers against short-term market fluctuations and can be relatively easily shed or reinforced. Thus employees in those parts of the organisation will tend to be employed on short-term or temporary contracts. HRM organisations also tend to feature considerable outsourcing of non-core work.

Remuneration: traditional approaches to remuneration featured long pay scales characterising the hierarchical organisational structure mentioned above, and reflecting length of service rather than current contribution. Pay structures in such approaches would be usually agreed via collective bargaining, at least for non-managerial employees. The HRM approach to remuneration is more focused on rewarding contribution and is likely to be individually or team-based. This implies both the use of performance management and appraisal and the setting of base rates from the market rather than by means of collective agreements.

Recruitment: sophisticated techniques such as the use of psychometric testing, psychological profiling and assessment centres have often been used for recruitment and selection into senior executive posts, while much simpler and less costly methods usually sufficed for non-managerial employment. With HRM, these sophisticated tools are much more likely to be used for all employees, or at least core ones, with a view to selecting staff amenable to the organisation's culture and values.

Training and development: when employees are viewed mainly as a cost which should be minimised, commitment to training is usually negligible since employers typically fear that employees will be 'poached' by free-loading competitors who do no training themselves. An exception was often made, however, in industries with collective agreements on apprentice training.

In HRM there is a culture of continuous development of all core employees who are seen as the originators and possessors of the organisation's strategic competencies necessary for sustainable competitive advantage. Senior managers are not exempt, the directors and CEO receiving 'executive development'. This commitment would not be expected in the peripheral shells surrounding the core.

Employee relations perspective – that is, the dominant managerial perspective within the organisation. In the HRM model the employment relationship is much more individualised than when dealing with the workforce collectively. This is reflected in, for example, the absence of trade unions and the introduction of performance-related reward systems.

The unitarist nature of HRM would seem to discourage the formation of a pluralist organisational culture, but in practice there have been examples where HRM has been successfully adopted within a previously pluralist culture while maintaining the pluralist style of collective bargaining in employee relations. See for example Tayeb's account of the Scottish division of the American firm NCR (Tayeb 1998). But see also the empirical evidence from the Workplace Industrial/Employment Relations surveys in the UK (referred to in section 1.7) on the long-term decline of trade unionism in the UK.

The organisation of the function: traditionally personnel management was seen as a specialist function which, in many important respects such as dealing with employee relations issues, was separate from line management. This often led to the creation and maintenance of large, bureaucratic, personnel departments. The HRM model instead stresses that most people management, even employee relations, is actually just part of normal management, at least in its day-to-day aspects. Accordingly in the HRM model, where there are specialist HR departments, they will be small and highly specialised and their function is (1) to formulate HR policies and (2) to act as internal consultants to line managers. The line managers will implement most HR policy, only seeking the involvement of HR in particularly difficult issues.

Welfare role: in earlier approaches, such as personnel management, there were at least residual expectations of a welfare role, the personnel officer being the member of the management team who could be approached with personal problems (at least if these impacted on work). This always led to ambiguous perceptions of personnel management. There was no doubt that it was a management function with the primary objective of reducing and controlling labour costs (see 'Criteria for success' below), but many employees expected a fuller welfare aspect than was often given, and this was a principal reason for the ambiguity with which personnel management has often been viewed. Personnel managers often felt themselves to be 'the meat in the sandwich' caught between dissatisfied employees and unsympathetic management colleagues, neither of whom really understood what they were supposed to be doing. Marxist critics always saw personnel management as in any case reflecting the perceived contradictions of capitalism (Legge 1989), but even dyed-in-the-wool free-marketers could see the possibility of perceived inconsistencies in the role of PM and danger of conflicting expectations.

There is no explicit welfare role in the HRM model, although proponents might argue that with its unitarist culture it is no longer necessary. Critics would not agree. To the extent that individual employees still expect some sort of welfare role from HRM, despite academic prescriptions to the contrary, the function will be subject to the same perceptions of ambiguity as was personnel management.

HRM is held to a very different *criteria for success of the function* – that is, how the organisation judges the performance of the people management function. In the personnel management model, the organisation would judge the effectiveness of the function by how well it minimised unit labour costs; in HRM, effectiveness is judged by how well it maximises the use of the organisation's human resources (while still maintaining proper control of costs).

1.7 HRM IN PRACTICE

There is substantial empirical evidence that that significant changes in the practice of managing people in modern organisations have occurred over recent decades and that the HRM model as described above is the predominant paradigm, although few if any workplaces fulfil all aspects of the ideal model shown in Table 1.2.

Evidence of the adoption of key HRM practices in the UK has been authoritatively established by the series of Workplace Industrial Relations/Workplace Employment Relations Study (WERS) surveys. These surveys provide a nationally representative account of the state of employment relations, working life and the management of people inside British workplaces, and of how these have all been changing over a quarter of a century. The surveys were jointly sponsored by the Department of Trade and Industry (DTI), Acas, the Economic and Social Research Council (ESRC) and the Policy Studies Institute (PSI), and were conducted in 1980, 1984, 1990, 1998, 2004 and 2011. These were all large-scale, representative surveys.

The WERS surveys confirmed this shift from collectivism to individualism, with a marked decline in trade unionism, and a significant increase in the sort of approaches to participation and communication that are embraced by HRM, and are largely dependent on management initiatives such as team briefings, quality circles and newsletters. There was also evidence of organisational changes such as the increasing involvement of line managers in personnel activities; human resource matters were often incorporated in wider business plans. By the end of the twentieth century, Cully et al (1999) could conclude that (people management) practices consistent with an HRM approach were 'well entrenched in many British workplaces' (Cully et al 1999). Later WERS surveys confirmed a continuing trend in this.

Many organisations operated a 'flexible organisation' with a 'core' of key employees and a 'peripheral' workforce of other workers who typically enjoyed less secure and less attractive terms and conditions of employment. Selection processes for core employees increasingly supplemented the well-established techniques of interviews, application forms and references with personality, competency and performance tests, and used these over a wider range of employees. The use of performance appraisals greatly increased, as did off-the-job training. New methods of work organisation were widely adopted, often described as 'high-performance', 'high-commitment' or 'high-involvement' work practices. These were intended to enhance employee commitment and involvement, often by increasing employees' participation in the design of work processes and the sharing of task-specific knowledge. Most commonly these entailed teamworking, cross-training (or 'multiskilling') and the use of problem-solving groups. Additionally, the WERS surveys established that the UK trend for work culture to become more unitarist and less pluralistic was unremitting.

The 2011 WERS confirmed that organisational interest in employee engagement and high-involvement management had steadily increased as had employee commitment as measured by loyalty towards, and pride in, one's employing organisation and the sharing of its values (Van Wanrooy et al 2013).

So the empirical evidence seems clear. In most UK workplaces the management of people has been progressively moving closer to the ideal HRM model (see Table 1.2) over the last 30 years, and the most recent evidence suggests strongly that this is continuing. The UK is not unique in this, and giving due weight to local cultural and contextual factors, similar changes in the management of people have been happening worldwide in developed and developing economies.

1.8 STRATEGIC HUMAN RESOURCE MANAGEMENT (SHRM)

We saw above that one of the defining characteristics of the HRM model as it evolved from the 1980s is its strategic nature. Many authors and researchers emphasise this by using the term 'strategic HRM' or 'SHRM', which serves to focus attention above the operational level of specific HR techniques.

Armstrong (2014, p16) describes 'strategic HRM' as: 'an approach to the development and implementation of HR strategies that are integrated with business strategies and supports their achievement.'

Certainly the importance of strategy to HRM cannot be overlooked. Ulrich's first recommendation for the HRM function was that it should become a partner with senior and line managers in strategy execution (Ulrich 1998, Ulrich and Brockbank 2005).

1.8.1 THE UNIVERSALIST VERSUS CONTINGENCY DEBATE IN SHRM

One of the fault lines in the theoretical debates on strategic HRM has been an argument that in one form or another has run through all of management literature from the time of Taylor's 'scientific management' to the present day. This is whether there is one best way to manage – that is, is there a set of principles which, if applied correctly, will always bring better performance, or does it depend on the particular circumstances and factors such as the nature of the work and technology that is employed? This is sometimes referred to as the 'universalist versus contingency' debate.

Somewhere between the two extremes of universalism and contingency lies the 'best-fit' or 'configuration' view: there may or may not be eternal, universally applicable management techniques, but experience (sometimes supported by theory) shows that, given similar structures and contexts, successful organisations tend to employ the same methods or policies.

We see this debate in the arguments over whether there are specific 'bundles' of HRM practices which enhance performance. In reality, the debate in HRM is usually about the range and choice of techniques rather than one of absolute principle. There probably are some generic HR processes and general principles of people management common to all successful organisations (Boxall and Purcell 2006, p69). No one really doubts that it is best to be as systematic and accurate as possible in selecting people for work, for example, but there is much less certainty as to whether it is effective or even ethical to screen employees' personality profiles to select only those whom the organisation believes will conform to the company culture.

On the other hand, Huselid (1995) argued that there is sound evidence, gathered from over 1,000 firms in various (US) industries, for a universalist case for specific high-performance work practices impacting on firms' financial performance.

1.9 BEST-FIT MODELS

1.9.1 COMPETITIVE STRATEGIES AND SHRM

Michael Porter is arguably the most influential figure in business strategy. His book *Competitive Strategy*, which was first published in 1980, is, at the time of writing, reportedly in its 53rd printing and is available in 17 languages.

The need for organisations to find sustainable competitive advantage is central to Porter's work. He distinguished three 'generic' competitive strategies: differentiation, cost leadership and focus:

- *differentiation* – setting the company's products or services apart from those of its competitors through, for example, advertising, features or technology to achieve a product or service which customers perceive as unique, and so achieving a premium price

- *cost leadership* – being the lowest-cost producer while achieving normal prices
- *focus* – concentrating on one or more niche markets and pursuing either differentiation or cost leadership in each niche.

Somewhat controversially, Porter maintains that a firm must choose one and only one of these strategies (or at any rate each strategic business unit must) or it risks being 'stuck in the middle' with no sustainable competitive advantage and will be vulnerable to competitors.

Porter has his critics, of course, but an evaluation of his work is outside the scope of the present text. His relevance to strategic HRM is that one of the most influential 'best-fit' models of HR policies and practices – that of Schuler and Jackson (1987) – is based directly on his strategic prescriptions.

Schuler and Jackson identified a set of 12 behaviours that were needed to make competitive strategies work. For each, the differentiation strategy required the opposite from that needed for cost leadership. These behaviours were: the degree of creative, innovative behaviour; the focus on long-term behaviour; the degree of independent, autonomous behaviour; concern for quality; concern for quantity; capacity for high risk-taking; concern for results; preference to assume responsibility; flexibility towards change; tolerance of ambiguity and unpredictability; range of skill application; and degree of job or firm involvement.

Schuler and Jackson then explicitly linked these HR characteristics of the workforce to Porter's generic competitive strategies (Porter 1980).

According to Schuler and Jackson (1987), if a firm pursues a cost leadership strategy in Porter's terms it will be sufficient that the employees show a preference for predictable and repetitive behaviour with a low degree of flexibility and a narrow application of skill. They need only have a low concern for quality of the product. Employees need show little desire for responsibility and will probably have low feelings of involvement with their jobs or organisations. To support these employee behaviours and attitudes, the firm's human resource practices can exhibit low employee participation, with little job security and minimal training.

Conversely, if a firm follows a differentiation strategy, the employees will have to exhibit a high concern for quality and be creative and innovative, with a high degree of flexibility and wide application of skills. They will have to be willing to assume responsibility and will experience a high level of involvement with both job and organisation. To support these employee characteristics, HRM practices will have to maintain a much higher level of employee participation. Employee relations will be co-operative rather than hostile, and job security is likely to be high. Reward systems will be geared to individual and group performance.

1.10 BEST-PRACTICE MODELS OF STRATEGY AND HRM

Best-practice models of HRM are universalist in nature and assert that regardless of context or internal factors there is one best way of managing human resources which, if applied, will lead to better organisational performance.

Pfeffer identified a set of seven HR practices that would lead to what he termed 'competitive advantage through people' (consolidated from an original list of 16). These were: employment security, selective recruitment, self-managed teams or teamworking, high pay contingent on company performance, extensive training, reduction of status differentials, and the sharing of information (Pfeffer 1994, 1998).

In a large-scale study of US manufacturing companies across a range of industries and firm sizes, Huselid (1995) reported evidence that the use of specified high-performance work practices (HPWPs) was reflected in better firm performance as measured by reduced employee turnover, increased productivity and enhanced corporate financial performance. The HPWPs which were identified were in the areas of personnel selection, performance appraisal, incentive compensation, job design, grievance procedures, information-sharing, attitude assessment, labour–management participation, intensity of recruitment (as measured by the selection ratio), average number of hours' training per employee per year, and promotion criteria.

Huselid also specifically looked for evidence for internal and external fit in HR strategy (that is, a coherent HR strategy for the former and a link between the HR strategy and the corporate strategy for the latter), but reported (1995, p667) that:

> despite the compelling theoretical arguments that better internal and external fit will increase firm performance, I found only modest evidence for such an effect for internal fit and little for external fit.

However, he acknowledged that the theoretical arguments in favour of both internal and external fit remain 'compelling', and he called for further research before a firm conclusion could be reached. It must be said that we still await such conclusive evidence that would close the debate on best fit or best practice for good one way or the other.

Huselid also made a final comment (1995, p68) of significant interest, although it is seldom referred to in the HRM literature:

> Although traditional economic theory would suggest that the gains associated with the adoption of high-performance work practices cannot survive into perpetuity (because the returns from these investments will be driven toward equilibrium as more and more firms make them), the substantial variance in the HRM practices adopted by domestic [US] firms and the expectation that investment in such practices helps to create firm-specific human capital that is difficult to imitate suggest that at least in the near term such returns are available for the taking.

These are perhaps the two most widely known best-practice models, but there are many others, the most important of which is the US Department of Labor (1993), which Huselid based his work upon. Youndt *et al* (1996) reviewed the field.

We can see from the above that best-practice models are typically universalist prescriptions for HPWPs. These models typically emphasise the importance of employee selection, training, flexibility, performance management and incentive-based pay, but they neglect issues of collective employee relations. This perhaps reflects their North American origins and arguably decreases the possibility of true universalism when applied to countries such as those of Scandinavia or Northern Europe, which still enjoy a more vigorous tradition of employee representation and trade union influence than does the United States.

1.10.1 STRATEGIC CHOICE?

Boxall and Purcell (2006) hold that neither the best-practice nor the best-fit approach is completely correct. Their solution – which seems sensible in principle – is to think in terms of (a) some underlying general or generic processes of managing human resources that are universal and that can be applied regardless of context; while there is also (b), a 'surface layer' of policies and practices in any organisation which are influenced by contingent factors. The difficulty, of course, is in identifying the generic processes. Boxall and Purcell suggest recruitment as an example of the generic processes – but they do not offer a definitive list.

1.11 SOME KEY THEMES IN HUMAN RESOURCE MANAGEMENT IN THE TWENTY-FIRST CENTURY

In this section we outline some of the key themes of current interest in HRM. These are discussed in greater detail in Chapter 9.

1.11.1 HIGH-INVOLVEMENT OR HIGH-PERFORMANCE WORK PRACTICES

The WERS studies identified increasing interest in the UK in 'high-performance', 'high-commitment' or 'high-involvement' work organisation and practices which are believed to contribute to better individual, team and organisational performance.

These typically comprise:

- *high employee involvement practices* – such as self-directed teams, quality circles and sharing/access to company information
- *specific human resource practices* – such as sophisticated recruitment processes, performance appraisals, work redesign and mentoring
- *specific reward and commitment practices* – such as financial rewards for performance, family-friendly policies, job rotation and flexible hours.

International studies have also found evidence of the importance of high-performance working for organisational performance (ILO/IFTDO 2000).

The topic of HPWPs is discussed more fully in Chapter 9.

1.11.2 HRM AND CHANGE MANAGEMENT

We noted above that Ulrich and Brockbank (2005) specified as one of their key roles for HRM that of 'strategic partner', which in addition to business strategy had an emphasis on transformation and cultural change. We also saw that Torrington *et al* (2014) identified change management objectives as central to people management.

'The only constant is change' has become a cliché but reflects the acknowledgement now that the competitive global economy and continuous increasing technological advances are realities. Physical resources are relatively easy to change; human ones are much more challenging. HRM is often tasked with taking the lead and co-ordinating change across the organisation.

1.11.3 THE GLOBAL CONTEXT OF HRM: INTERNATIONAL AND COMPARATIVE HRM

There are two aspects to the global context of HRM: international HRM (IHRM) and comparative HRM (CHRM):

1 IHRM focuses on the degree to which multinational companies can or should practise uniform HRM policies and practices in all the countries in which they operate.

2 CHRM is concerned with the degree to which HRM, as practised in different countries (for example the USA, China and India), shows general similarities or difference.

The 'convergence–divergence' debate in IHRM asks to what extent HRM systems of developing countries are converging or diverging with respect to those in the developed world.

HRM researchers have examined whether Western-derived, global, standardised HR policies and practices can be successfully implemented in the context of developing countries. They have also tried to identify unique aspects of indigenous HRM policies and practices. The evidence suggests that managerial attitudes, values, behaviours and efficacy all differ across national cultures.

The term 'soft convergence' has been coined to describe the 'partial impact' of globalisation on HRM policies and practices (Warner 2002). This is typified by the implementation by multi-national companies (MNCs) of globally standardised HRM policies and practices but allowing for local adjustments. Under globalisation, international trade and finance places pressure on firms to standardise practices and policies to seek competitive advantage. But this standardisation is necessarily moderated by the inescapable local variations in factors such as demography, geography, economics, legal and political systems and national culture.

The recognition of this has brought many commentators to the conclusion that 'soft convergence' is the most that realistically can be expected and that the notion of total or 'hard convergence of HRM is a chimera' (Budhwar and Debrah 2010).

This topic is covered in more depth in Chapter 8.

1.11.4 NEW FORMS OF EMPLOYMENT

Societal and economic changes, such as the need for increased flexibility by both employers and workers, combined with technological developments, especially internet-driven social media, have resulted in the emergence of new forms of employment across developed economies. These are transforming the traditional one-to-one relationship between the employer and employee. They are often characterised by unconventional work patterns and places of work, or by the irregular provision of work. One example is 'crowd employment' in which the internet allows employers to access a 'virtual cloud of workers', such as Amazon's 'Mechanical Turk' platform (**www.mturk.com/mturk/welcome**).

These new employment forms have enormous implications for working conditions and the labour market and consequently for the practice of HRM.

1.11.5 HRM AND CORPORATE SOCIAL RESPONSIBILITY

Corporate social responsibility (CSR) has been defined as comprising 'actions that appear to further some social good, beyond the interests of the firm and that which is required by law' (McWilliams and Siegel 2001, p117).

The CIPD (2009) argues that the HR function is crucial to effective CSR:

Successful CSR strategies depend on building relationships with a range of stakeholders and getting buy-in across the organisation. Enlightened people management practices are key in delivering this, and CSR offers HR professionals many opportunities to make a strategic contribution to their business. This may mean reviewing existing policies and practices on, for example, internal communications, recruitment, induction, health and safety, diversity or training. One of the main conclusions from [CIPD research] was that CSR became an instrument of change in an organisation's behaviours, attitudes and performance, and this was where the HR function made its greatest contribution to the success of CSR initiatives.

1.11.6 ETHICS AND HRM

In what is perhaps a residual echo of the welfare role of traditional personnel management, HRM is often expected to be something of a guardian of organisational ethics, and to act as a guarantor of organisational fairness and justice for all employees.

'While HRM does need to support commercial outcomes ... it also exists to serve organisational needs for social legitimacy' (Boxall *et al* 2007). This means something more than just ensuring compliance with legal protection for employees with respect to health and safety at work and against discrimination in employment.

1.12 SUMMING UP

In today's and tomorrow's world, sustainable competitive advantage can only come from the skills, experience, creativity, imagination and brainpower of people. In the modern economy it is relatively easy to raise capital to fund a bright idea, but managing the human resources of an organisation to turn that idea into a business and achieve *sustainable* competitive advantage – how to create and build the next Google or Facebook or Apple – is the single most important management challenge in the twenty-first century.

HRM is now the dominant paradigm in people management. It seeks commitment from employees rather than compliance; it tends to be unitarist rather than pluralistic in its approach to employee relations; and it places great emphasis on taking a strategic approach to human resources.

In this chapter we have explored the nature of HRM and how it evolved and have looked at some of the key contemporary themes in the management of people in modern organisations. These themes are examined in more detail in later chapters.

EXPLORE FURTHER

Armstrong, M. (2014) *Armstrong's Handbook of Human Resource Management Practice*. 13th edition. London: Kogan Page.

- Chapter 1, 'The essence of human resource management'; and Chapter 2, 'Strategic HRM'.
- These chapters provide brief overviews of their topics, useful for quick reference and starting exam revision.

Boxall, P. and Purcell, J. (2006) *Strategy and Human Resource Management*. Basingstoke: Palgrave Macmillan.

- Chapter 1, 'Human resource management and business performance' – this is a scholarly introduction to HRM which makes explicit linkage to business performance.

Boxall, P., Purcell, J. and Wright, P. (eds) (2007) *The Oxford Handbook of Human Resource Management*. Oxford: Oxford University Press.

- Not to be confused with a practitioners' handbook such as Armstrong (2014) noted above – this, like Storey (2007) (cited below), is a collection of specialist chapters all by leading academics in the field, although Boxall *et al* has a wider disciplinary and international scope than Storey.
- Chapter 2, P. Boxall, 'The development of HRM in historical and international perspective' – a concise but thorough account.
- Chapter 7, D.E. Guest, 'HRM and the worker: towards a new psychological contract' – a discussion of how HRM helps to shape workers' attitudes and behaviour, especially their satisfaction and well-being; optimistic about the potential of HRM to improve the workers' lot.
- Chapter 8, P. Thomson and W. Harley, 'HRM and the worker: labor process perspectives' – something of a counter-argument to Guest's optimism in the previous chapter, an analysis from the Critical Management School.
- Chapter 26, J. Purcell and N. Kinnie, 'HRM and business performance' – a sceptical evaluation of the case that HRM's impact on organisational performance can be measured.

Storey, J. (ed) (2007) *Human Resource Management: A critical text*. 3rd edition. London: Thomson Learning. The third edition of a collection of essays by leading academics. This edition also has some useful short illustrative case studies.

- Chapter 1, J. Storey, 'Human resource management today: an assessment' – another scholarly introduction, this time with a flavour of the Critical Management School. Especially sceptical of the universalist approach.

Van Wanrooy, B., Bewley, H., Bryson, A., Forth, J., Freeth, S., Stokes, L. and Wood, S. (2013) *Employment relations in the shadow of recession: findings from the 2011 Workplace Employment Relations Study*. Basingstoke: Palgrave Macmillan.

- The latest in the WERS series. Perhaps of less immediate interest to management scholars or practitioners than it is to HR and employee relations specialists, but the study confirms the trend away from traditional personnel management and gives solid empirical findings on many aspects of how people are managed in the UK today.

CHAPTER 2

Employee resourcing

INTRODUCTION

In the opening chapter we noted that one of the key themes of HRM in the twenty-first century was the use of sophisticated HR practices in recruitment and selection. Recruitment and selection are two of the most important HRM activities in any organisation. In this chapter we will examine the general principles underlying these activities and look at some of the most widely used techniques. Organisations also have to manage the processes involved when employees leave the organisation, and these too are studied in this chapter. We additionally introduce the concept of 'talent management'.

These activities might be described as 'managing the human resource flow'. In the UK human resource management profession they are usually described as 'employee resourcing'. In North America the term 'staffing management' is often used.

LEARNING OUTCOMES

On completion of this chapter you should:

- understand how recruitment and selection may be best viewed as particular stages in a larger process of 'managing and developing the human resource flow'
- understand the main models of recruitment and selection of human resources
- have an appreciation of 'e-recruiting'
- understand the use of competency approaches in employee resourcing
- have an awareness of the strengths and limitations of the techniques most commonly used in selection, and an appreciation of the use of assessment centres
- have an appreciation of the issues involved in managing the exit of employees from the organisation
- have an understanding of the concept of 'talent management'
- understand the idea of diversity in human resource management (HRM).

HR specialists often talk about recruitment and selection as separate activities – 'recruitment' meaning the process of attracting people to apply for the job, and 'selection' being the final choice of a particular applicant for a specific position. (The North American term 'hiring' covers both and is sometimes more useful.) It is important that we remember that recruitment and selection do not occur in isolation from other managerial and organisational processes. They are key stages in what Beer *et al* (1984, p66) termed 'managing the human resource flow': 'The more dynamic the environment ... the more a corporation must be concerned with managing the flow of people in, through and out of the organisation.'

For the twenty-first century we can update this to say 'managing *and developing* the human resource flow'. Table 2.1 illustrates the key stages in this process.

Table 2.1 Managing and developing the human resource flow

Strategic level		Individual job/ person level	Actions/outcomes
Talent management for high-value (core) staff	Organisational development Human resource planning	Job analysis	Identifying the task requirements and criteria for job success
		Person specification	Identifying the attributes and experience the job-holder needs to achieve job success
		Recruiting	Attracting applicants for consideration for the position
		Initial screening	Examining applications to identify those most suitable for further consideration
		Selection	Interviews, testing and obtaining other information to assess applicants' attributes
		Initial induction and training	Induction to the organisation. If necessary, additional testing, assessment and training to fit the person for the job
	Continuous improvement	Performance management	Performance appraisal Rewards
		Learning and development	Knowledge and skill enhancement and development
		Promotion/transfer	
Rightsizing	Restructuring	Employee exit and/or job restructuring/ elimination	Employee job exit Employee *voluntary* organisational exit: resignation; retirement Employee *involuntary* organisational exit: redundancy; dismissal

Most of the topics shown in Table 2.1 are discussed in this chapter; however, performance management and reward management are covered in Chapters 6 and 7 respectively, while learning and development are dealt with Chapter 3.

We can see that decisions on recruitment and selection are embedded in a process of managing and developing the human resource flow through the organisation, entailing a range of HR practices, from analysing the key aspects of the job through to managing the exit of the employee from the job or organisation. This process itself is further embedded in long-term HR decisions and actions, and HR experts often talk about 'strategic selection', at least for core or key employees.

In the twenty-first century it is no longer sufficient just to hire the right staff – the HR talent must be managed and developed to achieve and sustain competitive advantage. This is not bad news for HR departments: *The Economist*, under the subheading 'The triumph of the HR department', could write (*A Survey of Talent*, 7–14 October 2006, p6):

Managing talent has become more important to a much wider range of companies than it used to be. One result has been that human resources departments which used to be quiet backwaters have gained in status. A survey by Aon, a consultancy, identified 172 HR executives who were among the five best-paid managers in their companies. That would have been unheard of a few years ago.

2.1 RECRUITMENT AND SELECTION

Before you can capitalise on the talent of your human resources, you have first to get hold of it. You must hire people with the knowledge, skills and abilities (KSAs) you require. Taking the long-term aspect, you want core employees who can continue to adapt and learn, so that there is a better probability that your organisation can sustain competitive advantage in the future. From that long-term perspective, capability and potential may be more important than current skills and knowledge.

How do organisations get the human resources they need? We can think of a number of ways organisations might do this.

We have to remember that ideally we want to be able to make quick and accurate decisions over whether an applicant can do the job effectively before committing the organisation to hiring them. Hiring is a costly business: the CIPD has estimated that the median cost of filling a vacancy in the UK is £2,000, rising to £7,250 for senior managers or directors when the associated labour turnover costs are also taken into account (CIPD 2015e). A wrong hiring decision is of course even more expensive – not only do you have to do it all over again to get it right, you have to bear the consequences of incompetent performance until you do.

2.1.1 PAST EXPERIENCE

Using experience would seem to be sensible in recruitment and selection. After all, we learn from experience, don't we? However, it can lead to difficulties when employed crudely. For example, a firefighter's job requires the potential for heavy lifting – even when equipped with the latest apparatus and technology – because the firefighter might still have to physically carry an unconscious adult to safety in life-threatening conditions. Traditionally it was thought that only men could be recruited for such a job since on average men are stronger than women. Leaving aside issues of illegal discrimination, this is misleading. It is strength not gender that will determine whether that aspect of a firefighter's job can be performed properly. Although on average men are stronger than women, some women are stronger than some men, and so some good applicants – perhaps the best – would be lost to the organisation if only men were hired.

This example also illustrates how 'experience' as well as being misleading in specific cases can reinforce unhelpful and unfair prejudices. Not so long ago it was thought that women were unsuited for politics and could not be members of the UK Parliament. But Britain now has its second woman prime minister. Also, at the time of writing the British army has just announced that women soldiers can serve in the front line in combat – something most people of earlier generations would have considered unthinkable.

2.1.2 MATCHING ATTRIBUTES

In this approach selection is made on the basis of attributes which the applicant must possess in order to do the job properly. It is assumed that these attributes can be assessed in some way prior to employment, and that such judgements can predict job success reliably. This model should avoid the difficulties noted with the common sense and experience model because the selection of individuals should ignore factors that are not relevant to job success, such as age, race, gender, residence or occupation of parents. In the example given above, organisations following this model would determine the level of strength necessary to do the firefighter's job, devise tests to measure the lifting ability of applicants, and then make the selection on the basis of the intrinsic abilities of individuals, not what group they belong to. Of course, a consequence of using this approach is that the organisation has to know in some detail what is required to do the job properly – the skills, knowledge, abilities and so forth – that is, it must identify the *criteria for job success*. This approach is capable of considerable refinement and can be highly sophisticated, using, for instance, a battery of psychometric and other tests. It is sometimes referred to as the 'selection paradigm', implying an ideal model of selection. However, as we will see shortly, it has not been developed to the point of becoming an exact science and no selection process, however sophisticated, is infallible.

2.1.3 THE COMPETENCY MODEL

Competency models are increasingly popular with organisations. In this model a 'competency framework' is established for the job to be filled. Depending on the type of competency model used, this framework will either be a list of abilities or characteristics or other inputs which are required (for example 'leadership') or it will consist of specific behaviours or other outputs that are necessary for job success (for example being able to read a balance sheet). Although the former is not so very different from the selection paradigm noted above, the latter specifies actual performance which must be achieved, and not just the potential to do so.

Armstrong (2014, p86) defined competency-based HRM as being:

> about using the notion of competency and the results of competency analysis to inform and improve the processes of performance management, recruitment and selection, learning and development, performance, employee development and employee reward.

2.1.4 COMPETENCY FRAMEWORKS

A competency framework is essentially a structured collection of competencies used by an organisation to frame and underpin activities (managerial or non-managerial). Professional bodies also may use competency frameworks to show the requirements for their qualified practitioners. The use of competency frameworks has become an increasingly accepted part of modern HR practice.

Employers' competency frameworks typically contain between 10 and 20 basic competencies which relate to a spectrum of roles across the organisation. In addition, some organisations have developed role-specific or technical competencies to address the problem that occurs when the basic competencies turn out to be inadequate for particular roles or jobs. More recently, some organisations have established organisational-cultural competencies which seek to reflect the ethos of the company itself, and these are concerned with ensuring that employees work in a way that is consistent with company culture.

The skill areas typically included in competency frameworks are: communication; managing people; team skills; customer service skills; having a results orientation; and problem-solving.

The main uses of competency frameworks from the organisation's point of view are to improve employee and organisational effectiveness by underpinning employee reviews/appraisals and achieving a better analysis of training and development, as well as enhancing career management and development.

Competency frameworks are now widely used to help select, appraise, train and develop staff. For example, in the recruitment process, competencies can contribute to the content of job or role profiles, any written or practical tests, and the job interview itself. Banks of potential interview questions can be developed which are directly linked to a role's competencies. Competencies, together with personal objectives or targets, can form the basis of the appraisal systems used by organisations. In this way, employers can measure how staff carry out their work through assessing their performance against personal objectives and the role's required competencies (CIPD 2015d).

It is argued that the main benefits of a competency-based system include the following:

- Employees have a well-defined set of behaviours required in their work and are clear about how they are expected to perform their jobs.
- The appraisal and recruitment systems are fairer and more open.
- Recruiters are able to assess transferable skills and identify required behaviours regardless of career background.
- There is a link between effective individual inputs to work and organisational performance.
- Processes are measurable and standardised across organisational and geographical boundaries.

The main criticism of competency frameworks is that because they require large amounts of information on jobs to be gathered and analysed, it takes time to produce or modify a framework. A further consequence of this is that competency frameworks are focused on the past and it can be difficult to keep them abreast of current and future job demands.

?   REFLECTIVE ACTIVITY 2.1

Consider how people are recruited into your organisation. Which of the approaches discussed above best describes the process involved?

Would another model give better results? If so, why?

This text is mainly concerned with the last two models of selection we discussed: matching attributes and competency, because these are the most appropriate ones for professional managers to operate. One of the key points to note is that in any systematic approach to selecting personnel, the selection decision is based on the organisation's making a prediction as to whether or not a particular candidate could achieve job success.

2.2 WHY WOULD ANYONE WANT TO WORK FOR YOU? EMPLOYER BRAND

An important part of strategic selection, especially for core employees, is developing the organisation's 'employee value proposition' – what it can offer that existing and prospective employees will value and which will encourage them to join or remain – and its 'employer brand' – the image as a good and attractive employer. Just as the marketing function seeks to create a brand for products that appeals to customers, an employer brand communicates what the organisation has to offer to potential and existing employees (CIPD 2016a).

The value proposition describes what an organisation stands for, what it requires from employees and what it offers in return as an employer. The 'psychological contract' between employer and employee should reflect the value proposition, as should its mission and values.

HRM IN ACTION: GOOGLE'S FOUR RULES OF RECRUITMENT

CASE STUDY 2.1

Yvonne Agyei, the tech giant's international HR head, on its unexpectedly process-driven hiring methods – and the search for 'Googleyness'

The popular perception of Google's recruitment process is a fun-filled mix of gimmicky games, endless interviews and mind-bending conundrums. But according to the Silicon Valley start-up's international HR head, there's a lot more humdrum science to it than you might expect.

At the Future Talent Conference in London, Yvonne Agyei – Google's Vice-President, People Operations – explained that recruitment was 'where we invest most as an HR organisation', with 60% of HR personnel dedicated to hiring. 'That's partly because we are growing significantly, but also it's just really important to get the right people in,' she said. 'All Googlers are responsible for hiring, and bringing in people we term "good for Google".'

HR, said Agyei, takes the lead in all recruitment, with hiring managers unable to make actual hiring decisions: 'We intentionally take away that power. We don't want people to hire their friends, and we don't want to compromise on quality. It's tempting to bring someone in just because you want bums on seats.'

The quest to banish nepotism and increase accountability has led to a rigorous recruitment paper trail. All interviews take 45 minutes, following which detailed feedback is sent to a hiring committee, including questions and verbatim responses and interviewers' impressions, as well as the candidate's CV and academic background.

The committee is responsible for rubber-stamping hiring decisions, and can also request further interviews if it feels questions haven't been relevant or probing enough. Google became notorious for averaging around nine interviews per hire, but Agyei said it was now deploying a 'rule of four' to streamline its processes: 'You must make a decision within four interviews – you ought to have enough information on anyone by then.'

But what is Google actually looking for, and how does it know when it's found it? Agyei outlined four key attributes every employee should have:

1. General cognitive ability – an assessable level of intelligence, often tested through logic-based questions, though these are grounded in technical realities rather than the abstract brain-teasers that have become legendary in Silicon Valley.

2. Role-relevant knowledge – the least important attribute, according to Agyei, who said Google would be happy to hire someone who ticked their other boxes but needed to be taught technical capabilities.

3. Leadership – the ability, or potential, to manage is essential in all roles, said Agyei, because even someone hired into an entry-level position might be leading within a year or two given the fast-paced nature of the business. 'Plus, we are a really flat organisation and you're likely to be in meetings with people more senior than you. You need to be able to offer your opinions.'

4. 'Googleyness' – this intangible quality 'isn't the same as cultural fit', said Agyei. It is best explained as a sense that the hire is 'good for Google' and that they have a particular tolerance for ambiguity. Engineers, for example, are hired into a general pool and won't be told

where they will work (and who they will be led by) until they have accepted an offer. The business believes Googleyness is what makes people work well together, and is investigating whether it can quantify and account for this quality among its most successful teams.

Source: Robert Jeffery, *People Management*, 4 March 2016.

？ REFLECTIVE ACTIVITY 2.2

1 Does Google's approach to recruitment satisfy the CIPD's 'five key standards' (see Table 1.1)?

2 How does your organisation's approach to recruitment and selection compare with Google's? Would you say it was more effective than Google's or less? Why?

2.3 JOB ANALYSIS, JOB DESCRIPTIONS AND PERSONNEL SPECIFICATIONS

The first step in the process of managing and developing the human resource flow (Table 2.1) is a decision about what the job is and what qualities are needed for its effective performance. At one extreme, job analysis may reveal that the requirements of the job are such that most of the employable population is capable of performing it adequately with appropriate initial training, and if so, hardly any effort at selection is warranted. At the other extreme – for example, the selection of astronauts – the job may call for a set of qualities that are rarely found in a single person within the population, and so demand a highly sophisticated (and expensive) selection procedure.

In any event, before hiring, the organisation should have identified the criteria for job success and the characteristics required of the job-holder in order to achieve this success. This is true whether the job is stacking cans on a supermarket shelf, being a member of a multi-skilled autonomous work team or, indeed, that of an astronaut.

The process of job analysis should result in the production of a job description. These are best kept as brief as possible but will typically include the job title, the overall purpose of the job, reporting relationships and the main activities, tasks and duties.

The person specification for the job, also sometimes described as the job or role specification, is to identify the knowledge, skills and abilities the employee needs to undertake the job competently.

2.4 RECRUITMENT AND SELECTION (HIRING)

If we remember that recruitment and selection are parts of a connected system of managing and developing our human resources (Table 2.1), we can appreciate that decisions taken in these earlier stages will impact on later stages. For instance, if after establishing the requirements for job success we then lower the specified standards in terms of skills, knowledge or abilities for job success, we will inevitably have to either accept a lower level of performance in the job or take some form of remedial action at a later stage – for example initial training – both of which would incur additional costs to the organisation.

Decision-makers in the recruitment and selection process must try to make rational choices, for which they need information. Decision-makers ideally should limit their information-gathering to procedures in which the usefulness of the additional information justifies the cost of gathering it. However, this is not an exact science and organisations usually have no idea whether the cost of using, say, a particular psychological test is justified. Common sense should be applied: a poor chief executive might destroy the firm, so nobody doubts the wisdom of gathering as much useful and relevant information as possible, even if this is expensive and time-consuming. But would you really spend as much time, effort and money in choosing a new caretaker?

In essence, the information gathered in the selection process is used to predict likely success on the job if the individual is to be employed. All such predictions are liable to error, because no selection process can give wholly accurate predictions of future success.

HRM DILEMMA 2.1

If we raise the bar, we reject more candidates who could do the job.

Two kinds of decision error may occur in every selection process, however constituted:

1 'false positives' or erroneous acceptances, where applicants are selected but prove to be inadequate, and

2 'false negatives' or erroneous rejections, where applicants who would have performed adequately are rejected.

Employing organisations are more concerned about false positives because they lead to incompetent performance and expensive mistakes. Accordingly, it makes sense for such organisations to raise entry requirements to reduce the probability of false positives – even though this inevitably increases the probability of false negatives. The consequences of this are that a greater number of applicants who are actually capable of doing the job will be erroneously categorised by the selection process as not meeting the required standards and so be rejected.

In other spheres the question of false negatives may be of more significance – for example in education, where (ideally) there is concern that opportunities should be equitably distributed. Where there are no funding constraints a college might deliberately lower entrance requirements for a programme. This would result in increased failure rates overall if academic standards were kept at the same level as before, but would reduce the number of false negatives. It would give a greater number of capable applicants the educational opportunity, at the cost in this case of increased false positives – students who are accepted on the programme but who are discovered not to have the capabilities to succeed in it.

2.5 STRATEGIC SELECTION

The selection decision has always been important. We noted above that wrong selection decisions always incur costs to the organisation, both from the damage an incompetent employee might do, and of simply having to go through the process of hiring someone else. The more senior the employee, the greater the effects of incompetence: an office worker might lose data and even some customers, but an inept CEO could destroy the firm. The better an organisation's overall selection process, the better it should perform collectively, and this has obviously always been true. However, HRM literature suggests that the selection decision now has even greater importance for organisations:

- Changes in the labour market have brought about a more diverse workforce. This increases the pool of available talent but also raises questions of fairness and equality which must be addressed, not only to ensure legal compliance but to exploit fully the talent available in the market.

- In the light of the increasing need for multi-skilled flexible workforces and teamworking, selection becomes less a matter of matching an individual to the fixed requirements of a clearly defined job – immediate skills and experience may be less important than adaptability, willingness to learn and ability to work in a team. In a word, modern organisations typically need fewer employees, but these must be of a higher calibre than was often the case in the past. There are fewer and fewer unskilled and low-skilled jobs in advanced economies.
- The need to establish a close relationship between corporate competitive strategies and HRM has produced the concept of 'strategic selection' in which the selection system supports the overall current and future business strategies. As we saw in Chapter 1, this underpins the whole idea of HRM as an approach to managing people.

For these reasons organisations are now more likely than in the past to use relatively costly techniques that previously would have been reserved for senior high-salary positions, such as psychometric testing or assessment centres, for selection for ordinary jobs.

> **?   REFLECTIVE ACTIVITY 2.3**
>
> Think about how you were appointed to your present job. Clearly, the right decision was made! But as a professional manager, how would you rate the effectiveness of the process?
>
> What could you do to make it more efficient in the future?

2.6 SOME COMMON SELECTION TECHNIQUES

The most common predictors used in the selection process are interviews, tests, information from application forms or letters, curricula vitae (CVs) or résumés, and references from previous employers (CIPD 2015f).

The use of information technology ('e-recruitment') has obviously impacted on recruitment and selection as with most other management processes. While early predictions of its revolutionary effect on practice seem to have been overstated, at least at the time of writing (Torrington *et al* 2014), online sources such as company websites and social media are widely used by recruiting organisations, but typically in combination with traditional media such as newspaper and journal advertising. There are also concerns about privacy and security of data if organisations trawl social media for information about candidates.

2.6.1 THE INTERVIEW

The interview is widely used and heavily relied upon, probably because of low cost, high perceived applicability and just general familiarity. There is, however, a large body of evidence that its reliability and validity are surprisingly *un*impressive. The difficulty is that although we can make real – and worthwhile – attempts to improve our effectiveness at interviews (see below), there are limits to what can be achieved. The problem is intrinsic to the technique: people are just not very good at making decisions in such contexts.

Limitations of the selection interview process

Interviewers pay too much attention to first impressions, and information obtained early in the interview has a disproportionate effect on the final outcome. Interviewers tend to compare candidates with ideal stereotypes and are prone to falling for 'contrast effects' by which a candidate's performance is unconsciously exaggerated by the interviewer in comparison with that of a previous applicant (for example after a very good candidate the next one may look poorer than they actually are). Interviewers are also liable to be influenced by 'halo effects' by which one characteristic of the candidate overshadows others – for example what school or university they attended. This effect can be positive or negative.

Interviewers also make decisions very early. One classic study in Canada found that in a series of 30-minute interviews, the interviewers made their decisions on the suitability of a candidate in an average of four minutes! This raises the question: what were they doing for the other 26 minutes? And the answer is almost certainly that they were seeking information to rationalise or support the decision they had already privately made.

Organisations will never abandon interviewing as a selection tool. No sensible organisation hires anyone without first seeing them in person, but many seek to improve its usefulness by using it in a more systematic way, and also by supplementing it with the use of tests or other techniques designed to obtain more relevant information about the candidate.

Some hints for interviewers

It is possible to improve the effectiveness of one's interview technique. Prior to conducting it, develop a 'game plan' for the interview to cover building rapport with the candidate, obtaining information, providing information (salary and other rewards, of course, but also main terms and conditions of employment, pension, sick pay, and so on) and answering questions. This should be based on current job information. A plan is particularly important for panel interviews in which a team of people jointly conduct the interview:

- Outline the game plan to the applicant at the start of the interview.
- Try to put the applicant at ease.
- Follow a common format for all applicants.
- In general, avoid leading and closed questions.
- Provide a realistic and specific description of the job and organisation.
- The applicant should do most of the talking (aim for, say, 75%).
- Develop active listening skills.
- Develop skills to observe non-verbal communication.
- Make notes during the interview and complete your record of it immediately after it.
- Be fully informed of all relevant legal, policy and ethical issues.
- Get feedback on the subsequent job performance of successful applicants so that you have some basis for assessing the usefulness of your interviewing in predicting job success.

The information obtained from selection interviews may often be supplemented by information obtained by other means, which may include psychological tests.

2.6.2 PSYCHOLOGICAL TESTING

Psychological testing involves a varied set of instruments which are usually categorised as intelligence tests, ability and aptitude tests, and/or personality tests. The latter are the most controversial but are generally viewed as being popular, especially in the case of recruitment for 'greenfield sites' (that is, completely new enterprises).

It has been estimated that there are over 5,000 psychological instruments available in the English language. Pearn *et al* (1987) commented that the question of the usefulness of personality assessment was probably the most controversial subject in occupational psychology. A review of the available evidence in the USA (Schmitt *et al* 1984) suggested that ability and aptitude tests have only a modest degree of predictive accuracy as far as job performance is concerned, personality tests being even less successful (although ability and aptitude tests could give better results than unstructured interviews).

In response to concern about the abuse of psychological tests, the CIPD has issued guidance on the subject (CIPD 2015f). This recommends the use of chartered psychologists to administer and interpret tests, invokes the observance of strict confidentiality, and stipulates the necessity to provide feedback for applicants.

Remember: a poor test, or a good test which is poorly administered, is much worse than no test at all.

2.6.3 ASSESSMENT CENTRES

An assessment centre is a procedure (not a location!) that uses multiple assessment techniques to evaluate employees for a variety of manpower purposes and decisions. The assessment centre approach may use techniques such as tests, questionnaires and the use of background information. Information is gathered in a standardised and controlled manner on behaviour that is representative of future job behaviour. The assessment centre method is used with particular success as a method for potential evaluation and management development.

Assessment centres typically feature:

- the use of multiple assessment techniques
- the use of simulations and work sampling
- observation by multiple observers
- assessment by trained assessors
- the separation of observation and evaluation.

2.7 SO HOW EFFECTIVE IS SELECTION?

Muchinsky (1986) summarised the effectiveness of selection techniques as follows:

- No single method was simultaneously high on validity, fairness and applicability and low on cost: so a series of trade-offs was necessary.
- The single method that came closest to the ideal was biographical information ('biodata'), but while high on validity and applicability and low on cost, it was only moderate on fairness.
- Techniques that scored highest on validity were assessment centres, work samples and biographical information.
- Interviewing was low on validity, moderate on fairness, high on applicability and low on cost.
- Personality tests were moderate on validity, high on fairness, low on applicability and moderate on cost.
- Assessment centres were high on validity, high on fairness, low on applicability (beyond management grades) and high on cost.

2.8 RECRUITMENT AND SELECTION IN PRACTICE

As noted in Chapter 1, the findings of the Workplace Employment Relations Study surveys in the UK reinforce the view that many organisations operate a 'flexible organisation' with a 'core' of key employees and a 'peripheral' workforce of other workers.

It is beyond the scope of the present text to offer a detailed discussion of exactly why most organisations pursue flexibility. It is the accepted economic wisdom adopted not only by national governments but also by international organisations such as the International Labour Organization (ILO) and the Organisation for Economic Co-operation and Development (OECD) and supranational entities such as the European Union (EU) that flexible labour markets are a prerequisite for economic growth in a competitive global marketplace (Eurofound 2010).

The selection process usually involves the use of interviews, application forms and references. Personality or competency tests, although used less often, have gained in importance in the search for greater objectivity in selection, despite continuing debate about their validity and reliability. Performance or competency tests are routinely used in many workplaces and are more likely to be used when recruiting core employees, irrespective of their occupation.

L'ORÉAL: THEIR PEOPLE ARE WORTH IT

CASE STUDY 2.2

L'Oréal is the world's number one beauty company, present in 130 countries (in five continents), employing over 77,000 people globally and 3,500 in the UK and Ireland. By 2020 the group aims to recruit one billion new consumers globally as part of its universalisation strategy.

Pivotal to the group's success is its culture of innovation and entrepreneurialism. The belief that people rather than processes fuel ideas is a mantra that allows L'Oréal to attract and retain the best talent.

Catrin Roberts, recruitment director for L'Oréal UK&I, explains: 'We find talent are equally attracted to our position as industry leader of 28 different beauty brands, as they are to our fast-moving innovative culture. We're clear we want people who are bold, daring and creative – people who have an innovative flair and believe "nothing is impossible".'

Alongside world-leading brands, L'Oréal realises that part of the company's attraction and retention strategy are its CSR commitments. The group's sustainability commitment for 2020 – 'Sharing beauty with all' – revolves around producing, living and developing sustainably. Clear targets have been set

for 2020 to reduce CO_2 emissions by 60%, to enable 100,000 people from underprivileged communities to access work and to give employees access to health care, social protection and training, wherever they are in the world.

'People are becoming savvier about CSR. They want to know what we're committing to, and what we're doing to give back to our communities. We support over 250 charities at L'Oréal UK&I alone,' explains Negin Lankarani, graduate and intern manager.

Diversity plays a huge part in L'Oréal's ability to recruit a range of talents, with the company believing that a diverse workforce is key to promoting a creative and innovative environment. The company actively works to attract a gender balance by supporting the Male Undergraduate of the Year Programme, encouraging an agile approach to working, and it also works with the Army Career Service to offer individuals work experience opportunities to support their integration back into the world of work following serious or life-changing injuries. As Negin Lankarani states, 'it's not about a one-size-fits-all approach, it's about offering a whole range of different initiatives to create an inclusive environment ... that's what our experienced hires as well as our interns and graduates want and expect from us.'

L'Oréal also strives to create opportunities for young people coming from diverse social and academic backgrounds through industrial placements, internships and graduate management trainee schemes.

Every year they recruit over 100 industrial placements, including summer internships, and over the last two years they have offered over 70% of the management trainee places to previous interns. The management trainee scheme is a 12-month rotational programme where individuals get to experience different divisions and functions within the business. All management trainees have a structured training programme and receive an HR sponsor throughout their time on the programme. Their

performance and development on the scheme is frequently tracked, ensuring that top talent is recognised and retained.

L'Oréal offers tailor-made career paths across 28 of its international brands because, as Catrin Roberts explains, 'people have different needs and wants at different points in their career and as a company we need to be flexible and agile to meet the individuals' needs.' Career paths are tailored to meet people's competencies and aspirations to promote mobility within country as well as at group level across the different divisions and functions. Regular appraisal of performance, where technical skills, key job accountabilities and behavioural competencies are evaluated, is fundamental to supporting individuals with their next step and designing a development plan that supports their longer-term career aspirations.

Source: CIPD (2015a)

? REFLECTIVE ACTIVITY 2.4

Case Study 2.1 states that:

'Pivotal to the group's success is its culture of innovation and entrepreneurialism. The belief that people rather than processes fuel ideas is a mantra that allows L'Oréal to attract and retain the best talent,'

and:

'Career paths are tailored to meet people's competencies and aspirations to promote mobility within country as well as at group level across the different divisions and functions. Regular appraisal of performance, where technical skills, key job accountabilities and behavioural competencies are evaluated, is fundamental to supporting individuals with their next step and designing a development plan that supports their longer-term career aspirations.'

Choose a role for a young graduate appointee to the company (it may be any key role: HR, marketing, finance or whatever). Outline a competency framework for the role that reflects the company's stated culture and aspirations and that can be used for recruitment and performance appraisal and development (you may find it useful to refer to Table 2.1).

2.9 THE 'GIG ECONOMY'

We mentioned new forms of employment in Chapter 1. Social and economic developments, such as the need for increased flexibility by both employers and workers, have resulted in the emergence of new forms of employment across Europe. These are changing the traditional one-to-one relationship between the employer and employee. They are characterised by unconventional work patterns and places of work, or by the irregular provision of work. The term 'gig economy' is often used to describe the growth of these new employment forms. The impact of the 'gig economy' is discussed in greater detail in Chapter 9.

? REFLECTIVE ACTIVITY 2.5

What are the pros and cons of the gig economy as far as HRM is concerned?

REFLECTIVE ACTIVITY 2.5 ANSWER GUIDANCE

The journal *Personnel Today* recently asked, 'What does the gig economy mean for HR?' and concluded that the key challenges for HR were:

- managing a talent pool and developing an employee value proposition that works across a blend of permanent and portfolio workers
- how to integrate contract terms and conditions into a cohesive, seamless whole and offer pertinent benefits and rewards – and become an employer of choice for 'gig workers'
- ensuring that the right technology is in place to automate joining and leaving processes and ensure they are smooth and easy to manage so as not to increase the HR administrative burden
- working out what risk management and governance ground rules should be put in place for portfolio staff working for multiple employers, including rivals
- managing quality control and ensuring that contracts do not simply end up going to the cheapest rather than most reliable and/or best bidder
- line managers operating beneath the radar without being aware of working time, health and safety, and minimum wage legislation.

And see HRM in Action 2.2: 'Are bike couriers self-employed?'

 HRM IN ACTION: ARE BIKE COURIERS SELF-EMPLOYED?

CASE STUDY 2.3

Bike courier challenge could start chain of more employment status claims

How to draft freelance contracts accurately (and stay out of court)

The concept of the 'gig economy' has now entered the mainstream, as an ever-increasing number of workers take on both short- and long-term freelance work rather than spending all their time working for one business.

The arrangement can bring dividends for both parties: the worker has the flexibility to deal with personal

commitments while the business gets a skilled worker without the cost of a permanent employee. But there can also be risks, particularly if the contract or legal label the parties use does not reflect the working arrangements accurately. There can also be tax consequences.

These risks were highlighted recently when it was reported that four bicycle couriers were taking their employers to a tribunal in a bid to prove they have been wrongly categorised as self-employed. As short-term contracts and flexible working become increasingly popular options, it has never been more important for businesses to ensure that a 'worker' is correctly categorised, as any mistakes are likely to be viewed dimly by a tribunal. HR should review contracts regularly and seek advice if there is any uncertainty, as this can be a complex area.

When considering engaging someone to carry out occasional work, businesses need to give careful thought to what form of contract is appropriate. There are three basic options. The business can treat the recruit as an employee, a worker, or as a self-employed contractor.

Employees have the most extensive legal protection, including against unfair dismissal. Businesses should use this option if they want the individual to have to accept work if it is offered to them. In some cases, this may be in the form of a zero-hours employment contract, which imposes no obligation on the business to offer work ('exclusivity clauses' barring zero-hours employees from working for other employers are no longer enforceable). However, these contracts have become increasingly controversial over the last few years, so there are reputational issues to consider when using them.

Workers are obliged to carry out work personally and have some key employment rights, such as the minimum wage, paid holiday and whistleblowing and discrimination protection. They also need to be paid via PAYE. Many casual workers and freelances fall into this category.

Self-employed contractors' rights are mainly determined by their contract (although in some cases they have discrimination protection).

The key distinction between a worker and an employee is that a worker is not obliged to accept work offered. So a worker's contract should specify that the business is not required to offer the worker any work (or any particular shift or project) and that the worker may work for other organisations when not carrying out work under the agreement. There should be an agreed mechanism for offering and accepting work, and the contract should include an explanation of the worker's status (for example, that they are a casual worker and not an employee) and confirm that the employer's grievance and disciplinary procedures do not apply to them.

Holiday entitlement and pay for occasional workers can be tricky. Workers accrue holiday at the rate of 12.07% of the hours worked. The business may not want workers to take holiday during a short-term project, so an alternative is to pay workers in lieu of the accrued holiday when the contract terminates. The contract should include a holiday request approval process for longer assignments.

Self-employed contractors' contracts should specify that they are not employees or workers, and are in business on their own account, providing services to clients/customers. Having services provided through an individual's own company may protect the business against tax liability. If employers use this structure, they may need a separate agreement with the individual setting out confidentiality, intellectual property assignment and restrictive covenant terms.

The contract should specify the required level of service and a timeframe and any key milestones for the project. Employers should consider including a substitution clause allowing them to sub-contract the work (including a right of veto over a proposed substitute, if appropriate). There should also be an indemnity from the consultant against any tax liability, any employment or worker-status-related claims, and any breaches of the agreement by them. Employers should consider requiring contractors to hold their own general commercial insurance, third party or professional indemnity insurance, depending on the type of services involved. It's preferable for the consultant to be responsible for their own equipment and expenses.

Source: *Personnel Management*, 10 May 2016.

2.10 INTERNATIONAL RESOURCING

The HR function in international organisations has to meet a series of challenges in resourcing for the global economy (CIPD 2013):

- It has to work within an international system while dealing with local needs.
- Talent is sourced globally and diverse workforces must be integrated.
- Globalisation spurs international mergers and acquisitions with consequent challenges for harmonising organisational cultures and HR policies and practices.
- Talent management and learning and development have to be organised globally.
- There is likely to be an increasingly diverse range of expatriate assignments.
- Increasingly diverse national labour markets.

International HRM is discussed more fully in Chapter 8.

2.11 TALENT MANAGEMENT

The consultancy firm McKinsey is credited with coining the expression 'war for talent', by which it meant the increasingly competitive market for key employees in the knowledge economy. 'Talent management' combines the traditional responsibilities of recruitment and selection with development activities which include 'succession planning'. In one sense it is the twenty-first-century version of an old description of the function of personnel management: 'getting the right person in the right job at the right time' – but now the 'right person' is likely to possess key skills and knowledge, hold considerable market value and require (and demand) continuous development. Talent management is another of the HRM activities which applies to the core but probably not the periphery.

Definitions vary, but within the UK HR profession the emphasis is certainly on the management development and succession planning areas. We can see that talent management straddles both recruitment and selection, and learning and development, but is predominantly 'future-focused'.

The CIPD defines key terms in talent management as follows:

- Talent consists of those individuals who can make a difference to organisational performance, either through their immediate contribution or in the longer term by demonstrating the highest levels of potential.
- Talent management is the systematic attraction, identification, development, engagement/retention and deployment of those individuals who are of particular value to an organisation, either in view of their 'high potential' for the future or because they are fulfilling business/operation-critical roles (CIPD 2015b).

The business case for taking a strategic approach to talent management is now seen as persuasive by many organisations. Increasingly, competitive global markets, skills shortages, demographic trends, corporate governance issues and business strategy are all seen as main drivers for increased interest in talent management. Its meaning has evolved to cover a range of HR areas, including organisational capability, individual development, performance enhancement and succession planning.

2.12 EMPLOYEE EXIT AND RELEASE

2.12.1 GENERAL CONSIDERATIONS

The employee relationship may end voluntarily when the employee chooses to leave the organisation to take up a position elsewhere, or it may finish at the end of a person's career by retirement at an agreed age, or the person may have to leave involuntarily through ill health, dismissal or redundancy. Some authorities argue that employee exits are increasingly likely to be involuntary as competitive pressures from technological advances and globalisation continually force firms to reduce costs even when profitable.

All HR issues regarding employee exit must be dealt with in the framework of relevant current employment legislation. We do not deal in detail with employment law in this text.

2.12.2 THE ROLE OF THE HR FUNCTION IN ORGANISATIONAL RELEASE

The HR function is normally given the task of managing organisational release. When this is dealing with involuntary release it can be a hard and stressful duty. There are ethical and professional considerations. Managers have no choice, of course, about taking part in organisational redundancy or 'downsizing' programmes, but they can make an important contribution to managing the process in such a way as to minimise both the individual distress and trauma that redundancy can cause and the organisational damage that can result from ill-considered or badly implemented dismissals. Professionally, HR managers are obliged to ensure that dismissal and redundancy policies and practices are in line with legal requirements, codes of practice and relevant company policies. They can also argue for policies and actions that minimise unnecessary redundancies, and can emphasise the need to handle dismissals and redundancies sensitively. They can advise line managers on the approach to adopt, provide training, help them communicate decisions to employees and other stakeholders, and provide counselling and outplacement services to the staff who will be affected.

2.12.3 DISMISSAL

Some degree of legal protection is afforded to employees in most developed economies, but the nature and degree obviously differ from country to country. One of the prime HRM functions is to ensure that the organisation is legally compliant in dealing with employee issues – and in none more so than dismissal.

Any society which allows legal protection for employees will also provide a means of redress through the courts, or quasi-legal institutions such as the UK's employment tribunals, for the employee who has been 'unfairly' or illegally dismissed. In investigating any allegation of unfair dismissal such bodies will typically seek answers to two fundamental questions: 'Was there sufficient cause for dismissal?' and 'Did the employer act reasonably in the circumstances?'

Dismissals are usually held to be fair when the employee acted in a way that constituted misconduct. Actions such as theft or fighting at work, or being drunk, are termed 'gross misconduct' and might justify summary (that is, immediate) dismissal without any further warning. In most other cases, however, employers will have to show that they followed some reasonable procedure which informed the employee of their unacceptable misbehaviour and gave them some opportunity to respond positively. Poor work performance on one occasion is very unlikely ever to be regarded as reasonable grounds for dismissal, for instance. Other reasons might include the employee's being unable to fulfil their contract of employment by reason of incapacity – and this can cover the employee's skill, aptitude or health (either physical or mental). This most often occurs when some change in a person's health renders incapable a previously capable employee. Effective recruitment and selection procedures should screen out all applicants who lack the capability to do the job in the first place.

2.12.4 REDUNDANCY

'Redundancy' is the term used when employees are dismissed not because of any issue with their performance or capability but because their jobs are no longer required by the organisation. As with the general case of dismissal, most societies have legal requirements that organisations must comply with in terms of, for example, giving employees adequate notice, negotiating with trade unions, and paying compensation to employees who are made redundant.

There are other managerial considerations to note. One of the most damaging aspects of redundancy to an organisation is the effect on those who are *not* made redundant. The 'survivors' may feel very vulnerable to future job cuts and the most employable may well seek other work before that happens – so you can quickly lose a lot of your best people, who are just the ones you want to hold on to.

Managing the redundancy process

As noted above, 'downsizing' is one of the most demanding areas of people management. Managers should first ensure that legal requirements have been met – for example, requiring consultation with the employees concerned and/or their representatives. The information made available at any consultative meeting should cover the reasons for the redundancy, the steps the organisation has taken to reduce the number of redundancies to a minimum, and the arrangements that will be made for redundancy payments. There will probably be media interest in large-scale and/or sensitive redundancies and management should be prepared to deal with this.

Managers must also ensure that the redundancy selection procedure has been applied fairly and is legally compliant – for example, it is not discriminatory. Selection for redundancy on the basis of length of service – sometimes called 'last in, first out', or LIFO – is the easiest and most obviously objective method of selection for redundancy. Those with the shortest length of service in the organisation will be selected first. Until recently this was the most commonly used criterion for redundancy, but its popularity is now declining as more employers become concerned that selection on length of service alone can have a detrimental effect on the firm's skill base. It is reasonable for employers to try to retain a workforce balance in terms of ability, so an individual's skill and knowledge are reasonable considerations, provided that they are assessed objectively and clearly defined from the outset of the selection process. The precise choice of factors and their relative weighting should be determined according to the current and future needs of the business.

All individuals affected by the redundancy process should be personally informed by interview, and managers should be appropriately trained and supported by HR specialists in handling this.

CLANSOFTWARE LTD

CASE STUDY 2.4

ClanSoftware Ltd is based in the west of Scotland and is part of a US-owned multinational. It specialises in the provision of information technology and software solutions for clients in the public and private sectors in the UK and Europe.

The company has grown rapidly in recent years and has earned the reputation of being able to provide for its clients bespoke total information solutions that have proved to be both competitive and reliable. To deal with the increased demand for its products, the company recently had to expand its sales force

very rapidly. Pressure on the sales director was such that she often cut corners in hiring the new staff, frequently relying on word of mouth and the industry grapevine to find 'good' people. However, some problems quickly emerged:

1 Successful sales staff have been 'poached' by other companies in the UK and Europe.

2 Less successful sales staff have not been hitting their sales targets. Because of other sales staff leaving, the company has been reluctant to

release these lower-performing employees and their managers are often unwilling to put pressure on them to improve their performance in case they leave too.

Sales staff are typically graduates with computing, finance or sales backgrounds. Their work is highly pressurised, because they have to deal not only with potential clients but also with software engineers who develop the solutions based on client specifications. Timescales for delivery are always tight. After-sales service is required, and this is also provided by the sales staff. Because of the pressures of the job, very attractive reward and bonus packages are available.

Question

You have been employed by the company as a consultant to address the resourcing problems with the sales staff. What would you propose?

CASE STUDY 2.2 ANSWER GUIDANCE

The case study suggests that the company:

- has not fully thought through what knowledge, skills and aptitudes (KSAs) it expects in its sales staff, or what it is able to offer new staff in terms of a total remuneration package (which includes financial as well as other rewards)
- may not be applying the most appropriate recruitment techniques to ensure that the right people are selected.

It would be necessary first to review the numbers of sales staff needed, given the business projections and sales targets of the company over, say, the next five years, and the typical sales figures expected of experienced sales staff. Some attention ought to be paid to the scalability of its sales targets – that is, are these expected to grow each year, or is there a 'steady state' position, or a rising trend, plateau and decline forecast? This should reveal the number of sales staff needed over the period. The figure will have to be compared with the numbers currently employed and an analysis undertaken of current staff turnover and staff performance indicators.

We should then turn to the role of the salesperson, the duties to be performed, the conditions under which the job is expected to be performed, and the KSAs needed. After that, the criteria for job success must be established and appropriate performance indicators developed. This job analysis should lead to the production of a job description and person specification.

We must then establish a systematic recruitment process that will be either the 'matching attributes' model, or the 'competency' model as defined earlier in this chapter.

Of course, the above procedure would be relevant for new staff we wished to employ. For the existing sales staff we should carry out other HR functions to help ensure that the high-performers stay and that the lower-performers are brought up to acceptable levels of performance. Both types of performance will be required here. Stabilising the existing sales workforce would be a first priority, because that would then give us an indication of the staff-resourcing issues that remain.

2.13 RESOURCING AND DIVERSITY

People are not alike: everyone is different. Diversity therefore consists of visible and non-visible factors, which include personal characteristics such as sex, race, age, background, culture, disability, personality and work style. Harnessing these differences will create a productive environment in which everybody feels valued, their talents are fully utilised and organisational goals are met (CIPD 2010b).

In many developed countries concerns about equal opportunities for women and for racial and ethnic minority groups started to find legal expression in the 1960s when governments passed laws that required employers not to discriminate on grounds of sex or race in employment matters, including pay. Other grounds such as disability or age or sexual orientation came to be included once a culture of acceptance of equal opportunities began to grow in society.

It became obvious that although a legal framework for equal opportunities was essential and achieved real progress in reducing discrimination, it had inevitable limitations in terms of producing equality of outcome.

Although the business case against discrimination was always a sound one, the original impetus for equal opportunities legislation was largely moral and social: to make a fairer and better world. These concerns are still with us, of course, and as the limitations of legislation became apparent there were calls for organisations to go beyond legislative minimum standards. Because the economy has become increasingly globalised over the past 25 years – workforces, customers and other stakeholders all becoming more diverse – organisations are now urged to positively adopt diversity in their HRM.

And it seems that no matter how big your organisation is, you really do have to take issues of diversity seriously.

In February 2007 Wal-Mart – the world's biggest retailer and owner of the Asda supermarket chain – faced the biggest sexual discrimination case in US history when an appeal court ruled that the firm had to face a class-action lawsuit involving around 1.5 million women, who claimed that the retailer discriminated against them in terms of pay and promotion.

2.13.1 THE DEFINITION OF DISCRIMINATION

Discrimination literally means distinguishing between people and therefore treating some differently from others. This is not always unlawful or bad management practice – for example, people are paid different wages depending on their status and skills. However, there are certain grounds on which an employer cannot lawfully discriminate against an employee. There are also other areas such as harassment and bullying of employees which might fall short of illegality but which are nonetheless both unethical and inefficient management.

If an employer treats an employee less favourably than another for an unlawful reason, the employee can take action against the employer. If an employer treats the employee unfairly for any other reason, this is not unlawful discrimination, just bad management.

2.13.2 TYPES OF DISCRIMINATION

Legislation protects employees from discrimination of different types.

Direct discrimination

Direct discrimination happens when an employer treats an employee less favourably because of, for example, their gender or race. (So it would be direct discrimination if an ordinary driving job was open only to male applicants.) In the UK there is legal protection on the basis of the 'protected characteristics' of age, disability, gender reassignment, marriage and civil partnership, pregnancy and maternity, race, religion or belief, sex, and sexual orientation.

Associative discrimination is an aspect of direct discrimination in which someone is discriminated against because they have an association with someone with a particular protected characteristic – for example, discriminating against someone because they are a carer for a disabled person.

Perceptive discrimination is another aspect of direct discrimination where the discrimination occurs because the discriminator thinks a person possesses a protected characteristic even if they do not. For example, if a manager discriminates against an employee because they think the person holds certain religious beliefs, this is perceptive discrimination even if in fact the person does not hold those beliefs.

Indirect discrimination

Indirect discrimination is when a condition that disadvantages one group of people more than another is applied to a job. For example, saying that applicants for a job must be clean-shaven puts members of some religious groups at a disadvantage. However, the law does allow employers to discriminate indirectly if they can show a good reason for retaining the condition. For example, the condition that applicants must be clean-shaven might be justified if the job involved handling food and it could be shown that having a beard or moustache was a genuine hygiene risk.

Harassment and victimisation

Harassment means offensive or intimidating behaviour – sexist language or racial abuse, for example – which aims to humiliate, undermine or injure its target.

Victimisation means persistently treating somebody less favourably than others through spite.

2.13.3 WHY BOTHER ABOUT DIVERSITY?

There are three reasons why managers should be concerned with issues of equality and diversity at work: the moral case, the legal case and the business case.

The moral case

Managers have a moral obligation to treat all employees fairly and equally as fellow human beings. Managers are in a position of some power over their staff and they should not abuse it by showing favouritism or prejudice. Most managers would subscribe to this, and no organisation would wish to acquire a reputation for being immoral or unethical towards its own employees.

Ensuring that all employees at work have equal rights is an important aspect of fair treatment at work. Equal opportunity will remain an important issue given the increasing diversity of the workforce in all developed economies (Van Wanrooy *et al* 2013, p116).

The legal case

Most countries have legal obligations not to discriminate on grounds of gender, race or religion. Other criteria are also often specified. For example, in the UK employees have legal protection against discrimination on the basis of age, disability, gender reassignment, marriage and civil partnership, pregnancy and maternity, race, religion or belief, sex, and sexual orientation. The Equality Act 2010 consolidated nine previously specific pieces of anti-discrimination legislation.

Additionally, there was also legal protection for workers to prevent them from being dismissed or treated less favourably than other workers because of working part-time or on a fixed-term contract.

This degree of protection for employees is fairly typical of most developed economies.

The business case

Any instance of discrimination means that the optimum use of the organisation's human resources has been impaired. Another consideration, noted above in connection with the moral case, is that quite apart from any legal sanction that might be applied, if a firm gets a reputation for discrimination, not only will that seriously affect the morale of its own employees, who will fear being discriminated against personally, but it will hurt its standing with customers and other stakeholders, including investors, and with potential recruits.

The limits of legislation

Although legislation is recognised as essential in achieving equality at work, it has been found to be not sufficient and its limitations have become increasingly evident.

2.13.4 MANAGING DIVERSITY

Employers should follow a three-stage process to provide equality of opportunity:

- Formulate an explicit equal opportunities policy.
- Implement the policy.
- Monitor the policy to ensure its effectiveness in practice.

In the UK the Equality and Human Rights Commission publishes advice for employers on how to comply with their legal responsibilities.

The 2011 WERS survey found that 77% of all UK workplaces (and 99% of public sector workplaces) had a written, formal equal opportunities policy or a policy on managing diversity, and 92% of UK employees in establishments were covered by such a policy – but 72% of workplaces neither negotiated, consulted nor informed employee representatives over equal opportunities. Most (75%) workplaces' written equal opportunities policies explicitly mentioned gender, ethnic group, disability, religion or belief, age, or sexual orientation.

HRM IN ACTION: HOW CHANNEL 4 TRANSLATED ITS ON-SCREEN DIVERSITY INTO WORKPLACE INCLUSION

CASE STUDY 2.5

It's the television channel that brought us the first lesbian kiss with *Brookside*; the first black sitcom, *Desmond's*; and round-the-clock coverage of the 2012 Paralympics – so you're probably thinking Channel 4 has got its diversity agenda sorted.

But amid increasing pressure to improve diversity across the UK media, Adam Lancaster, learning programme specialist at Channel 4, had to ask: are the channel's successes on-screen reflected off-screen, through its employees? 'It's easy to think we're really good at this because we are Channel 4 – but we need to be a lot better than we are,' says Lancaster. Last year, the broadcaster launched its 360° Diversity Charter, setting itself the target that, by 2020, the workforce would be reflective of the UK population when it comes to gender; black, Asian and minority ethnic; sexual orientation; and disability.

To communicate its commitment to improving diversity on- and off-screen, a list of 30 planned activities were published publicly, with targets ranging from 'ensure 15 per cent of the production team or crew are from an ethnic minority or have a disability', to 'ensure a female holds an executive role on every entertainment programme'. Channel 4 also launched 'Born Different', an e-learning project designed to bring to life the scale of the challenge to its 800 in-house staff.

'The hardest sell wasn't so much "why are we doing this?" People understand the benefits and importance of diversity,' says Lancaster. 'It was more a question of "aren't we already really good at this?"'

He admits the organisation had to be candid with its staff when communicating its current position on diversity. With a ratio of 53 women to 47 men, Channel 4 was overrepresented by female employees. And while 6% of the UK population class themselves as LGBT, just 2% of the channel's staff reportedly fell into this category.

The Born Different online training modules were created with the help of learning consultancy Acteon, and combine a range of text, graphics, video and audio to provide interactive fast-paced scenarios, scrolling stories, practice role-play sessions, 'talking head' accounts, quizzes and a bank of further reading and resources. L&D specialists partnered with the wider HR team, and a further 20 to 30 members of Channel 4 staff, to hone the messaging and create a bespoke learning campaign designed not only to communicate the broadcaster's aims, but also to provoke a reaction.

'It had to be an authentic and realistic portrayal of what colleagues would see in real life,' says Lancaster. 'E-learning can sometimes be too passive if you don't challenge people enough.' But there is a fine line between creating a programme that genuinely feels 'Channel 4-y' and not scaring off new recruits, or getting the organisation into legal hot water, he adds. 'At Channel 4, we make an effort not to be too politically correct. You can get away with saying stuff here that you wouldn't in other organisations, but that isn't an excuse to cross that line.'

While the e-learning programme wasn't compulsory (rather 'heavily recommended'), Lancaster says staff had to feel compelled to complete it, and personally involved in the campaign for it to have the intended effect. 'It was important that it wasn't just a bunch of HR bods sat around a table telling people how to be more diverse. So the message became: how can you have an impact on diversity within your role, and within the building, and what does that actually mean to you?'

A process of self-declaration helped to gather the relevant data needed to base the campaign on. 'Often, people don't bother to fill in those forms you get when you start a new job because they don't realise the positive impact of self-declaring,' Lancaster says. Every new starter at Channel 4 is now asked to divulge a personal profile including gender, sexual orientation, religion, ethnicity and disability, while current staff are encouraged to regularly check and update their personal information.

'Diversity is a massive topic, but understanding what is going on internally, and where the Channel 4 population is really at, allowed us to understand where we should be spending our time and focus,' says Lancaster. This year, the organisation will be focusing its efforts on increasing its representation of disabled employees, from 1.9% of the workforce to 6% by 2020.

Further face-to-face diversity and inclusion training for managers, recruitment workshops and diversity breakfast sessions were created off the back of the Born Different programme, helping to keep the issues relevant and campaign momentum going. Two staff-initiated employee networks – one for LGBT colleagues and another for women – are now helping keep the L&D team on its toes with their suggestions for achieving the channel's ambitious targets.

By tracking the training completion rates, and the level of detail updated in the employee information profiles as a result, the HR team was able to determine whether the launch had resonated with the whole of the workforce. As Lancaster concludes: 'We might have come up with 30 aims, but how we execute those is down to everybody across the business.'

Source: Grace Lewis, *People Management*, 30 March 2016.

KEY ISSUES IN RESOURCING

In this chapter we have been concerned with 'employee flow' through the organisation; in particular, with how the organisation obtains the human resources it needs and how it manages the exit of employees. We first discussed some basic underlying principles involved in recruitment and selection, and two important findings soon emerged. First, recruitment and selection should be seen as stages in a wider process of managing the human resource flow. This is because decisions made at the recruitment or selection stages will inevitably impact on later activities, such as need for training and level of job performance. Second, organisations should recruit using a model based on initially identifying the criteria for job success and then systematically seeking applicants with the necessary qualities to achieve that success. We noted that in the twenty-first century capability and attitude were often more important than the possession of particular knowledge or skills at the time of recruitment. A competency framework is often useful in recruitment and selection. Some of the most commonly used selection techniques were examined. We introduced the concept of talent management, which in a sense bridges recruitment and selection and employee development.

The 'war for talent' – the increasingly competitive market for key employees – has become an important aspect of employee resourcing. Many organisations now employ 'talent management' strategies, at least for their core employees, which combine the traditional responsibilities of recruitment and selection with development activities and succession planning.

All employees will eventually leave the organisation, and this process also has to be managed. After some general considerations of the question of dismissal we examined some of the issues surrounding redundancy and how that can be managed.

Legal compliance with discrimination legislation is obviously obligatory and is a key responsibility of the HRM function, which should take a corporate lead on the issue. But day-to-day compliance demands that line managers and supervisors are aware of company policies and procedures and must be trained accordingly.

Compliance is necessary but is not enough. You are not going to win the war for talent if potential key employees shun you because they believe that they will be discriminated against in any way. Organisations that want to succeed must ruthlessly eliminate any discrimination in the workplace and build a genuine culture of valuing diversity.

Useful websites

CIPD: **cipd.co.uk**

British Psychological Society: **www.bps.org.uk**

Acas: **www.acas.org.uk**

EXPLORE FURTHER

Armstrong, M. (2014) *Armstrong's Handbook of Human Resource Management Practice*. 13th edition. London: Kogan Page.

● Chapters 16–20, 'People resourcing' – useful outlines of strategic resourcing, human resource planning, recruitment and selection, employer brand and talent management.
● Chapter 50, 'Selection interviewing skills'.

Boxall, P., Purcell, J. and Wright, P. (eds) (2007) *The Oxford Handbook of Human Resource Management*. Oxford: Oxford University Press.

● Chapter 14, M. Orlitzky, 'Recruitment strategy'.
● Chapter 15, N. Schmitt and B. Kim, 'Selection decision-making'.

Storey, J. (ed.) (2007) *Human Resource Management: A critical text*. 3rd edition. London: Thomson Learning.

● Chapter 6, P. Iles, 'Employee resourcing and talent management'.

CHAPTER 3

Learning and development

INTRODUCTION

HRM places much greater emphasis on development than did earlier people management paradigms, and, at least in principle, extends this to all core employees regardless of hierarchical position.

The term 'learning and development' is often the preferred description for this HR function, although 'employee development' and 'human resource development' are also often used. Recently, 'talent development' has become a common term among HR professionals to describe the 'high end' of learning and development.

Learning and development interventions can span external education and in-house activities, both formal and informal. There has been a cultural change in most developed economies over the past few decades in that the intention in development now is often to facilitate learning and personal development rather than to impose formal training on individuals.

There is also greater emphasis on informal learning at all levels, including self-development, which formerly might have been taking place in many instances but was virtually never recognised. There are limits to this, of course, and it would be wrong to suppose that conventional, structured training has no place in the modern workplace.

Two other fashionable development initiatives are coaching, which is a non-directive form of development aimed at improving workplace performance, and mentoring, which aims to transmit knowledge, skills and experience in a broader sense than simply improving job performance.

Traditionally, and for very obvious reasons, development activities are among the most vulnerable to cutbacks when organisations need to reduce their costs.

LEARNING OUTCOMES

On completion of this chapter you should:

- understand the terms used to describe the various learning and development interventions, both formal and informal
- understand the general principles of learning used in in this field
- understand the concepts of single- and double-loop learning
- have an appreciation of the main learning and development methods used in organisations
- appreciate the concept of the 'learning organisation'
- understand the idea of talent development.

Traditionally, learning at work was divided into more-or-less mutually exclusive domains for (1) managers (and other professionals) who might receive 'development', and (2) non-managers, who were 'trained'. Traditionally in the UK firms did minimal training and development anyway, fearing that the money spent would be wasted because the employees would undoubtedly be poached by competitors. Although there were some striking exceptions, until the late 1980s most UK firms did little or no management development at all, and the self-development that was in many cases taking place was seldom recognised.

The nature and types of the most common learning interventions are shown in Table 3.1.

Table 3.1 Nature and types of learning interventions

Nature	Type	
	Formal	*Informal*
Off-the-job	Externally provided accredited education – for example, MBAs, NVQs, professional qualifications	Voluntary, accredited education
	Externally provided training courses	Voluntarily attended training courses (for example foreign language classes)
On-the-job	Practical supervised work periods on apprenticeship schemes Placements in trainee management programmes	Learning partnerships Coaching Mentoring Peer relationships Action learning Self-development Self-development groups Learning logs

We should bear in mind that whatever learning intervention is contemplated, the question of evaluation is crucial; this is discussed later in this chapter.

3.1 DEFINITIONS

Training is defined as a set of planned activities on the part of an organisation to increase job knowledge and skills, or to modify attitudes and social behaviour, to achieve specific ends which are related to a particular job or role.

Learning is a relatively permanent change in knowledge, skills, attitudes or behaviour that comes through experience. We may say that learning happens inside the person, whereas training is something that is given to a person in the sense that it is a planned experience that is expected to lead to learning.

Development describes the continuing improvement of an individual's effectiveness in terms of their role or profession beyond the immediate task or job.

Education means the process of personal growth in abilities and attitudes which might take place independently of its application to work, and is therefore a broader experience than training or work-related learning and development.

3.2 A BRIEF OVERVIEW OF LEARNING PRINCIPLES

Detailed discussion of the psychological mechanisms underpinning learning theory is outside the scope of the present text. The interested reader is referred to the relevant chapters of Landy and Conte (2007) for further reading.

However, on the basis of the research that has been conducted on the various theories of learning, certain rules or guidelines have emerged regarding efficient learning which are useful to HRM. These include:

- the principle of 'distributed practice' – that is, breaking the learning experience up into manageable chunks for the learner
- praising the learner for correct responses, so reinforcing the learning
- training individuals to perform entire task units as a whole
- giving results of the training performance to the learners
- providing opportunities for practising the skills developed during training.

3.3 LEVELS OF LEARNING

There seem to be two levels of learning that occur in the modern organisation.

The first relates to obtaining knowledge in order to solve specific problems based on existing premises. The second is concerned with establishing new paradigms, mental models or perspectives. These two levels of learning have been termed 'single-loop' and 'double-loop' learning respectively (Argyris and Schön 1978, after Ashby 1940). The metaphor is drawn from the field of cybernetics. Single-loop learning may be compared with the action of a thermostat which is used to control temperature (for example of a refrigerator), where the thermostat scans and monitors the environment (the temperature inside the refrigerator), compares the information it obtains with operating norms (the range of acceptable temperatures inside the refrigerator), and initiates any appropriate action (if the temperature is too high, the thermostat switches on the refrigeration unit to reduce the internal temperature until it is within the acceptable range). The thermostat then proceeds to scan the environment again, setting up a continuous loop of activity. In double-loop learning, a 'single loop' operates as before, but here in addition the 'operating norms' themselves may be questioned (is refrigeration the best way to preserve fresh food in the short term for domestic use?) and if necessary altered, thus creating a 'double loop'.

Firms should be constantly seeking to improve their product offerings, whether these are physical goods or intangible services. Quality circles and autonomous work teams encourage workers to seek improvements continually in production and design as they deal with the everyday problems of production and delivery. This should encourage continuous learning and result in steady, incremental improvements which we can think of as the outcomes of single-loop learning – basically, learning how to do the same things better and better. Every so often, however, a worker, or a team of workers collectively, might have a sudden flash of insight which leads not to an incremental refinement but to a radical rethinking of a process or feature of the product. This discontinuous change would be an example of 'double-loop' learning. For example, if a manufacturer, Acme Mousetraps, develops a new, more efficient way of producing its traditional mousetraps, this can be explained as a collective example of single-loop learning. However, if the development team produce a new way of controlling or removing unwanted small mammals which does not require the use of traps at all, this might be an example of double-loop learning.

Radical innovation relies on double-loop learning, and in the 'knowledge economy' one of the key goals of the learning and development function is to help build a culture in which double-loop learning can flourish.

3.4 KOLB'S LEARNING CYCLE

Kolb and his colleagues (1971) identified a four-stage learning cycle, which has been hugely influential in people development in HRM, especially in management development. The four stages are:

1   concrete experience

2   observations and reflection

3   formation of abstract concepts and generalisations

4   testing the implications of the concepts in new situations.

The learning experience runs in sequence from 1 through to 4 (see Figure 3.1):

1   The individual takes note of some concrete experience. This could be part of a planned learning intervention, such as a skills demonstration, or it might be accidental – they may suddenly realise that something has occurred.

2   The individual thinks about, or reflects upon, the experience and its significance.

3   The individual constructs some mental model to explain what happened and why. This will allow the individual to generalise about where and how the experience may recur.

4   The explanation is tested out in some new situation.

Figure 3.1 The Kolb learning cycle

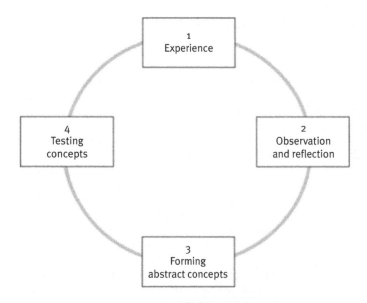

Of course, Kolb's work has not been without its critics. For instance, Holman *et al* (1997), Vince (1998) and Reynolds (1999) have argued that the emphasis on experiential learning is at the expense of psychodynamic, social and institutional aspects of learning. It remains, however, one of the most influential models of learning.

3.4.1 LEARNING STYLES

The effectiveness of learning will vary from stage to stage of Kolb's cycle among different people. Some will learn most effectively at the first stage; others at the second, third or fourth. This has led to the concept of *learning styles*. Honey and Mumford (1989) identified a set of four learning styles, each of which suggested a preference for a particular stage of the Kolb cycle. The cycle should always be completed by the learner but the learning style will dictate which part of the cycle is most important for a particular person. These learning styles are:

- 'Activists' tend to learn best from the experience stage: they prefer to take action – for example hands-on learning or role-playing.
- 'Reflectors' tend to learn most from the second stage, observation and reflection.
- For 'theorists', learning is most effective at the third, abstract conceptualisation stage.
- 'Pragmatists' learn best from trying out the new skill or knowledge in actual work situations, so they benefit most from the fourth stage of the Kolb cycle.

The theory of learning styles implies that, ideally, a trainer might design each learning intervention according to the learning style of the individual learner. Clearly, there are limits to this in practice, but learners can be encouraged to identify their learning style and thus increase awareness of the strengths and weaknesses in their own learning processes. Activists, for example, can be alerted to the fact that they may tend to skip abstract conceptualisation and might neglect full testing of their new skills or knowledge in the workplace. Theorists can be reminded to get 'hands on' in the learning intervention, and so on. Honey and Mumford have produced a questionnaire which helps learners to identify their own particular learning style.

The theory of learning styles is not unproblematic: Coffield *et al* (2004) identified 71 different models of learning styles, 13 of which were judged to be influential. So caution is indicated, but the Honey and Mumford set of learning styles, as linked to the Kolb learning cycle, is certainly widely used and frequently cited in the learning and development literature.

3.5 TRANSFER OF LEARNING

From the organisation's perspective, by far the most important issue is that of transfer of learning – that is, whether the knowledge, skills, attitudes or behaviours learned will be available and used 'back on the job'. This is a critical issue in the evaluation of the effectiveness and utility of a learning programme, and for formal learning interventions such as conventional skills training where the intention is to impart specific knowledge or skills, or to develop certain attitudes, there can be little value from the organisation's point of view in learning which does not carry over to the job situation.

Some general rules have been established to increase the probability of transfer of learning:

- Maximise the similarity between the learning situation and the job situation.
- Provide as much experience as possible with the task being taught.
- Provide for a variety of examples when teaching concepts or skills.
- Label or identify important features of a task.
- Make sure the general principles are understood.
- Make sure that the learned behaviours and ideas are rewarded in the job situation.
- Design the learning content so that the learners can see its applicability.

3.6 EXPLICIT AND TACIT KNOWLEDGE

In almost all occupations, there are skills that will be picked up in the course of performing the job which cannot be acquired through training, only through experience. When training new staff, it is important to distinguish what can be trained – such as the use of equipment and a fixed knowledge base – from what cannot. For example, medical students can be trained in how to take a patient's blood pressure correctly and effectively, but a good 'bedside manner' can only come with experience and observing skilled doctors dealing with their patients. To use the current jargon, we can train people by imparting 'explicit knowledge' but we cannot easily train people in 'tacit knowledge'. We discuss this later in this chapter in a section on knowledge management.

3.7 SOME COMMON LEARNING AND DEVELOPMENT METHODS

Action learning was originally introduced for management development but is now widely used at all organisational levels. Groups of people work together to find practical solutions to real work problems. Instructors act as facilitators, encouraging participants to learn from each other and reflect on the experience.

Blended learning is a combination of multiple approaches to learning. Typically, a combination of technology-based materials and face-to-face sessions are used together to deliver instruction.

Case studies are detailed examinations of real-life situations written up and presented for educational purposes. Students typically work in groups to analyse each case and then to answer set tasks. They are very commonly used in management development.

Coaching and mentoring. Coaching is a non-directive form of development which focuses on improving performance and developing individuals' skills and giving feedback on a person's performance. Coaching should be delivered by trained personnel, who usually are drawn from outside the organisation. Mentoring is similar to coaching but the mentor is usually an experienced senior member of staff, though not the person's line manager. The emphasis in mentoring is less focused on the person's current job or role than in coaching, but more on their future development and career within the organisation. In HRM, coaching and mentoring are seen as key line manager skills.

Continuing professional development (CPD) is a continuous process of personal growth by which individuals improve their capability at work and realise their full potential. It is achieved by developing a range of knowledge, skills and experience which goes beyond initial training or qualification, and which maintains and develops professional competence. Many professional bodies such as the CIPD now insist on CPD as a condition of continued membership.

'*Corporate universities*' have been established by some large companies for the delivery of management education. They are more than just in-company training departments and have been defined (Meister 1998, p38) as a:

> centralized strategic umbrella for the education and development of employees ... [that] is the chief vehicle for disseminating an organisation's culture and fostering the development of not only job skills but also such core workplace skills as learning-to-learn, leadership, creative thinking and problem-solving.

E-learning is learning that is delivered, enabled or mediated using electronic technology for the explicit purpose of learning and development in organisations.

Instruction may be defined as the use of a highly structured teaching method to teach specific skills. Usually its format corresponds to a physical demonstration followed by supervised practice of the skills concerned.

Joint development activities are collaborations between employing organisations and academic institutions. They can include: project work by which managers deal with work problems while receiving consultation/tutoring from the institution; consortia of companies running programmes with schools (for example 'company MBAs'); and reciprocal secondments between institutions and industry.

Lecturing is giving a structured talk, usually longer and more formal than a presentation, normally accompanied by visual aids and handouts of key points. A lecture may be combined with audience participation in a discussion, a question-and-answer session and/or group exercises/activities.

Outdoor training comprises team exercises involving physical and mental tasks in challenging external environments. They are very popular in corporate team-building, believed by advocates to teach leadership and team- and self-development skills in addition to teamworking.

Role-playing is the enactment of roles in a structured context. This method is very useful for practising interpersonal skills.

Self-development is concerned with helping people to understand their own personal learning and development processes, and by doing so to assume greater control of, and responsibility for, their own development. There is an emphasis on longer-term development, as distinct from specific study or learning, and a stress on setting one's own goals and methods of achieving them. This technique can be applied to groups in which participants are encouraged to support each other. Self-development is frequently, but not exclusively, applied to managers and professionals.

Simulations/business games are group exercises or case studies, usually now computerised, in which the participants are asked to make certain choices and the computerised system gives them the 'result' of their decisions.

3.8 DEVELOPING PEOPLE IN PRACTICE

The CIPD 2015 *Learning and Development Survey* (CIPD 2015c) reported that the most commonly used learning and development practices in the UK were (1) on-the–job training (47% of responding organisations), (2) in-house development programmes (46%) and (3) coaching by line managers or peers (32%).

Other practices identified were e-learning courses; external conferences, workshops and events; off-the-job instructor-led training; blended learning; formal education courses; and coaching by external practitioners.

Judgements on the effectiveness of these practices did not always correspond with their popularity, however, as shown in Table 3.2.

Table 3.2 Reported frequency and effectiveness of learning and development practices

Learning and development practice	Most commonly used (% of respondents)	Most effective (% of respondents)
On-the-job training	48%	47%
In-house development programmes	46%	34%
Coaching by line managers or peers	32%	40%
E-learning courses	29%	12%
External conferences, workshops and events	27%	15%
Off-the-job instructor-led training	27%	20%
Blended learning	19%	19%
Formal education courses	17%	12%
Coaching by external practitioners	12%	16%

Source: CIPD (2015c)

The survey found that three-quarters of responding organisations used learning technologies, defined as the broad range of communication and information technologies (CIT) such as online or mobile learning. Their use in learning and development was expected to increase in the future, but face-to-face delivery methods remained dominant and many learning and development professionals lacked confidence in their own ability to obtain the full benefits of learning technologies.

Eighty per cent of responding organisations reported that they would be carrying out leadership development in the following 12 months, principally: equipping line managers to improve performance; changing the organisational culture; and encouraging strategic thinking.

?   REFLECTIVE ACTIVITY 3.1

Referring to Table 3.2, which learning and development methods are used in your organisation? Which is the most commonly used? How effective would you say the interventions are? What needs to be improved?

The CIPD survey defined talent management as:

> the systematic attraction, identification, development, engagement, retention and deployment of those individuals who are of particular value to an organisation, either in view of their high potential for the future or because they are fulfilling a business/operation-critical role (CIPD 2015c).

    HRM IN ACTION: TARMAC

CASE STUDY 3.1

Why Tarmac is ditching its traditional image and embracing fresh talent

'We have some women – particularly in operational roles – who are highly adaptable and flex their behaviours and language to fit into a male-dominated environment. But we don't want the women in our company to behave like men – what's the point?'

Serge Colin, who became group HR director at Tarmac – a building materials firm employing 7,000 workers in more than 300 sites across the UK – in 2013, is on a mission to shake off the company's conventional image and appeal to the talent of the future. Diving through reams of notes, he's explaining the four challenges faced by his female employees – as identified by the 10% of Tarmac's women who were recently interviewed for a qualitative report.

Needing to be 'one of the lads' (as the women put it) is the final one on his list, which also includes persistent perceptions of a 'men's club', the need to compromise on work–life balance to reach the top and expecting more support from managers.

Colin is keen to make Tarmac a more attractive proposition for a young, diverse pool of talent. 'We know we have an ageing population and we are a traditional business, so preparing for the future is a key challenge,' he says. Its youth programme, launched in 2013, sees nearly 100 graduates and apprentices hired into the company every year. 'But the challenge goes beyond recruiting them; we have to figure out how to retain and motivate this "digitalised" generation within a business that is seen as traditional.'

A core part of Tarmac's HR strategy has been to reinvent its employer brand, which is now represented by the strapline 'make your mark'. 'We need to create this emotional connection with the younger generation, which we're doing by showcasing stories of people who joined us as graduates or apprentices and have developed their long-term careers with us,' says Colin. Tarmac is also working closely with several schools to shed light on what a career with them could look like – especially for girls.

But attracting the new 'digitalised' generation isn't without its challenges. 'We have to adapt our ways of working and our work environment. This is hard work,' says Colin. 'But it's an essential part of our future resourcing strategy.'

Colin and his 60-strong HR team identify gaps in the organisation's skills through an annual capability planning process, which compares its current skillset against its long-term objectives. The secret to its success – as with so many HR projects – is engagement with line managers. 'Fundamentally, it's not an HR process – it's a business process,' says Colin. 'It happens in every business unit and every function.' Talent mapping and succession strategies are also taken into account, and the overall plan's success is measured through key performance indicators (KPIs).

In fact, measurement is a passion for Colin, who started his 28-year HR career at a time when the profession was just starting to shift from the procedural to the strategic. 'Anything we do in HR must be measured. If we cannot measure – forget it. We're wasting our time,' he says. 'If you want the HR function to be credible, like finance, you need to drive it though the KPIs.'

When it comes to learning, Tarmac has partnered with management schools at several universities to develop its bespoke leadership academies for senior leaders, middle managers and front-line managers. 'It's our ambition to give our managers the competencies they need to lead and develop their people in a business where line managers were traditionally technical experts,' says Colin. There's also significant investment in line managers' coaching skills, to support new talent and the embedding of the 70:20:10 learning principle. 'They need to understand that it's okay for staff to be spending time on the Discovery Zone, our online learning platform, within their working hours – that learning is a part of work, not separate to it,' he adds.

And upskilling the HR team itself – particularly in terms of its organisation development expertise and coaching skills – will be key to Tarmac's long-term future, says Colin, who is working with the CIPD to design an internal HR excellence academy. 'We need to stop being traditional in the way we deal with the HR role. We should be transformational in everything we do – everything should be embedded in the future, not only in the now.'

Source: *Personnel Management*, 24 May 2016.

3.9 THE PROCESS OF FORMAL LEARNING INTERVENTIONS

By 'formal' we mean a learning intervention that is wholly or mainly planned and structured. Of course, such an intervention may include areas in which informal learning is to be encouraged – for example managers may be encouraged to keep learning logs and CPD plans within a structured management development programme – but the overall intervention will be organised from the start with clearly identified learning objectives in terms of the knowledge, skills, attitudes or behaviours to be attained as a result of the intervention.

To assess the impact of a learning intervention, we usually need to know something about the status of the learners' relevant knowledge, skills and abilities (KSAs) before development takes place, so we should obtain baseline pre-intervention information. Similarly, after the intervention has taken place we need some post-intervention information. Finally, since the purpose of the intervention is to improve job performance, we should also seek information about how the learning and development has transferred to on-the-job behaviour.

There is thus a four-stage process for any formal learning intervention:

1   Identify the development need.

2   Design the development activity.

3   Undertake the development activity.

4   Evaluate the development intervention.

This process is sometimes termed the training cycle.

The stages in the process are described in more detail below.

3.9.1 NEEDS ANALYSIS

We need to know the requirements of a job or role before we can know what constitutes good performance in doing it. In learning and development a particular form of job analysis is used which, by convention, used to be termed *training needs analysis*. In the light of the changes in people development already referred to in this chapter, in this text we will use the terms 'needs analysis' (NA) or 'learning needs analysis' (LNA) to describe this activity.

The needs analysis provides a set of learning objectives for the development programme. These objectives might include adding *knowledge*, developing specific *skills* or helping to form specific *abilities* (KSAs). 'Knowledge' is the information needed to perform the work, 'skills' are attributes which are required, and 'ability' refers to the physical, emotional, intellectual and psychological aptitudes necessary to perform the work.

The objectives have a double role. First, they guide us towards what learning principles and training methods should be used. Second, they provide a means for assessing whether the learning intervention has been successful.

The impetus for training is usually an identification of a need for improvement.

A job, task or occupational needs analysis is an examination of the actual duties and responsibilities that compose the job/task/occupation concerned. The question asked is, 'What KSAs are required for successful performance of the duties?' In practice, a needs analysis consists of a combination of activities. Often there is a job description based on some earlier and perhaps less systematic job analysis. After reading this and any other relevant documentation relating to the job, the analyst will discuss the job with a supervisor or manager responsible for the staff concerned. This will allow the analyst to identify critical terminology, qualify important job dimensions, develop questions for interview and identify things to look for when observing the job. The analyst will typically observe several employees undertaking the task or job. Finally, the analyst may arrange interviews with other job-holders and/or distribute questionnaires for them to complete.

3.9.2 WHO NEEDS LEARNING INTERVENTIONS?

There are primarily two possible groups:

- present job-holders who are performing below standard
- new appointees who are about to take up the job or role.

For the first group the most obvious method for identifying weaknesses in job performance is via job appraisal or performance management.

Other groups to be considered for learning interventions include apprentices, graduate trainees and those on similar long-term structured education/development programmes (including management development schemes). In some cases, employees returning from employment breaks because of, for example, maternity leave, long-term absence, expatriate assignments, and so on, should also be considered.

? REFLECTIVE ACTIVITY 3.2

Consider this: training current staff and training new staff are likely to be very different processes. Why is that?

REFLECTIVE ACTIVITY 3.2 ANSWER GUIDANCE

Training new starters usually provides opportunities for new learning, but training experienced workers often involves eliminating old habits. So in addition to learning, the experienced incumbent often has to unlearn old methods or attitudes.

3.9.3 THE IMPORTANCE OF LEARNING OBJECTIVES

On the basis of the needs analysis it should be possible to specify some objectives or goals for the training programme: what levels of KSAs would you like the trainees to have after the training intervention that they did not have before? Learning objectives for job incumbents are usually tailored to identified, specific deficiencies in the employee's performance and they are often negotiated with the individual employee as a result of a performance appraisal. Learning objectives have several important uses. They represent information for both the learner and the facilitator about what is to be learned; they help to motivate the learner; and they allow evaluation of whether the learning intervention has been completed satisfactorily.

3.9.4 EVALUATING THE LEARNING INTERVENTION

Learning and development is ultimately about adding value to the organisation's human resources, or, in other words, increasing its human capital. Assessing whether this has been achieved requires the systematic evaluation of learning and development interventions.

The best-known model for evaluating a learning intervention is that developed by Kirkpatrick (1967). This operates at four levels: trainee reactions, learning reactions, behavioural change and results.

Trainee reactions correspond to participants' evaluations of the usefulness of the learning intervention. It will be familiar to many readers from the ubiquitous 'happy sheet' or questionnaire doled out after company training events. The questionnaire typically asks the participant to rate their overall impression of the event, their perceptions of the trainer, and the extent to which the course and the trainee's own objectives have been met. Such an exercise clearly tells us nothing about how much has been learned, or whether what has been learned will be translated into better job performance, but it is not without some usefulness and is inexpensive and easy to obtain.

Learning reactions represents a level of evaluation that seeks to assess how much knowledge has been imparted to the trainee as a result of the intervention. This might be assessed by a written test, and again this can be inexpensive and relatively quick and easy to obtain.

Behavioural change is the third level of evaluation in Kirkpatrick's model. Specifically, the question is whether the training or learning intervention has resulted in observable changes in the trainee's behaviour on the job. Such assessment cannot be quick, cheap or easy, although an effective performance management system should obtain the information required. Of course, changed behaviour will not always equate with improved job performance.

Results represent the final level of evaluation. Has there been a measurable improvement in the trainee's job performance? This is the ultimate measure of the effectiveness of the learning intervention but it is often difficult to obtain, especially when the intervention has been in complex areas such as managerial or professional effectiveness. Even in more straightforward cases, such as physical skills training, it is often difficult to isolate the effects of the intervention from those of other extraneous factors.

?   REFLECTIVE ACTIVITY 3.3

Reflect on a recent learning and development intervention which you have experienced. Try to evaluate it according to Kirkpatrick's model.

3.10 INFORMAL LEARNING

So far we have discussed formal, structured learning interventions where the objective is to facilitate the acquisition of specific knowledge or skills, or the particular modification of abilities. Informal or experiential learning is quite different in nature, being unplanned and indeed unplannable in detail. It is the learning that the individual acquires from the experiences of doing the job, from working in the organisation and from just thinking and reflecting on the work done. Informal learning may sound somewhat airy-fairy, but a US Department of Labor (1993) report found that people learned 70% of what they know about their jobs informally through processes which were not structured or sponsored by their employing organisation.

To be effective, informal learning requires a level of employee motivation, confidence and capability. Employers who wish to encourage informal learning strive to create a climate which is supportive and to impart basic learning skills ('learning how to learn') to their people.

3.11 ORGANISATIONAL LEARNING AND KNOWLEDGE MANAGEMENT

The manufacturing-based industrial society of the post-war period has been evolving towards a more service-based society and, more recently, an 'information society'. The leading management thinkers of the late 1990s agreed that the manufacturing, service and information sectors would be based on knowledge in the future and that business organisations will evolve into knowledge-creators in many ways. Peter Drucker was one of the earliest writers to foresee this transformation, and he is credited with inventing the terms 'knowledge work' and 'knowledge worker' in the early 1960s. We are entering the 'knowledge society' in which the basic economic resource is no longer capital, or natural resources, or labour, but is knowledge, and in which knowledge workers will play a central role (Drucker 1993). The organisation has to be prepared to abandon knowledge that has become obsolete and learn to create new things through (1) continuous improvement of every activity; (2) the development of new applications from its own successes; and (3) continuous innovation as an organised process. Drucker (1993, p24) recognised the importance of tacit knowledge when he argued that a skill (*technē* in ancient Greek) could not be explained in words but could only be demonstrated through apprenticeship and experience.

3.11.1 ORGANISATIONAL LEARNING

The concept of the 'learning organisation' was defined by Pedler, Burgoyne and Boydell (1991) as: 'An organisation, which facilitates the learning of all of its members and continuously transforms itself.'

This leads to a continuous process of organisational transformation, the end-points of which cannot be planned with any certainty. The cumulative learning of individuals leads, over time, to fundamental changes in assumptions, goals, norms and operating procedures, not simply as a reaction to external pressures but based on the organic growth in knowledge of the people who compose the organisation.

Senge (1990) proposed the 'learning organisation' to overcome 'organisational learning disabilities'. To build a learning organisation managers had to (1) adopt 'systems thinking'; (2) encourage 'personal mastery' of their own lives; (3) bring to the surface mental models and challenge them; (4) build a 'shared vision'; and (5) facilitate 'team learning'. Systems thinking was the key integrating 'discipline' of the five.

Nonaka and Takeuchi (1995, p45) argued that Western organisational learning theories still used the metaphor of individual learning and failed to deal adequately with the idea of knowledge creation. They also considered that rather than relying on 'artificial' interventions such as organisational development programmes to implement double-loop learning, it should be a continuous activity of the organisation – not a special and difficult task that requires outside intervention.

In their theory of knowledge Nonaka and Takeuchi adopt the traditional definition of knowledge as 'justified true belief', but they add that whereas traditional Western epistemology has focused on 'truthfulness' as the essential attribute of knowledge and emphasises the absolute, static and non-human form of knowledge, they consider knowledge 'a dynamic human process of justifying personal belief towards the "truth"' (Nonaka and Takeuchi 1995, p58).

Most writers on knowledge management draw on Polanyi's (1966) distinction between tacit knowledge and explicit knowledge. Tacit knowledge is personal and context-specific and therefore hard to formalise and communicate. Explicit or 'codified' knowledge refers to knowledge that can be transmitted in formal, systematic language. Polanyi contends that human beings acquire knowledge by actively creating and organising their own experiences, and that knowledge that can be expressed in words and numbers thus represents only the tip of the iceberg of the entire body of knowledge: 'We can know more than we can tell,' as Polanyi famously put it (1966, p4). In traditional epistemology, knowledge derives from the separation of the subject and the object of perception: human beings as the subject of perception acquire knowledge by analysing external objects. In contrast, Polanyi contends that human beings create knowledge by involving themselves with objects – that through self-involvement and commitment, or what Polanyi called 'indwelling', scientific objectivity is not the sole source of knowledge, and much of our knowledge is the fruit of our own purposeful endeavours in dealing with the world.

Such arguments may not convince everybody, but it is certainly the case that the ideas of knowledge management have had an enormous influence on management thinking.

3.11.2 KNOWLEDGE CONVERSION: INTERACTIONS BETWEEN TACIT AND EXPLICIT KNOWLEDGE

Nonaka and Takeuchi assume that human knowledge is created and expanded through social interaction between tacit knowledge and explicit knowledge, a process they call 'knowledge conversion' (1995, p59). They postulated four modes of knowledge conversion as these two types of knowledge are combined, which they termed respectively 'socialisation', 'externalisation', 'combination' and 'internalisation'.

Socialisation: from tacit knowledge to tacit knowledge

Socialisation is a process of sharing experiences and thereby creating tacit knowledge such as shared mental models and technical skills. An individual can acquire tacit knowledge directly from others without using language. Apprentices learn their trades from their masters, and on-the-job training uses much the same principle in business and management. Experience is thus the key to acquiring tacit knowledge.

Externalisation: from tacit knowledge to explicit knowledge

Externalisation is a process of articulating tacit knowledge into explicit concepts by means of metaphors, analogies, concepts, hypotheses or models. This utilises metaphor following Nisbet's (1969) argument that what Polanyi terms tacit knowledge may be expressible, to a degree, by means of metaphor. Successful creative design seems usually to work this way; Nonaka and Takeuchi give a number of interesting industrial design examples (1995, pp64–7).

Combination: from explicit knowledge to explicit knowledge

Combination is a process of systematising concepts into a knowledge system, combining different bodies of explicit knowledge. Nonaka and Takeuchi thought an MBA education one of the best examples of this (1995, p67).

Internalisation: from explicit knowledge to tacit knowledge

Internalisation is a process of embodying explicit knowledge into tacit knowledge and is closely related to 'learning by doing'. When experiences through socialisation, externalisation and combination are internalised into individuals' tacit knowledge bases in the form of shared mental models or technical know-how, they become valuable assets.

 HRM IN ACTION: CATERPILLAR 'THINKBIG' PROGRAMME FOR DEALER SERVICE TECHNICIANS

CASE STUDY 3.2

This is a two-year programme to develop technicians' competence in supporting company products using advanced (and advancing) technologies. It combines classroom instruction with on-the-job working, lab work and experience of real-world problem-solving with customers. Graduates receive a bachelor's degree in science and technology.

A two-yearly international ThinkBIG conference for dealers, technical colleges and Caterpillar representatives is held to share ideas, develop new programmes and share best practice. (**www. deltacollege.edu/div/astech/cat/ program.html**)

The company has also introduced its 'ThinkBIGGER' programme, which is an additional two-year programme focused on management opportunities. (**www. pittstate.edu/department/auto/bas-degree/cat-thinkbigger.dot**)

HRM DILEMMA 3.1

In Chapter 1 we noted some new forms of employment. One of these was 'ICT-based mobile work' (information and communications technology), where employees can do their job from any place at any time, supported by modern technologies, also known as 'crowdworking'.

How can an organisation ensure necessary learning and development, for example for upskilling, for a 'virtual cloud of workers'?

What are the implications for the 'social and ethical responsibility' standard of the CIPD professional framework?

3.12 MANAGEMENT DEVELOPMENT

The CIPD defines management development as 'the structured process by which managers enhance their skills, competencies and/or knowledge, via formal or informal learning methods, to the benefit of both individual and organisational performance' (CIPD 2014).

Managers learn in many ways, including experientially, and many organisations combine formal and informal approaches. Handy *et al* (1988, p12) proposed a clear distinction between 'business education' and 'management development'. By 'business education' is meant the formal or academic knowledge base required for management, as is typically provided by an external source such as a university, business school or commercial college. The attainment of such education is primarily the responsibility of the individual manager. Business education cannot by itself qualify one for management, but can only be a prelude to it. 'Management development' largely takes place within the organisation and should be seen as a combination of experience, training and education which, although usually initiated by the organisation, requires the active co-operation of the individual, and for which both organisation and manager share joint responsibility. Twenty years on, Handy's distinction still has much to commend it, although organisations are very much more likely now to actively support their managers in acquiring business education, either paying the fees for external MBAs and the like or setting up their own 'corporate universities'.

One of the key changes in management development in the UK and in many other countries in the past 30 years has been the growth in management education at university level. In North America this provision was evident for most of the twentieth century, but it was only in the latter decades of the century that most other countries took the academic education of managers as seriously as did the North Americans. Indeed, it was mainly the continuing success of the US managerial and entrepreneurial culture which brought about this change. The CIPD estimates that by 2006 there were over 100 higher-education institutions in the UK that offered undergraduate and postgraduate courses, around 20,000 first degrees and 11,000 higher degrees (mainly MBAs) being awarded every year. Over 80% of MBAs were awarded for distance learning or part-time study. Some of these MBA graduates will have been sponsored by their employers, but others will have decided to study for themselves as part of their own programme of career development. Edinburgh Business School currently offers one of the largest distance learning MBA programmes in the world with, to date, over 10,500 graduates working in over 150 countries (**www.ebsglobal.net**).

Some large UK companies have followed the US lead in setting up 'corporate universities' which supply in-house many of the formal courses and programmes for their people development, including management development, which previously would have been supplied by external academic institutions.

3.12.1 THE OBJECTIVES OF MANAGEMENT DEVELOPMENT

The choice of management development approach and methods will depend on the strategic outcomes that the organisation is pursuing, such as performance, attitude and adaptability.

Improving managers' expertise in specific areas such as marketing, finance, production or HRM is usually highest on most companies' agendas for management development, followed by giving individuals experience to prepare them for senior management positions. Management development is also used either as a catalyst for organisational change or to help build a new culture following a major change, such as a large-scale merger or acquisition. Management development can also be a key factor in building a learning organisation in which there is a climate for continual learning. In this case the emphasis is away from structured programmes and taught courses and towards enhancing opportunities for self-development via methods such as action learning, on-the-job training, career breaks, secondment to temporary 'taskforces' and e-learning.

3.12.2 METHODS OF MANAGEMENT DEVELOPMENT

It is recognised that a good deal of management development takes place on the job and that planned job experience and career succession can play vital roles in the process. Line managers should be involved in the development of their subordinates.

In the UK the most common formal methods of management development are external courses, attending seminars and conferences, attending in-company training to develop individual skills, attending in-company training to develop organisational skills, and pursuing external formal qualifications such as MBAs (Thomson *et al* 2001, p144).

The most popular informal methods in the UK are in-company job rotation, job observation, on-the-job training, mentoring and coaching (Thomson *et al* 2001, p149).

3.12.3 CONDITIONS FOR SUCCESSFUL MANAGEMENT DEVELOPMENT

There is a consensus in the literature (Storey *et al* 1997, p43) that management development is most effective when:

- it is recognised by the organisation as a strategic business activity
- the design of management development programmes recognises the nature of managerial work
- the programme is tailored to fit the needs of the individual managers on it
- education, training, selection, career planning, reward systems and managerial evaluation are recognised as all being part of a connected system
- evaluation is itself a vital part of the system of development.

CASE STUDY 3.3

TRAINING ACADEMY: PHYSICIAN HEAL THYSELF?

The company Training Academy is a part of a German holding group specialising in personnel and organisational development and training, including virtual training, e-learning and other IT solutions for learning as well as coaching, and talent management.

The company considers that having well-qualified people is the backbone of the

organisation and is crucial for the competitiveness of the company. It is necessary to have up-to-date skilled employees because they sell 'knowledge' and training. The company believes that having a general overarching concept and budget for employee training makes it easier for the employees to get and conduct training, and enable continuous improvement.

The company aims to give the employees more job autonomy and give them the feeling that their opinion is taken seriously. Therefore the general structure was changed and a new management line was added to give small teams more workplace responsibility. The new team structure changed the whole management structure, being the guarantee for more autonomy and self-responsibility of the employees.

Exercise

Drawing on the principles of learning and development which we have discussed in this chapter, devise a company-wide training strategy for employees of Training Academy, whose role is to deliver face-to-face training to clients in their own workplaces.

CASE STUDY 3.1 ANSWER GUIDANCE

This case involved elements of work organisation (flexibility, self-managed teams), learning and reflection (continuous improvement), and workplace partnership (integrating tacit and strategic knowledge).

The overall training concept

Continuous training of the employees is very important for the company. In 2013 the company implemented an overall training programme and budget for every department to make it easier for the employees to get the training they need to keep them up to date. There are now no costs for the departments, but the employees still have to reconcile with their manager. Within a yearly appraisal interview, individual personnel development measures are identified and agreed upon. There is also a hotline giving advice on which training course fits best or is possible. A multi-channel learning concept was developed: for example, it is possible to learn English during working time and at home via smartphone or while traveling (e-learning). An interactive tool was developed consisting of video and audio sequences, reading and writing exercises and on-site courses.

Team leader and small teams (12–15 employees)

In 2013 there was a comprehensive structural change: launching new departments, closing and combining different departments. Team leaders replaced some former heads of department, with the aim of having small teams with more self-responsibility at the workplace. The addition of team leaders gave the employees more autonomy, encouraged better involvement of the employees, and facilitated workplace-directed decisions made by both employees and managers.

Employee survey and participation system

Every two years an employee survey takes place. Since the beginning of this initiative more than ten focus teams (depending on the agreed personnel and organisational developments) were set up to transfer the results of the surveys into active measures, giving the employees the opportunity to develop bottom–up solutions. Controlled by the managers, most of the measures developed by the employees were implemented (if they were not too expensive): such as health management (medical examinations, massages, and so on) and care points for critical situations such as work overload, and unmanageable time schedules (at the workplace or within a department). A fair improvement system was established; money for the best solutions is given to the employees.

So who benefits?

By keeping the employees up to date on professional and technical issues, the company stays competitive and has a better customer focus. The employees' voice is based on a suggestions system, small teams and individual training. These workplace innovations allow an optimal usage of employees' competences and capabilities at the workplace by the team structure.

The employees benefit from the top-down workplace innovations: having been accepted and adopted by employees, a win–win situation for employees and management is created, especially by bottom-up structures (care points, self-responsible teams, and so on). Employees' competences are continuously updated and their competences are relevant for the company development and products.

Source: Eurofound (2015).

KEY ISSUES IN LEARNING AND DEVELOPMENT

The term 'learning and development' covers terms such as 'employee development' and 'human resource development' as well as older terms such as 'training' and 'management development'.

HRM places much greater emphasis on development than did earlier people management paradigms. In principle this extends to all employees, regardless of their position in the organisational hierarchy, but in practice is focused on core employees. New forms of more individualised employment may put many employees beyond the reach of development.

Talent development is often a preferred term among HR professionals to describe the 'high end' of learning and development.

Learning and development interventions cover external education and in-house activities, both formal and informal.

The intention in employee development now is often to facilitate learning and personal development rather than to impose formal training on individuals.

There is also greater emphasis on informal learning at all levels, including self-development.

EXPLORE FURTHER

Armstrong, M. (2014) *Armstrong's Handbook of Human Resource Management Practice*. 13th edition. London: Kogan Page.

- Chapters 21–24, 'Learning and development' – the basics on individual and organisational learning and development, plus management development.
- Chapter 52, 'Learning and development skills'.
- Chapter 67, 'Planning and delivering learning events toolkit'.

Storey, J. (ed) (2007) *Human Resource Management: A critical text*. 3rd edition. London: Thomson Learning.

- Chapter 7, A. Felstead, 'Measure for measure: mapping the terrain of the training, learning and skills debate'.

CHAPTER 4

Employee relations

INTRODUCTION

'Employee relations' is the term now normally used to describe the policies and practices an organisation uses in dealing with its employees, and the systems of rules and mechanisms by which organisations and employees interact with each other. The term usually implies collective relations such as collective bargaining with trade unions or staff associations, and the resulting agreements, but it also includes policies and procedures which operate at small-group or individual level – for example disciplinary and grievance procedures.

As the traditional, collectivised forms and institutions of employee relations decline in influence, albeit at different rates in different countries, the focus for many organisations is shifting towards ensuring employee engagement and commitment.

LEARNING OUTCOMES

On completion of this chapter you should:

- understand the nature and importance of conflict in employee relations
- understand the nature of negotiations in the context of employee relations
- understand the purpose and nature of both grievance and disciplinary procedures
- be able to describe the process of traditional collective bargaining and agreements
- be familiar with the main forms of industrial action
- understand the nature of 'new employee relations'
- understand the concepts of employee engagement and employee voice.

4.1 WHAT DOES EMPLOYEE RELATIONS MEAN TODAY?

There has been a marked decline in trade union membership and influence in the UK and most other developed economies over the last 20 years. Far fewer employees in the UK are now covered by collective bargaining in the original sense. Union influence is increasingly confined to the public sector and to traditional industries, and where it is present it is very much weaker than in the decades immediately following the Second World War. This has been the trend in the USA and many other countries also, although there are international variations – for example, trade unions remain relatively strong in continental Europe and Scandinavia.

But having said all that, even in the UK in the twenty-first century, collective bargaining remains an important part of the management process in some industries and many parts of the public sector.

Taking the international view, in every nation the nature and structure of the legal framework within which employee relations takes place and the national culture itself will profoundly affect the way employee relations is conducted.

By 2005 the CIPD could report (CIPD 2005, pp3–4) that from the manager's viewpoint:

> in general [the employee relations agenda] is no longer about trade unions. There is more emphasis on direct communication, managing organisational change and involving and motivating staff. Issues about work–life balance and the war for talent reflect a changing workforce with changing expectations. Employers have to come to terms with these changes in managing the employment relationship.

The same CIPD report (p1) stated that:

> managing the employment relationship remains central to good HR practice. The emphasis of employee relations continues to shift from institutions to relationships, but employee relations skills and competencies are still critical to achieving performance benefits. The focus now needs to be on gaining and retaining employee commitment and engagement.

Acas concluded in 2011 that traditional frameworks and assumptions surrounding employment relations were outdated. These assumptions were predicated on large traditional workplaces where employees worked under permanent contracts of employment with a single employer and employee relations were mediated by negotiation with trade unions (Acas 2011).

It is not just the emergence of HRM that has brought this about. Globalisation, with the emergence of the new economic superpowers of China and India, the rise of new industries exploiting new technologies, the fragmentation of workplaces, the changing composition and expectations of workforces and the shift towards more individualised work relations have all played a part.

Traditional, collectivised models of employee relations bring little to the understanding of problems where, for example, activities are contracted out to a separate employer; or in start-up companies or SMEs where informality in work relations is a core cultural aspect; or where global corporations have to manage international supply chains in which different countries have different conceptions of social justice and human rights. And they may have little power to deal with the problems that new forms of employment bring for employee rights and protection.

For some HR practitioners and authorities, employee relations is really becoming all about employee engagement (CIPD 2016b).

In Chapter 1 we introduced the idea of 'perspective' in people management and outlined the three most important for our purposes – namely, unitarist, pluralist and radical or critical. We noted that the HRM model is really unitarist in its culture but that it is often successfully applied in a pluralist milieu. There is no doubt, however, that in countries such as the UK and the USA, where trade union power has declined, employee relations is significantly less collectivised than was the case several decades ago. As early as 1990 the Workplace Employment Relations Study reported a significant decline in trade unionism in the UK, accompanied by a considerable increase in HRM-style initiatives in participation and communication, such as team briefings, quality circles and newsletters, replacing the more traditional collective methods. There was also evidence of the increasing involvement of line managers in HR activities which had previously been reserved for specialist personnel management departments. The later Workplace Employment Relations Study surveys have confirmed these trends in the UK (Van Wanrooy et al 2013).

Most countries have legal frameworks which give statutory rights to employees, both individual – for example, protection against unfair dismissal – and collective – for example, the right to trade union membership and recognition, and ensuring legal compliance on the part of the organisation is a vital responsibility for HR managers. The actual rights and responsibilities of both parties may vary widely from country to country – a point that multinational companies have to bear in mind when framing their HR strategies and policies.

Collective bargaining by trade unions and employers' organisations was supported by public policy in most free-market economies after 1945. A long-term decline in recent decades was followed by further pressure in many countries after the financial crisis of 2008. The International Labour Office (ILO 2015a) concluded that only deliberate policy choices by governments could maintain or increase the coverage of collective bargaining.

The ILO has also argued that collective bargaining is particularly important in reducing the vulnerability of workers employed in non-standard forms of employment, such as part-time, temporary and agency working (ILO 2015b).

Where traditional formal employee relations processes such as collective bargaining have declined, HRM initiatives such as more direct methods of communication between management and workers might be expected to take their place. However, the empirical evidence on this is mixed and greater communication may often mean more one-way communication from management rather than genuine dialogue. In their analysis of the WERS 2011 data, van Wanrooy et al (2013) concluded:

> Consultation with unions has not filled the space created by the decline in bargaining. And structures for non-union representation have failed to materialise. ... it appears more managers were content to directly inform staff, rather than representatives, about change.

> The growth in the use of direct communication methods has continued and is now almost ubiquitous. The increasing preference managers have for communicating directly with employees is manifest in the widespread use of briefing methods either at the workplace or team level. But the use of two-way communication methods which may give employees more voice, such as staff surveys and suggestion schemes, has not increased.

4.2 DEALING WITH CONFLICT

We use the term 'conflict' widely in employee relations. It does not always mean a breakdown in the working relationship, although that can be a consequence of conflict. We mean any situation where there is a significant difference in objectives or interests between management and the workforce, whether it is a collective difference about pay rates or major terms of employment, or individual differences about a particular work situation.

So the issue of conflict and how to deal with it is important for managers, both at the level of the individual or small group – for example by means of disciplinary and grievance procedures – and at the larger scale, handling disputes with trade unions or staff associations which represent collectively some significant section of the workforce.

4.2.1 GRIEVANCE AND DISCIPLINARY PROCEDURES

The 2011 Workplace Employment Relations Study (WERS) concluded that 'conflict at work [in the UK] is manifested through individual rather than collective disputes' (Van Wanrooy et al 2013, p152).

Some 19% of UK workplaces reported the raising of formal grievances in the preceding 12 months, a slight (1%) reduction since the 2004 WERS. The most common types of grievance were unfair treatment by managers or supervisors (39% of managers reported this type of grievance); pay, terms and conditions of work (30%); and bullying and harassment from colleagues or managers (23%).

The same survey found that in 41% of workplaces disciplinary action had been taken against an employee in the previous 12 months, with a mean of 4.8 disciplinary sanctions applied per 100 employees. These figures showed no significant differences from 2004. In 2011, the most common actions were formal verbal warnings (66%) and formal written warnings (63%).

The most common reason for an employer taking disciplinary action in 2011 was poor performance (59% of workplaces reported this, an increase from 47% in 2004).

Most managers would agree that it is inevitable that there are issues of grievance- and discipline-handling in most organisations. Notwithstanding the unitarist culture of most HRM models, few managers really expect that the interests of both employers and employees will always coincide. These interests are expressed in the parties' respective legal rights and responsibilities, but also in the informal expectations they have of each other.

Employees expect that employers will treat them reasonably, fairly and consistently, and that action will be taken against them only on the basis of just cause and after proper and thorough investigation. Employees will feel they have a right to pursue a grievance if these expectations are not met.

Employers expect employees to perform their duties and tasks in a satisfactory manner in accordance with their legal obligations and organisational policies and procedures. If the employees' performance is not satisfactory, employers will consider that they have the right to apply disciplinary action.

HR has an important role in resolving such differences and so assisting the effective running of the organisation. Apart from ethical and legal considerations, if grievance and discipline cases are dealt with properly, we assume that employee dissatisfaction should be reduced and motivation increased, with consequent improvements in individual, team and organisational performance. If the employment relationship is working in any sort of reasonable fashion to begin with, it is usually seen by both sides as an ongoing relationship that should survive the resolution of any one dispute, whether individual or collective.

As we saw in Chapter 1, a key characteristic of HRM is the devolution to the line manager of most day-to-day people management. This includes handling grievances and discipline with minimum HR specialist input, at least initially, so it is now perceived as crucial that all line managers be trained to handle grievance and disciplinary cases properly.

If an employment tribunal investigates the dismissal of an employee, it will test the issues of fairness and reasonableness by considering whether the procedures that were applied by the employer conformed to the concepts of natural justice. From the employer's point of view, the main purpose of procedures is to ensure that standards are maintained and legal compliance is adhered to.

Good grievance and disciplinary procedures typically are set in stages, and on the principle that issues should be dealt with as close to their origin as possible. Not all actions have to go through all these steps, however, since the first instance of severe misconduct may merit disciplinary action much more punitive than that of, say, a verbal warning. For example, fighting in the workplace and being drunk at work are both classed in almost all circumstances as 'gross misconduct' justifying immediate dismissal, as may be the refusal to carry out a reasonable and legitimate instruction from a superior. But the general principle is always to deal with issues at the lowest level possible given the nature of the inappropriate behaviour.

It may be surprising but it is a fact that in the UK employment tribunals still report cases in which the employer has failed to conduct a proper and fair investigation before taking disciplinary action against an employee. It is the employer's responsibility to ensure that any disciplinary action is taken only after a full and proper investigation of the facts has been conducted. Line managers need appropriate training in handling grievance and disciplinary matters. HR experts are still usually involved in both, but not necessarily in person, at least at initial stages. The line managers will need access to expert HR advice, however, whether or not HR personnel themselves are present.

? REFLECTIVE ACTIVITY 4.1

Find out what the disciplinary and grievance procedures are which operate at your place of employment (or some other workplace with which you are familiar). If there are neither, outline what you think the procedure(s) should be.

REFLECTIVE ACTIVITY 4.1 ANSWER GUIDANCE

If an organisation lands in court or in some legal sub-forum (such as the UK system of employment tribunals) to defend its actions in respect of any grievance or disciplinary matter, there are five tests that will be applied to the employer's actions: fairness, reasonableness, consistency, operating with just cause, and operating within the law. Grievance and disciplinary issues are usually regarded as linked and often share common procedures to avoid the perception that one is being given greater status or importance than the other by the organisation. Useful advice on the handling of grievance and disciplinary matters, both from the employee's point of view and that of the employer, and also advice on employee relations issues more generally, can be found on the Acas website: **www.acas.org.uk**. Acas is a publicly funded body whose remit is to 'improve organisations and working life through better employment relations'. It has produced a Code of Practice for Disciplinary and Grievance Procedures.

 WHAT HAPPENS WHEN GRIEVANCE AND DISCIPLINE OVERLAP?

CASE STUDY 4.1

The following case draws attention to a challenge often faced by managers: how to deal with an employee raising a grievance during the course of a disciplinary procedure.

Cynics may observe that grievances are lodged sometimes with the objective of delaying a disciplinary process. Nevertheless, this scenario raises the issue of whether the disciplinary process should be adjourned or should continue and, if it continues, on what basis.

Is this a grievance?

Employers need to analyse the specific nature of the issue being raised. The employee may style it a 'grievance' but it may actually be:

- a representation that should be considered by the employer when deciding the result of the disciplinary process
- about a disciplinary decision already made and, therefore, constitute an appeal rather than a separate grievance
- entirely unrelated to the disciplinary process.

The Acas Code

If the disciplinary and grievance processes do genuinely overlap, what is the way forward?

The Acas Code of Practice on Disciplinary and Grievance Procedures says (paragraph 44): 'Where an employee raises a grievance during a disciplinary process, the disciplinary process may be temporarily suspended in order to deal with the grievance. Where the grievance and disciplinary cases are related, it may be appropriate to deal with both issues concurrently.'

Although this provides some guidance, it does little more than emphasise that employers need to be flexible.

The non-statutory Acas guide, *Discipline and Grievances at Work*, makes more specific recommendations. It says that it may be appropriate to suspend the disciplinary procedure where, for example:

- the grievance relates to an alleged conflict of interest on the part of the manager holding the disciplinary meeting
- bias is alleged in the conduct of the disciplinary meeting
- the organisation has been selective in the evidence it has supplied to the manager holding the meeting, or
- there is possible discrimination.

Options

Arguably, there are three possible options:

1 The disciplinary process continues regardless of the grievance, and the grievance is dealt with separately and in parallel with the disciplinary process.

2 The disciplinary process is adjourned pending completion of the grievance process (including any potential appeal).

3 The disciplinary process is conducted by a different person, where practicable, if the grievance concerns the person conducting it, while the grievance is considered separately.

Case law

One further possible scenario was demonstrated in the decision of the Employment Appeals Tribunal (EAT) in the case of *Samuel Smith Old Brewery (Tadcaster) v (1) F Marshall (2) P Marshall*. Here the subject matter of a grievance preceded the disciplinary process, rather than the other way round.

The claimants were pub managers. One of them failed to implement the proposed reduction in staff hours and then raised a grievance about the issue. The allocation of pub staffing hours was determined at the discretion of the employer. The brewery revised its proposed hours reduction but the employees refused to implement it until the grievance process had been exhausted. The employer's response was to institute disciplinary proceedings. This led to the employees' dismissal for gross misconduct – for deliberately refusing to carry out lawful instructions – after they failed to attend the relevant meetings.

Judgment

The employment tribunal concluded that dismissal was within the range of reasonable responses but found that the managers had been deprived of their rights to pursue a grievance appeal and had therefore been unfairly dismissed.

On appeal, the EAT found it difficult to see how the decision to dismiss for a failure to comply with reasonable instructions could be outside the range of reasonable responses simply because the grievance appeal was delayed. It felt this would only be unfair in the rarest of cases. And there was no absolute rule that a disciplinary hearing could not proceed until a related grievance had been completed. So the tribunal's decision was overturned.

Flexibility

The lodging of a grievance does not require employers to postpone connected disciplinary proceedings automatically. Employers must consider each particular case on its facts, be prepared to be flexible where circumstances demand, and avoid adopting prescriptive rules about what happens when disciplinaries and grievances do truly overlap.

Source: Charles Wynn-Evans, *People Management*, 27 April 2010.

A useful starting point for this topic is Walton and McKersie's (1965) classic account of negotiations and negotiating behaviour. Walton and McKersie define formal negotiations in terms of *four* distinct systems of activity with their own identifiable tactics. These are:

- distributive bargaining
- integrative bargaining
- attitudinal structuring
- intra-organisation bargaining.

Attitudinal structuring refers to the negotiator's attempt to get the 'opponent' to see things their way during the bargaining process, while intra-organisational bargaining is concerned with the bargaining that necessarily has to take place on occasion between the negotiator and their 'constituents'. Both of these are really subsidiary to the major processes – distributive and integrative bargaining – and will not be examined here.

4.3.1 DISTRIBUTIVE BARGAINING

Walton and McKersie coined the term 'distributive bargaining' to refer to the 'normal' kind of bargaining which takes place where it is necessary to resolve conflicting interests but in a context in which both parties stand to benefit from a continued relationship. They therefore recognise that there exists a level of 'mutual dependence', bounded by lower and upper limits of possible demands. Within this range, there is an actual bargaining range which represents an area within the limits previously indicated, since neither side would seek to push the other to extremes for fear of risking the maintenance of their valued long-term relationship. Thus negotiators strive for *targets* but will take an entrenched position with regard to *resistance points*.

The resistance point is a function of the negotiators':

- lowest estimate of what is needed to secure agreement
- most pessimistic assumptions about what is possible, and
- least favourable assumptions about their bargaining skill.

The target point is a function of the negotiators':

- highest estimate of what is needed
- most optimistic assumptions about what is possible, and
- most favourable assumptions about their bargaining skill.

An effective negotiation enables each party to identify the 'bargaining parameters' between them and to reach an agreed settlement within these parameters.

So, for example, in typical wage negotiations, management's bargaining range runs from its ideal settlement point (what it would ideally like) to its resistance point (the point beyond which it will not go), with a target point of favourable and realistic expectation somewhere between the two. Similarly, the unions also have a bargaining range between their ideal settlement and resistance points (and also with a target point). The two bargaining ranges are not identical (different resistance and ideal settlement points), but if negotiations are to be at all possible there will have to be an overlap, and this overlap is bounded by the two sides' resistance points, which thus form the bargaining parameters.

Example

Acme Widgets plc, a mid-level technology manufacturer, starts its annual pay negotiations with the Widget Engineers' Union. Acme management would ideally like to give no pay rise to its employees because the market is becoming increasingly competitive and, although Acme is profitable, it is suffering continuous pressure on its profit margins and is always seeking to cut costs. However, it knows that this would be completely unacceptable to the workforce, who will expect a pay rise at least equal to the rise in the cost of living as established by the Government's published rate of inflation for the previous year, which is 3%. Management know that they could just afford a maximum pay rise of 10%, but this would adversely affect the balance sheet and be extremely difficult to sell to shareholders. Benchmark settlements in comparable industries are running at 4% to 5% on average. Management have therefore privately set a target of 4%.

In this case, then, the bargaining range will be between 3% – which is the resistance point of the union side – and 10%, the resistance point of the employer.

The more equal the balance of power between the two parties, and the more skilled the negotiators, the more likely it will be that a settlement is reached somewhere between the two sides' target points.

Negotiation is not confined to traditional pay bargaining. Managers who have no responsibility for pay may still have to negotiate with trade unions or other employee groups on issues related to work (CIPD 2005).

4.3.2 INTEGRATIVE BARGAINING

This is essentially concerned with problem-solving. Because the interests of both parties are identical or coincidental, both parties stand to gain in absolute terms at best or lose very little at worst. Walton and McKersie suggest certain types of problems are inherently more conducive to integrative bargaining – for example, job security, mutual gains efficiency schemes, and participation and involvement arrangements.

The integrative process can be seen in essentially problem-solving terms, involving a number of stages:

* identifying the problem
* searching for alternative solutions
* preference ordering of solutions and selecting a course of action.

Each stage involves tactics that are necessarily different from those of the distributive model and, in turn, require the maximum exchange of information: a thorough and accurate gathering of information about alternatives and their consequences, for both parties. Whereas the distributive 'atmosphere' might be characterised by concealment, devious tactics and aggression, successful integrative bargaining requires openness, trust and a motivation on behalf of both parties towards solving the problem.

Both types of bargaining suggested by Walton and McKersie would reflect the origins of the term *negotiation*. The Latin verb *negotiari* means 'to carry on business' and is defined (*The New Shorter Oxford English Dictionary*) as:

> a process or act of conferring with another or others to arrange some matter by mutual agreement, a discussion with a view to some compromise or settlement.

More specifically, to 'bargain' – which is derived through an old French verb meaning 'trade', 'dispute' and 'hesitate' – is defined (*ibid*) as being:

> to discuss the terms of action, negotiate, seek to secure the most favourable terms, haggle.

These dictionary definitions give a good flavour of what we mean by negotiations or collective agreements between an organisation and a trade union.

Negotiation has also been defined (Kennedy *et al* 1984, p12) as:

> a process for resolving conflict between two parties whereby both modify their demands to achieve a mutually acceptable compromise.

4.4 COLLECTIVE BARGAINING

Collective bargaining is the traditional term for the process by which pay, terms of employment and working conditions are mutually negotiated between employees, as collectively represented by trade unions or staff associations, and employers. Collective bargaining can also take place at industry level, where the employers are also represented collectively. In this case industry or national agreements will typically be supplemented by local agreements negotiated subsequently with individual employers.

As noted above in this chapter, collective bargaining remains an important part of the management process in some industries and many parts of the public sector. Where there has been a tradition of collective bargaining, it lends legitimacy to agreements on pay and conditions of employment.

Certain conditions are necessary for collective bargaining to operate:

● Both management and the workforce are organised. This implies the existence of trade unions or some other sort of association representing the employees.
● There is formal recognition of the trade unions or other employee association(s) by management.
● There is mutual agreement to negotiate in good faith and to keep agreements that are reached.

And even in the USA some traditional large industries are still engaged in very large-scale collective industrial relations – for example, the car manufacturing industry. But increasingly, this looks like the past and not the future.

There are some particular characteristics of the negotiating process in employee relations that should be kept in mind:

● The parties are not involved in a one-off negotiation (like, say, buying a car) and usually need, and want, to continue working together after the negotiation or bargaining has been completed.
● The negotiation is usually about more than one issue – for example basic pay *and* some aspect of working conditions or some other benefits.
● Negotiations are actually conducted by a small number of representatives from each side and agreements reached by them will require endorsement from the parties themselves. So when trade union negotiators reach agreement with management on some issue, they normally have to seek approval from the wider membership of the union by means of a ballot. Similarly, management negotiators may have to seek endorsement from their board of directors.
● On each side, priorities, strategies and tactics must be established before the negotiations start with the opposite party, so there is always the possibility of internal conflict on each side.
● Once an agreement has been reached, there is joint responsibility to make it work.

4.4.1 EXAMPLES OF COLLECTIVE BARGAINING AGREEMENTS

'New style' agreements

A major feature of so-called 'new style' agreements is that their negotiating and disputes procedures are based on the mutually accepted rights of the parties expressed in a recognition agreement. The explicit objective is to move away from the traditional confrontational approach between management and unions in which both sides viewed the negotiating process as a 'zero-sum game' in which any advantage to one side could only be gained at the expense of the other. New-style agreements will typically include provision for single-union recognition (see below), single status, labour flexibility, the establishment of a company council, and a no-strike clause to the effect that issues should be resolved without recourse to industrial action. 'Pendulum arbitration' is often a feature of such agreements. This is where it is agreed beforehand that, in the event of a deadlock in negotiations, an arbiter is empowered to choose one or other side's proposal, which both sides must then accept. The rationale for this is that it encourages both parties to commence negotiations with responsible proposals since they know that in the event of an impasse an arbiter would be unlikely to support an extreme or unreasonable demand.

Single-union recognition

The existence of a number of unions within one organisation is frequently criticised because of the increase in the complexity of bargaining arrangements this brings and the danger of inter-union demarcation disputes. One answer to this problem is representation of all employees through a single union. These single-union agreements have a number of characteristics that were advantageous to management.

Single-union deals have the following typical features:

- a single union representing all employees, with constraints put on the role of full-time union officials
- flexible working practices – agreement to the flexible use of labour across traditional demarcation lines
- single status for all employees – what is termed the 'harmonisation' of terms and conditions between manual and non-manual employees
- an expressed commitment by the organisation to involvement and the disclosure of information in the form of an open communications system and, often, a works council
- the resolution of disputes by means of devices such as pendulum arbitration, a commitment to continuity of production, and a 'no-strike' provision.

Single-union deals have generally been concluded on greenfield sites, often by Japanese firms such as Nissan, Sanyo, Matsushita and Toyota. What cynics have termed a 'beauty contest' is often held by the employer to select the one union from a number of contenders.

Partnership agreements

A partnership agreement is one in which both parties (management and the trade union) agree to work together to their mutual advantage and to achieve a climate of more co-operative and therefore less adversarial employee relations. A partnership agreement may include undertakings from both sides. For example, management may offer job security linked to productivity, more involvement and better communications, and the union may agree to new forms of work organisation or work practices which offer more flexibility on the part of employees.

Five key values for partnership are:

- mutual trust and respect
- a joint vision for the future and the means to achieve it
- continuous exchange of information
- recognition of the central role of collective bargaining
- devolved decision-making.

Research in the United States indicated that if these matters were addressed successfully by management and unions, companies could expect productivity gains, quality improvements, a better motivated and committed workforce, and lower absenteeism and staff turnover rates.

The UK Department of Trade and Industry and Department for Education and Employment report *Partnerships at Work* (1997) concluded that partnership was central to the strategy of successful organisations. A growing understanding that organisations must focus on customer needs has brought with it the desire to engage the attitudes and commitment of all employees in order to effectively meet those needs, says the report. The five main themes or 'paths' identified by the report are:

- shared goals – 'understanding the business we are in'
- shared culture – 'agreed values binding us together'
- shared learning – 'continuously improving ourselves'
- shared effort – 'one business driven by flexible teams'
- shared information – 'effective communication throughout the enterprise'.

4.5 DISPUTE RESOLUTION: CONCILIATION, ARBITRATION AND MEDIATION

The aim of collective bargaining is, of course, to reach agreement to the satisfaction of both parties. Negotiating procedures provide for various stages of 'failure to agree', and often include a clause providing for some form of dispute resolution in the event of the procedure's being exhausted. The standard processes of dispute resolution include conciliation, arbitration and mediation.

Conciliation is the process of reconciling disagreeing parties. It is carried out by a third party, in the UK often an Acas conciliation officer, who acts in effect as a go-between, attempting to get the employer and trade union representatives to agree on terms. Conciliators can only help the parties come to an agreement. They do not make recommendations on what that agreement should be. That is the role of an arbitrator (see below). The incentives to seek conciliation are the hope that the conciliator can rebuild bridges and the belief that a determined search for agreement is better than confrontation, even if both parties have to compromise.

Arbitration is the process of settling disputes by getting a third party – the arbitrator – to review and discuss the negotiating stances of the disagreeing parties and make a recommendation on the terms of settlement which is binding on both parties. The arbitrator is impartial, and employee relations academics or other figures recognised as experts in the industry concerned are sometimes asked to act in this capacity. Arbitration is the means of last resort for reaching a settlement where disputes cannot be resolved in any other way. Procedural agreements may provide for either side unilaterally to invoke arbitration, in which case the decision of the arbitrator is not binding on both parties. The process of arbitration in its fullest sense, however, only takes place at the request of both parties, who agree in advance to accept the arbitrator's findings. Acas will only act as arbitrator if the consent of both parties is obtained, conciliation has been considered, any agreed procedures have been followed to the full, and a failure to agree has been recorded.

Pendulum or *final-offer arbitration* increases the rigidity of the arbitration process by allowing an arbitrator no choice but to recommend either the union's or the employer's final offer – there is no middle ground.

Mediation is an approach to finding a result in a dispute which can be thought of as something midway between arbitration and conciliation – being weaker than arbitration but somewhat stronger than conciliation. It takes place when a third party (often Acas) helps the employer and the union by making recommendations which, however, they are not bound to accept.

4.6 INFORMAL EMPLOYEE RELATIONS PROCESSES

The formal processes of union recognition, collective bargaining and dispute resolution described above provide the traditional framework for employee relations insofar as this is concerned with agreeing terms and conditions of employment and working arrangements and settling disputes. But managers should always remember that within that formal framework, informal employee relations processes are taking place continuously, whenever a line manager or team leader is handling an issue in contact with an employee representative, an individual employee or a group of employees. The issue may concern methods of work, allocation of work and overtime, working conditions, health and safety, achieving output and quality targets and standards, discipline or pay. Line managers and supervisors handle day-to-day grievances arising from any of these issues and are expected to resolve them to the satisfaction of all parties without involving a formal grievance procedure. The thrust for devolving responsibility to line managers for human resource matters has increased the onus on them to handle employee relations effectively.

Creating and maintaining a good employee relations climate in an organisation may be the ultimate responsibility of top management, advised by HR specialists. But the climate will be strongly influenced by the behaviour of line managers and team leaders. The HR function can help to improve the effectiveness of this behaviour by identifying and defining the competencies required, advising on the selection of supervisors, ensuring that they are properly trained, and encouraging the development of performance management processes that provide for the assessment of the level of competence achieved by line managers and team leaders in handling employee relations.

4.7 INDUSTRIAL ACTION

The term 'industrial action' is ordinarily used to describe the sanctions which employees may resort to if bargaining or negotiation does not produce a result acceptable to them. The term is usually associated with strike action by employees against their employer – but that is only one form of industrial action. It should also be noted that employers/management have a range of sanctions that they too may resort to.

We will first consider industrial action in the sense of employee action.

There can be individual, unorganised forms of industrial action such as high labour turnover, deliberately poor time-keeping, high absenteeism, withholding of effort, inefficient working, time-wasting, sabotage and complaints. All these may of course occur with particular individuals who are dissatisfied with their employment regardless of the general employee relations situation in the organisation, but when they are exhibited by a large number of employees they may constitute deliberate, although unorganised, industrial action. Such behaviour is most likely to occur after collective industrial action has failed and employees have been obliged to accept an unpopular settlement.

Organised, collective action by employees can take a variety of forms. At its mildest, collective action could be 'going slow' or 'working to rule'. A 'go-slow' might involve workers in a breach of their contract whereas normally a 'work to rule' will not. In this form of industrial action employees obey the letter of managerial instructions, exploiting the fact that very often in full production rules may be bent and corners cut.

Overtime bans are rather tougher actions, exploiting management's use of overtime to provide flexibility in labour resources and costs. Very often an overtime ban can have an immediate and pronounced impact on production. It is a double-edged sword, however: it immediately hits workers' earnings.

Often work-to-rule, go-slow and overtime ban action are used tactically by employees and unions early in a dispute or negotiation to put pressure on management to modify their position.

The ultimate sanction possessed by employees is to strike – that is, to withdraw their labour.

Strikes are described as 'unofficial' when they take place without the support of the union concerned, and 'unconstitutional' when they occur without the agreed negotiating procedures having been followed.

Another form of industrial action by employees is the 'sit-in', which is a mass occupation of employers' premises, perhaps to protest at the proposed closure of a plant and/or to physically prevent removal of machinery or other property. A similar action is a 'work-in' in which, in addition to occupying premises, the employees continue production without management, perhaps in defiance of them. All forms of unauthorised occupation are likely to be illegal, however. Although employers may prefer in certain circumstances not to go to law about the matter – for example, when they wish to preserve or restore better employee relations in the future – such considerations are unlikely to be taken in the case of proposed closure, however, where the employers' concern will be disposal of property and equipment.

HRM DILEMMA 4.1

In the absence of traditional collective bargaining, and given the more 'unitarist' perspective of HRM compared with earlier models of people management, how can the HR function fulfil Ulrich and Brockbank's (2005) employee advocate role (see Chapter 1)?

4.8 EMPLOYEE ENGAGEMENT

'Employee engagement' is a term now widely used in HRM literature to encapsulate management's attempts to motivate staff and focus their commitment to the organisation. The CIPD (2016b) describes it as bringing together 'a range of earlier concepts, including work effort, organisational commitment, job satisfaction, shared purpose'.

Engagement can be seen as a combination of commitment to the organisation and its values plus a willingness to help out colleagues (organisational citizenship). It goes beyond job satisfaction and motivation. Engagement is something the employee has to offer willingly – it cannot be 'required' as part of the employment contract.

The idea is to encourage employees to choose to exercise 'discretionary behaviour' and exceed the literal requirements of their contracts of employment. Clearly, there are links to the psychological contract, which we touched on in Chapter 1. The idea of the 'employer brand' is also relevant. A strong employer brand will help in attracting and retaining employees, and engaged employees will help promote the brand and protect it from being damaged by poor levels of service or product quality.

As the mechanisms of traditional employee relations, such as collective bargaining, have diminished – although, as we have seen, not disappeared – there has been increasing interest in the importance of employee engagement. A catalyst for this was the Macleod report (Macleod and Clarke 2009). These authors concluded that employee engagement was necessary for organisational success and proposed four 'enablers' of engagement, which they described as factors that 'were commonly agreed to lie behind successful engagement approaches' (2009, p33). These enablers were: a strategic narrative; engaging managers; employee voice; and integrity.

The 'strategic narrative' is a clearly expressed account of the purpose of the organisation, its vision and how the individual contributes to that purpose. Employees need a clear line of sight between their job and the narrative, and to understand where their work fits in. A successful strategic narrative requires leadership and widespread ownership and commitment from managers and employees at all levels.

'Engaging managers' facilitate and empower rather than control or restrict their staff. They treat their staff with appreciation and respect and show commitment to developing, increasing and rewarding the capabilities of those they manage.

To achieve an effective and empowered 'employee voice', management must seek employees' views and listen to them. Employees must see that their opinions count and make a difference and they must be allowed to challenge management legitimately when appropriate. This culture of listening and of being responsive depends on effective, two-way communications.

'Integrity' means that behaviour throughout the organisation is consistent with stated values, which leads to a culture of trust and a sense of integrity.

Acas (2014) analysed data from the 2011 WERS to examine actual practice in the UK. Not surprisingly there were significant variations in terms of the enablers of engagement by industry and sector. Employees working in the public sector scored lower on the enablers than those working in the private or third sectors. There were also significant variations by the size of the employer. Employees in large organisations score lower both on the enablers and on organisational commitment than those in smaller organisations. There were also significant variations by employee group (for example gender, age and disability).

Macleod and Clarke's study relied on case studies and interviews with managers. Purcell (2010) examined empirical data from WERS 2004 and concluded that their factors were supported by the evidence. Acas (2014) tested the Macleod and Clarke model with data from WERS 2011, finding similar support. Acas also found that having shared values was strongly linked to organisational commitment, discretionary effort and a sense of achievement. This was interpreted as support the findings of Alfes *et al* (2010), which identified 'meaningfulness' as the most important driver of engagement for all employee groups. As they expressed it, 'having a meaningful job is the most important factor influencing levels of engagement. This is true of all types of worker in all kinds of job' (Alfes *et al* 2010, p2).

HRM IN ACTION: AN APP FOR EMPLOYEE ENGAGEMENT?

CASE STUDY 4.2

British Airways (BA) has developed an app it hopes will help its managers reconnect with employees.

BA believes in symbols: in the company's Heathrow headquarters, visitors can't miss a giant set of Boeing 747 landing gear parked in its main atrium, complete with tyres a metre high and eight-metre metal struts. But the company has faced big challenges in recent years, with well-publicised disputes with cabin crew over pay and conditions, and other airlines challenging BA's claim to carry the most international air passengers. However, management hope their efforts to engage employees, together with rising profits for parent company International Airlines Group, mean that the airline's glory days may be returning.

Maria da Cunha, Director of People and Legal, says that staff engagement will be at the heart of BA's recovery. She says: 'We're challenging people to find different ways of doing things, and to improve productivity and efficiency. And for that

we need highly engaged staff – people who, in times of disruption, are willing to give discretionary effort . . . research shows us that a good relationship between someone and their line manager is the greatest driver of that.'

BA is trying to put this into practice through a new engagement app currently being deployed to managers.

The airline had tried numerous initiatives over the years to boost employee engagement and motivation, but never with much success. So they decided to focus on an area where they knew they had problems and try to substantially improve engagement, and consequently motivation, there. The target was a group of 3,000 front-line managers each looking after teams of 20–30 people in airfields, driving passenger buses or refuelling planes. With team members who are mobile and working between day and night shifts, it can be challenging for managers to find opportunities to engage on a person-to-person basis.

And the company is employing technology to help them. Managers download an app, called 'My Team', onto company iPads. It is designed to guide the managers in the sort of individual and small group employee interactions that so often get lost in the day-to-day hurry of a competitive global business and especially with physically dispersed teams. 'My Team' shows the managers who is on each team and who is working that day or shift. An additional prompt appears next to any name with an 'event' that the manager needs to know about. BA's global employee engagement manager, Jim Eaton, explains, 'We know that recognition drives engagement, so we thought it would be useful to recognise some simple things that would prompt conversations and basic recognition. For example, it might be their birthday or someone's long service anniversary. Managers can use these prompts to plan what they're going to do that day, who they're going to see and who they need to have a conversation with.'

The app also gives managers access to a range of employee information such as holiday and attendance records, current training certificates and core competences. 'Mobile access means managers can get on with stuff that adds value, by spending less time doing admin and more time with their team,' Eaton says.

Da Cunha adds: 'Before we introduced the app, some people were telling us that their managers were great at having regular catch-ups, while others were saying: "I never see my manager unless there's a problem." The app makes people more visible and ensures managers are talking to their team members regularly, whether or not there's a problem.'

Information on individual employees' training and skills also helps generate conversations about future training and development opportunities and requirements. One of the most valuable elements of the app is a coaching conversation guide called 'Time with my Manager', which Eaton describes as, 'Fundamentally, it's relationship-building – coaching one-to-one.' He sees it as a way to start coaching discussions about a team member's contribution and their role in the business, as well as finding out what obstacles their manager could remove to help them.

Before any manager can download the app, they are asked to attend a short skills session where they learn how to use it in the most productive way.

The company claims early results are positive, with 86% of managers saying it has helped them give team members more recognition, while almost half report that they're spending more face-to-face time with people. Da Cunha says that early results and enthusiastic comments from managers have 'given me the confidence that we were right to invest in it because it's having a significant impact on managers' ability to do their jobs'.

There are already plans to roll the app out to other areas of the company, such as customer services and engineering, and once it's scaled up it could reach 10,000 BA staff.

Source: Claire Churchard, *People Management*, 24 November 2015.

4.9 EMPLOYEE VOICE

Employee voice is an employee relations concept that is closely linked to and underpins engagement. It comprises two-way initiatives which directly involve employees in exchanging information with managers, replacing or supplementing traditional, indirect means of communication such as joint consultation. It seeks to promote engagement and higher performance at work.

The CIPD defines employee voice as 'the means by which employees communicate their views on employment and organisational issues to their employers' (CIPD 2016c).

Employee voice implies two-way communication between employees and management. The mechanisms that provide employee voice can be classed as 'upward problem-solving' and 'representative participation' (CIPD 2016c).

Upward problem-solving techniques are initiated by management and operate directly between managers and employees rather than through employee representatives. Such techniques include:

- digital media such as email, and social networks to spread and share information
- two-way face-to-face communications between managers and employees – for example, by regular meetings every few weeks
- suggestion schemes, under which employees put ideas to management, who then reward those whose ideas are implemented
- attitude surveys, to measure staff satisfaction with particular aspects of work
- working groups, which are groups of employees brought together to discuss practical work issues such as quality or work organisation.

Representative participation refers to schemes in which employee representatives meet managers on a regular basis, and range from partnership schemes to some 'traditional' employee relations vehicles such as European works councils, joint consultation and collective representation (which may be – but which is not necessarily – trade union representation).

These are the main formal mechanisms of employee voice. All these mechanisms are formal. But informal mechanisms – in effect, simply having a word about a problem to a manager who listens and takes action if necessary – can be a very effective form of voice. Informal mechanisms may be relatively more important in smaller organisations, where fewer formal structures are needed.

4.10 INTERNATIONAL COMPARISONS

The 2009 European Company Survey (Eurofound 2010) covered the 27 EU states and three candidate countries: Croatia, the Former Yugoslav Republic of Macedonia, and Turkey. Taking the 30 countries together, it found that some 37% of establishments had an institutional form of employee representation at the workplace (that is, trade union representation and/or a works council) and that this covered more than 60% of employees. The data showed large national differences, however, and economic sector and company size were also important factors in explaining the incidence of an institutional employee representation at the workplace.

In one group of countries, which included the Nordic countries of Sweden, Denmark and Finland, plus Belgium, Spain, France, Luxembourg, Romania and the Netherlands, a majority of the establishments had an institutional form of employee representation at the workplace, more than 70% of the employees being covered in this manner. Countries in the south of Europe tended to have a lower incidence and coverage, Portugal and Greece revealing the lowest rates in this regard. The UK was in a middle group, which had averages between those of the other two groups.

Incidence and coverage of institutional employee representation were both highest in public services and lowest in private services. Public services, and education in particular, had the highest probability of having a recognised form of employee representation. This pattern was confirmed in most of the countries and was particularly pronounced in Bulgaria, Germany, Romania, Slovenia and Slovakia. For example, the employee coverage of the German works council type is over 40% in private services, above 60% in industry, and reaches 80% in public services.

Company size matters most and, perhaps unsurprisingly, it seems that in all countries the larger the establishment, the greater is the need to have employee representation. It is interesting, however, that the lowest incidence was found in small establishments of 20–49 employees and not in micro-enterprises of 10–19 employees. The reasons for this are not clear. Being a subsidiary of a larger organisation or having foreign ownership also increased the odds of having an institutional form of employee representation.

The interested reader may be directed to the survey for full details of its findings.

An example of a collective agreement between employers and employees in the German metal industry can be found at: **www.eurofound.europa.eu/observatories/eurwork/ articles/industrial-relations/collective-agreements-concluded-in-the-metal-industry**

TURBULENT TIMES IN AIR TRANSPORT

CASE STUDY 4.3

This case study deals with the following topics: collective bargaining, atypical forms of employment, employee relations institutions and legal frameworks.

The European air transport industry is going through turbulent times. A series of recent collective disputes has put the spotlight on aspects of working conditions and the terms and conditions of the employment relationship, particularly social protection.

Air transport has been in the news in recent years as strikes and difficulties in social dialogue across the EU have strained relations between the sector's unions and companies. Disputes in the different countries have revolved around pay and working conditions, restructuring and planned redundancies, collective agreement 'cherry-picking' and foot-dragging over entering into agreements.

In 2014, the air transport sector employed around 440,000 workers across Europe. The move towards a single market has resulted in the gradual liberalisation of the industry, but has also led to a continuous fall in employment.

The issues under debate in the sector are complex and numerous. Recently the social partners in the European civil aviation sector – the European Transport Workers' Federation (ETF), the European Cockpit Association (ECA) and the Association of European Airlines (AEA) – and the European Commission commissioned an extensive study on atypical employment in aviation.

The survey found that atypical employment (defined as 'all forms other than the standard open-ended contract') was largely connected with low-cost airlines. It showed that the labour market for pilots was highly age-segregated (younger pilots are much more likely to fly for low-cost carriers) yet very dynamic, with considerable movement by pilots in search of better terms and conditions of employment. Around half of the survey's 6,000 respondents had changed their employer at least once and, of these, 60% had changed employer more than seven times. The study underlined the risks created by these trends in terms of worker well-being and client safety. It also drew attention to the lack of regulation in the sector to tackle these specific issues:

'... civil aviation legislation does not take into account the prevalence of different forms of atypical employment and outsourcing in the rapidly changing civil aviation industry. Moreover, social legislation is not able to tackle the new phenomena, leaving room for elaborate subcontracting chains and elaborate social as well as fiscal engineering. As a result, the competition nowadays is a true race to the bottom, which affects fair competition and workers' rights as well as raises important issues in the field of safety and liability' (Jorens *et al* 2015).

A recent ruling by the German legal sickness insurance funds on 3 November 2015 illustrates this point. The ruling stated that pilots assigned to Ryanair via a third company and defined by the company as self-employed should in fact be considered salaried employees (in Germany). Their employment status was effectively considered to be 'bogus self-employment'.

EU-level policy

Following an extensive stakeholder consultation, the European Commission planned to adopt two measures by the end of 2015: an 'aviation package for improving the competitiveness of the EU aviation sector'; and a 'social package'. As part of this initiative, the European Parliament issued a resolution on 11 November 2015 which emphasised that 'to boost the EU's air transport economy, the EU needs to ensure a level playing field, while upholding high safety and social standards'.

On 20 October 2015, the European Commission released an action plan for safer aviation prepared by a taskforce led by the European Aviation Safety Agency (EASA) following the tragedy of Germanwings flight 9525, which crashed in France in March 2015 as a result of pilot suicide. Among other things, the taskforce recommended:

- Pilots should undergo psychological checks before beginning employment; random drug and alcohol testing for flight crew should be introduced; a European aeromedical repository should be set up.
- In addition, representatives of airlines (staff and employers) signed a European Corporate Just Culture Declaration on 1 October 2015 in the presence of the European Commissioner for Transport, Violeta Bulc, to 'promote a just culture and boost aviation safety'.

Recent collective disputes in European air transport

Disputes over wages and working conditions

As well as 'traditional' wage-related disputes, such as those in the Czech

Republic and Norway, other aspects of working conditions sparked conflict. These included work intensity and related working time demands at SAS in Sweden, working time flexibility at SAS in Norway, and flight safety at Cargolux in Luxembourg.

A number of the other reported conflicts have similarities with the most recent Lufthansa case, in which new collective agreement provisions on early retirement were the main point of contention. Lufthansa's pilots took strike action at the beginning of September, but regional courts could not agree about the legality of the strike. On 9 September 2016, the court in Hessen ruled the strike unlawful, arguing that the pilot's union Vereinigung Cockpit (VC) was not disputing the collective agreement but was attempting 'to circumvent the restructuring plans of the company'. VC went to the constitutional court to challenge this ruling; at the time of writing, the court's decision was still pending. Meanwhile, the regional labour court at Darmstadt ruled that a five-day strike by members of the cabin crew union, the Independent Flight Attendant Organisation (UFO), was legal, while the Dusseldorf labour court ruled against it (in Germany). On 25 November, UFO called off the planned strikes (in Germany) because a breakthrough had been made in the negotiations.

There were disputes in Romania over the social protection of employees. Air traffic controllers contested, among other things, the possibility of being moved to other positions after the age of 55. The issue of how pensions would be dealt with after the transition to a different employment status are still to be resolved. This issue also concerns firefighters employed at a Norwegian airport and Swedish SAS cabin crew. The latter recently sued their union (Unionen), claiming it had overstepped its authority by agreeing to significant pension cuts for its members which would deprive many cabin crew of a substantial portion of their earned pensions.

Disputes over restructuring and redundancies

The longest strike in Air France's history took place in autumn 2014 when pilots went on strike for 14 days at an estimated cost to the company of €500 million, with more turbulence to follow. On 30 April 2015, the company informed the central works council of its plans to cut 800 jobs by 2017. At the beginning of October 2015, a further cut of 2,900 jobs was announced following the failure of negotiations with the pilots over increasing their working time. Air France management had asked the pilots to increase their productivity by about 17%. The National Union of Airline Pilots' (SNPL) counter-proposals would, according to management, result in an increase of only 2–4%. This deadlock resulted in industrial action, during which angry workers were alleged to have resorted to violence. Negotiations to cut job losses are pending with unions but the management insists that a reduction of 1,000 positions by 2016 cannot be avoided. Negotiations are continuing over the remaining 1,900 positions. SNPL has claimed that Air France's financial difficulties are linked to the traffic rights offered by the French government to airlines from the Persian Gulf, increasing pressure from competitors.

In Portugal, the continuing privatisation process at national carrier TAP Portugal has sparked collective action. The National Union of Civil Aviation Personnel (SNPVAC), which represents around 90% of TAP's 2,500 cabin crew, left the General Workers' Union (UGT) in March, after other unions negotiated an agreement with the government and called off industrial action in December 2014. TAP pilots, who want a share in the forthcoming privatisation, led a ten-day strike in May 2015, but public opinion and the other TAP trade unions opposed this strike. The pilots say the government reneged on a deal agreed in 1999 that they would receive a stake should the airline be privatised. The government

estimated that the stoppage affected 300,000 passengers and cost €70 million.

Disputes over 'cherry-picking' of collective agreements and reluctance to negotiate

In Finland, a dispute between two unions, the Finnish Cabin Crew Union (SLSY) and the Finnish Aviation Union (IAU), and the Union of Service Sector Employers (PALTA) dragged on throughout the spring and up to the end of May 2015. This dispute included several threatened strikes and one executed strike over ground services at all major Finnish airports. The dispute was about which collective agreements applied to ground-handling and cabin crew staff at Airpro, a subsidiary of the former civil aviation authority Finavia, which is now run as a publicly owned company. There was a valid company-level collective agreement and two further existing sector-level agreements which in theory covered ground-handling and cabin crew services. Airpro's customers in ground-handling and cabin crew services are mainly low-cost airlines, and IAU and SLSY have accused Finavia of 'collective agreement shopping'. They claim the company is supporting low-cost airlines at the expense of workers by 'cherry-picking' the cheapest applicable agreement. The company-level agreement offers lower wages and does not take the special features of cabin crew services into account. With help from the national conciliator, the dispute was finally settled in May. The details of the settlement have not been disclosed, but the applicability of the company-level collective agreement remains as it was before the dispute.

Another case worth highlighting in this context is one involving Ryanair in Denmark. The Federation of Employees in the Service Trade (Serviceforbundet), representing cabin crew, tried to enter into collective bargaining with the company but it refused to do so. In turn, the Danish Confederation of Trade Unions (LO) brought the case to the Danish

Labour Court. The court subsequently ruled in favour of the unions, ruling that Ryanair had to recognise the legal right of Serviceforbundet to issue notice of industrial action in support of specific demands on collective bargaining negotiations to establish the working conditions of cabin crew at Ryanair bases in Denmark. This verdict made it possible for other unions affiliated to LO, whose members deliver services such as fuel, catering and baggage-handling to Ryanair, to call sympathy strikes. Such strikes would have prevented Ryanair from flying out of Copenhagen. The verdict attracted great interest because it confirmed that Danish cabin crew, working from a Ryanair base on Danish territory, are covered by Danish labour law. Ryanair had claimed that it was a company registered in Ireland and the working terms of all its employees, wherever they were based, were regulated by Irish civil law. The Union of Civil Servants (ST) announced a sympathy strike (in Sweden) when Ryanair announced plans to relocate to Sweden, but the strike was averted when Ryanair instead moved to Lithuania.

Exercise

As an individual exercise, draft an appreciation of the employee relations situation in the European air transport industry and make recommendations to unions, employers and governments.

For a study group or class exercise, the case may be used as the basis for a debate, for example: 'This House supports (or deplores) present developments in employee relations in the European air transport industry.'

CASE STUDY 4.2 ANSWER GUIDANCE

Commentary from Eurofound (2015)

The recent conflicts have to be seen in the context of an industry under intense pressure from a number of interrelated factors. These include commercial competition and related restructurings; the threat of 'easy' relocation; the growing difficulty of regulating atypical employment and increasing 'bogus-self-employment' in a fundamentally multinational industry; a highly age-segregated labour market; and an increasing gap between a highly organised workforce in some segments of the sector and non-organised workforces in others.

The Ryanair case demonstrates the effect that a single market with low entry and exit barriers can have on industrial relations. The threat of relocating an airline's base, as has happened in this particular case, can eliminate a trade union's bargaining power or even prevent the organisation of workers in the sector, particularly in the newly emerging parts of it.

In the European Commission's recent public consultation on improving the competitiveness of the EU aviation sector, cabin crew unions suggested that collective agreements could be negotiated across nations. Responding to this consultation, many airlines reiterated their support for upholding labour standards.

There is a need for a level playing field in terms of social standards. Wages, statutory labour and social standards are an important part of the business. To ensure this in the future, all companies and their employees stationed in the EU must be subject to the same rules and they must be enforced.

Assuming that a weakening of industrial relations can impact on labour standards, pay, the quality of working conditions and ultimately on flight safety, this challenges the national and European regulators, governments and social partners to avoid a 'race to the bottom' in which all parties would lose.

Source: Eurofound (2015) *Turbulent times in air transport: Recent collective disputes and the 'race to the bottom'* (www.eurofound.europa.eu).

KEY ISSUES

Employee relations is the term now normally used to describe the policies and practices an organisation uses in dealing with its employees, and the systems of rules and mechanisms by which organisations and employees interact with each other. The term implies collective relations such as collective bargaining with trade unions or staff associations, and the resulting agreements, but it also includes policies and procedures which operate at small-group or individual level – for example disciplinary and grievance procedures.

Traditional, collectivised forms and institutions of employee relations have declined in influence, albeit at different rates in different economic sectors and countries, and the focus for many organisations today is shifting towards ensuring employee engagement and commitment.

Organisations try to manage conflict at the level of the individual and the small group by means of grievance and disciplinary procedures, and at the collective level with employee relations systems and agreements. Negotiation can be seen as a process for resolving conflict between two parties whereby both modify their demands to achieve a mutually acceptable compromise. Within any formal framework, informal employee relations processes take place continuously.

Nowhere is the changing nature of the employment relationship in the twenty-first century seen more starkly than in the question of employee relations. This changing relationship is examined further in Chapter 5.

EXPLORE FURTHER

Armstrong, M. (2014) *Armstrong's Handbook of Human Resource Management Practice*. 13th edition. London: Kogan Page.

- Chapters 29–34, 'Employee relations' – an overview of the employee relations framework and processes; employee voice and employee communications.
- Chapter 53, 'Negotiating skills'; Chapter 58, 'Managing conflict'; Chapter 64, 'Employee engagement toolkit'.

Van Wanrooy, B., Bewley, H., Bryson, A., Forth, J., Freeth, S., Stokes, L. and Wood, S. (2013) *Employment Relations in the Shadow of Recession: Findings from the 2011 Workplace Employment Relations Study*. Basingstoke: Palgrave Macmillan.

The following chapters give the most comprehensive picture available of UK practice in the key areas of employee relations.

- Chapter 3, 'Employment and flexible working'.
- Chapter 4, 'The involvement of employees in workplace change'.
- Chapter 5, 'Pay and rewards'.
- Chapter 8, 'The quality of employment relations' (covers conflict and dispute resolution).

Boxall, P., Purcell, J. and Wright, P. (eds) (2007) *The Oxford Handbook of Human Resource Management*. Oxford: Oxford University Press.

• Chapter 12, M. Marchington, 'Employee voice systems'.
Boxall, P. and Purcell, J. (2006) *Strategy and Human Resource Management*.
Basingstoke: Palgrave Macmillan.

• Chapter 8, 'Managing employee voice in unionised and non-unionised firms'.
Storey, J. (ed) (2007) *Human Resource Management: A critical text*. 3rd edition.
London: Thomson Learning

• Chapter 10, M. Marchington and A. Cox, 'Employee involvement and
participation: structures, processes and outcomes'.

CHAPTER 5

HRM and the design of work

INTRODUCTION

In HRM the terms 'work design' and 'job design' are frequently used. Michael Armstrong defined these terms as follows:

> Work design is the creation of systems of work and a working environment that enhance organizational effectiveness and productivity, ensure the organization becomes a 'great place in which to work' and are conducive to the health, safety and wellbeing of employees (Armstrong 2014, p136).

> Job design specifies the contents of jobs in order to satisfy work requirements and meet the personal needs of the job holder, thus increasing levels of employee engagement (Armstrong 2014, p145).

Armstrong proceeds to quote Wall and Clegg (1998, p265):

> Jobs are created by people for people. Whether deliberately or by default, choices are made about which tasks to group together to form a job, the extent to which job holders should follow prescribed procedures in completing those tasks, how closely the job incumbent will be supervised and numerous other aspects of the work. Such choices are the essence of job design.

LEARNING OUTCOMES

On completion of this chapter you should:

- have an appreciation of the concept of division of labour
- know what is meant by job design
- understand the principles of 'scientific management'
- know about developments in job design following scientific management, and especially the principles of the autonomous work group and the Toyota production system
- understand the principles of team formation
- appreciate the team roles required for effective teamworking
- see why organisations seek flexibility in work patterns
- have some appreciation of the organisation of work beyond the team level: by function, by product, the use of the matrix structure, and divisionalisation.

The recognition of the importance of organisation in the efficiency and effectiveness of work can be traced back at least to Adam Smith in his concept of the division of labour. The first sentence of Smith's great work of 1776, *The Wealth of Nations*, reads:

> The greatest improvement in the productive powers of labour and the greater part of the skill, dexterity, and judgement with which it is anywhere directed or applied, seem to have been the effects of the division of labour.

The necessity of the division of labour has naturally been hugely multiplied by the enormous technological advances which have been made, and the resulting complexity of products and services which are now possible, since Smith observed his simple pin-makers in eighteenth-century Kirkcaldy. For example, the modern motorcar is composed of more than 20,000 individual parts, many of which require computer-assisted design and manufacture, while the computers and machines themselves each consist of many, many parts and software which need many engineers and programmers to produce – and so on.

But, as the example of the car shows, to make anything work, after division of labour must come reintegration or synthesis. The 20,000-odd parts of the modern car have to be assembled absolutely correctly if the car is to function at all.

So we can see that organisation of work is really fundamental to the modern technological world.

One of the principal tasks of management in any enterprise is to achieve the most effective combination of division and synthesis of work. That is why the organisation of work matters to executive management and investors. Why it matters to HRM is that unless the whole process, from conception through design to production, can be completely computerised, the division and synthesis crucially depends on, and intimately affects, human beings.

In this chapter we are concerned, first, with the 'micro-organisation' of work, from the level of the individual job to that of the group or team of related workers. We then examine the organisation of work at levels above the team or group. After that we look at patterns of work and flexibility, and finally at some aspects of change management.

5.1 SCIENTIFIC MANAGEMENT

The best known, and perhaps most influential, managerial initiative to achieve efficient division of labour and synthesis of work following the Industrial Revolution was what became known as 'scientific management', and was pioneered by an American industrial engineer, Frederick Winslow Taylor.

Taylor presented a paper called 'A piece-rate system' to the American Society of Mechanical Engineers in 1895, giving him a claim to be the world's first management guru. He certainly became one of the most notorious. He is probably the only management writer whose works were the subject of an examination by a US House of Representatives Special Committee, which occurred in 1911 (Aitken 1960).

Taylor (1911) established the following principles of what he himself called 'scientific management':

- a clear division of tasks and responsibilities between management and workers – management studying the work methods for each job, establishing the most efficient, and then dictating these to the workers
- 'scientific' selection and training of workers: matching suitable employees to the scientifically designed jobs
- the 'enthusiastic co-operation' of management and workers, secured by the use of economic incentives.

The use of this approach combined with high-speed, high-volume assembly lines at Ford's Highland Park plant in the USA led to typical work cycles of one to two minutes. This machine-driven variant of 'Taylorism' came to be known as 'Fordism'. Scientific management produced remarkable increases in productivity, but was usually deeply resented by the workforce. It became associated with poor industrial relations and increased absenteeism, ill health, employee turnover and sabotage. The 1911 House of Representatives hearing came about because of concerns that the intended use of scientific management techniques at a new US Navy arsenal would result in unacceptably hostile industrial relations in a vital military facility. In the event, Taylor's methods were not employed.

Despite these drawbacks, scientific management was widely accepted and applied throughout the twentieth century. Braverman (1974) demonstrated how Taylor's approach had been extended to clerical work. Recent analyses of Japanese car assembly methods ('Toyota-ism') reveal some similarities with Taylorism, as we shall see later in this chapter.

5.1.1 CRITICISMS OF SCIENTIFIC MANAGEMENT

At least since the time of the Hawthorne Studies (Roethlisberger and Dickson 1939), scientific management has been subject to criticisms that it assumed that the only motivation of the worker was economic; that it ignored workers' needs for feelings of achievement, job satisfaction and recognition; and that it neglected the importance of social relations and group psychology in the workplace.

However, it has been said (Buchanan 1994) that:

> Modern techniques of work design have been developed and applied in the second half of this century as antidotes to Taylorism. The impact of these alternative techniques has not been as powerful or pervasive as the influence of scientific management on management practice.

5.2 DEVELOPMENTS FOLLOWING SCIENTIFIC MANAGEMENT

The alienating and demotivation effects of 'scientific management' job design (Taylorism) led to attempts to re-humanise work to increase employees' motivation and performance. These efforts naturally focused on the characteristics of the work itself. Herzberg *et al* (1959) proposed that 'motivator' factors such as recognition and autonomy lead to job satisfaction (and hence motivation), while the absence of 'hygiene' factors, such as acceptable levels of pay, lead to dissatisfaction (and demotivation). Critics have argued that Herzberg is wrong and that research does not support his model, but Herzberg's work encouraged organisations to pursue 'job enrichment' by addressing 'hygiene' factors to produce an acceptable job context for workers and building motivators into jobs to increase satisfaction.

The principle of job enrichment was reinforced by Hackman and Oldham's (1980) job characteristics model (JCM) which proposed that five job characteristics – namely, task variety, autonomy, feedback, significance and identity – promote individual motivation, job satisfaction and performance through critical psychological states such as experienced meaningfulness.

The core proposition of the JCM has been supported by later studies (see Parker and Ohly 2010). One, Birdi *et al* (2008), examined the productivity of 308 companies over 22 years. They found that empowerment, broadly defined as giving significant operational management responsibility to individuals or teams, was associated with increased performance.

Parker and Ohly (2010) concluded that there was reasonably consistent and strong empirical evidence from such studies for the effects of job enrichment on attitudes and affective (that is, emotional) reactions, such as job satisfaction, although with more mixed evidence for the effects on performance.

JCM and job enrichment are mainly focused on individual jobs. In a study of coal miners, Trist and Bamforth (1951) observed that the introduction of a Taylorist work design in a particular mine destroyed the social support systems the miners relied on and this led to increased absenteeism and poor motivation. In a second mine, the miners managed to alleviate the destructive social effect of the new work processes by organising themselves into groups. Their studies led to a new model of work design, the autonomous work group, which we discuss in section 5.3.1. When we consider the idea of teamworking, the concepts of work design and job design overlap.

5.3 THE INFLUENCE OF MOTIVATION THEORY ON THE DESIGN OF WORK

Psychologists have been studying the motivation of workers for over 100 years, and the theories that have sought to explain employees' motivation have reflected the dominant psychological theories of their day. The earliest theories were based on the assumption that people had an 'instinct' to work. Later theories, such as those of Maslow (1943) and Herzberg (1966), introduced the concepts of 'needs', 'drives' and 'motives'. Behavioural psychology brought an emphasis on reinforcement of behaviour – that is, in this context, job performance.

The 'cognitive revolution' in psychology has been influential more recently. This approach reacted to extreme behaviourism, which had held that mental states were irrelevant to behaviour, by insisting that people's behaviour was affected by their conscious states and intentions. Goal theory provides managers with a workable technology to structure work – including more abstract and complex work such as management and professional activities – in a way that can apply the general lessons learned from the body of motivation theory.

It is fair to say that there is still no comprehensive and universally accepted theory of motivation, and our current understanding and practice of motivation and commitment are influenced to some degree by all of the various principal schools of thought since the time of Maslow at least. However, we must not doubt the immense influence that motivation theory has exercised on the organisation of work. Buchanan could comment (Buchanan 1994, p93) that:

> Maslow's influence is clearly stamped across the work design theories and practices of the latter half of the twentieth century.

For instance, the concept of the 'composite autonomous work group' or 'self-managing multi-skilled team' (see below), which was first developed by the Tavistock Institute of Human Relations in London, explicitly reflects Maslow's ideas.

A comprehensive discussion of motivation theory is beyond the scope of the present text. The interested reader may be directed to Landy and Conte (2007) for an up-to-date and accessible treatment of these theories.

5.3.1 SOME PRACTICAL CONCLUSIONS FROM MOTIVATION THEORY

Some useful general principles have been derived from the body of motivation theory:

- We should set goals whenever we can, and, where it is possible and sensible to do so, we should involve the employee(s) concerned in designing and agreeing the goals.
- Establishing agreed, specific and difficult goals ('stretch goals') leads to significant increases in employee performance.
- We should link rewards to performance wherever we reasonably can. The actual scheme or schedule of rewards is usually less important than having a clearly perceived link to performance.
- We should seek to increase employees' sense of self-confidence ('self-efficacy') that they can successfully perform the job or task.
- We should let employees know the level of performance that is expected of them, and give them accurate and timely feedback on their actual work performance.

- Giving positive rewards for good performance is more effective in motivating people than punishing them for poor performance.
- Perceived fairness or equity is important to the motivation of employees.

Practicalities of goal-setting

One of the first and best-known systems of goal-setting at work was 'management by objectives' (MBO). The phrase was coined by Peter Drucker. MBO was initially developed for organising managerial work, but it is now extensively used at all levels of organisations. When used properly it facilitates both the performance of management and the development of individual employees.

Drucker stressed the importance of involving employees in the setting of goals for themselves rather than managers simply imposing goals upon them. From the manager's point of view, the art of goal-setting is obtaining genuine employee input into the setting of goals which can 'stretch' the employee to improve their performance.

There is a widely known acronym that is helpful in reminding us how goals should be set at work: they should be 'smart' – that is, they should be:

- **S**pecific
- **M**easurable
- **A**ssignable
- **R**ealistic
- **T**ime-bound.

In other words, people should know exactly what they are being asked to achieve (that is, their goal is 'specific'). Their performance should be capable of being assessed against some criteria or standard of success ('measurable'), and this means looking for appropriate measures of performance whenever this is feasible. There should be no doubt or ambiguity about responsibility, whether individual or team ('assignable'). No one should be asked to undertake responsibility for any action that is intrinsically impossible or for which they are not capable (goals must be 'realistic'). All actions must be successfully completed by a stated time ('time-bound').

Of course, as any manager will tell you, it is not always as easy as that sounds. The great strength of the 'smart' approach is that it compels the manager to seek clarity and realism in what they are asking people to do, and this can be hard, time-consuming work, entailing considerable interaction with other people. Moreover, this requirement works both ways, up and down the organisation – no manager should accept a goal or objective themselves until they are happy with its 'smart' profile.

The degree of direction or participation which the manager employs in this process will depend on many factors, such as the degree of urgency, the complexity of the task and the expertise and knowledge of the individual or team undertaking the work.

? REFLECTIVE ACTIVITY 5.1

Write down the last three things you were tasked to do in your work. How smart were your goals?

Write down the last three activities you assigned to subordinates. How smart were these?

HRM IN ACTION: THE 'CRITICAL FEW'

When the present author was undertaking research into management development in firms in Scotland, one very well-known US technology firm explained to him their performance management and development system, which was known in the company as 'the critical few'. It was essentially MBO but with a neat twist relating to prioritising. It was described by the plant director as follows:

> A manager has to do 101 or maybe 1,001 things, but only a few – no more than half a dozen at most,

and often less than that – are *really* critical at any time. If these 'critical few' are done well, mostly the other ones either fall into place or don't matter much. The smart manager learns to think that way and to spot his or her 'critical few'. If you can't learn to do that, you'll get buried in this place.

This illustrates the importance of prioritising one's own work as a manager, but competent managers also assist their people to find their own 'critical few'.

The autonomous work group

The principles of the autonomous work group are expressed in the 'Tavistock work organisation model' (Trist and Bamforth 1951, Emery 1963). This specified that work should be organised in teams and that individual jobs should provide variety, a meaningful task, an 'optimum' work cycle, the worker's control over work standards, feedback of results, preparation and auxiliary tasks, the use of valued skill and knowledge, and a perceived contribution to the end product. The teams should provide workers with the means for communication and also promotion. A very important aspect of the Tavistock model is its freedom from the technology that is used in the work, so it is applicable in virtually all work situations.

Autonomous work groups were extensively used in Scandinavia, especially by the car manufacturers Saab and Volvo, and also elsewhere in Europe, including Scottish & Newcastle Breweries in Edinburgh. Autonomous work groups were not at first popular in North America, and in the 1970s job enlargement schemes were more accepted. The comparative lack of popularity of the autonomous work group with managers until the mid-1980s may be partly explained by its sophisticated theoretical basis and consequent complex language, and partly by its effect on the status and responsibilities of supervisors and junior managers. Until compelled to by the spectre of economic failure in global competition, most Western companies – workers as well as managers – were unwilling to make the revolutionary organisational and cultural changes that the adoption of the autonomous work group entails.

By the 1980s the increased competition from Japanese industries with team-based 'lean manufacture' reawakened Western, and especially American, interest in autonomous work groups. The management guru Tom Peters supported them (Peters 1987, p296):

> the modest-sized, task-oriented, semi-autonomous, mainly self-managing team should be the basic organisational building-block.

However, whereas the Tavistock work organisation model was a deliberate move away from Taylorist work principles and towards the self-actualising goal of the humanistic psychologists (Maslow 1943, Herzberg 1966), the Japanese team system explicitly contained some Taylorist aspects.

The Toyota production system

The Toyota production system (TPS) presents the paradigm case of Japanese work organisation – so much so that the word 'Toyota-ism' has passed into everyday management language. The TPS has been highly influential not only in manufacturing but also in services, including recently even the UK National Health Service, a work situation that you might think was about as dissimilar from a car manufacturing plant as could be imagined (see HRM in Action 5.2).

There are four main principles of the TPS (Adler *et al* 1997): 'just-in-time' production, flexibility, quality, and a combination of standardised work and continuous improvement.

'Just-in-time' (JIT) production aims to eliminate all work-in-progress (WIP) inventory. In addition to reducing the capital locked up in WIP, this helps to increase organisational learning by eliminating buffers of stock and WIP, and so exposing bottlenecks and problems in production. This then necessitates flexibility and participation from the teamworkers because they must solve problems in real time.

To aid flexibility, workers are typically organised in teams of four to six, and tasks are rotated within the team. Team leaders train workers, cover for absent team members and handle administrative tasks. Clusters of from three to five teams typically comprise a group, and group leaders are the first level of management.

The *jidoka* quality principle dictates that the production process should be as error-free as possible. Traditional manufacturing processes rely on quality-control inspectors to catch substandard parts at the end of the assembly line, but managers trust the workers to inspect their own work in the TPS. Workers are expected to catch faulty parts immediately, to avoid waste, and to find the causes of production problems. Workers are empowered to stop the assembly line whenever they fall behind or see a fault they cannot repair.

Standardised work and *kaizen*, or continuous improvement, together constitute the fourth component of the TPS. Each task is analysed and the most efficient method is specified in motion-by-motion instructions describing exactly how each job should be done. This is the 'Taylorist' aspect of Japanese work methods which seems to sharply demarcate it from the Western autonomous work group. Despite the use of these methods, TPS is not Taylorist in the normal sense of the word, however. It is the team members and team leaders who identify the best procedures for each job, whereas in Western Taylorist production systems it is industrial engineers who would design the work process and observe and time workers at specific jobs. And as we have just seen, workers are empowered to stop assembly lines on their own initiative – a radically *anti*-Taylorist concept. Workers are also encouraged to engage in continuous improvement of their work process and constantly make advances in 'best practice'.

Autonomous work group versus Toyota-ism

Hammarström and Lansbury (1991) compared the experience of Swedish car manufacturers which had adopted autonomous work groups with that of Toyota. Saab was forced to sell its car business in the late 1980s, and Volvo experienced troubles in the early 1990s that eventually meant it was bought by Ford – but their Japanese competitors thrived. No doubt the reasons both for the Swedish failures and for the Japanese success were complex and many-factored, but Hammarström and Lansbury concluded that for managers in many countries the Toyota approach appeared safe and more 'natural' than autonomous work groups as a means of production, and they questioned whether the Swedish model – and by extension the Western autonomous work group – could survive the impact of global competition.

CASE STUDY 5.2

HRM IN ACTION: NHS LOTHIAN'S 'LEAN VISION'

The *Scotsman* newspaper (26 October 2016) reported that a change management programme implemented by National Health Service Lothian, and which used the 'lean management' approach of the Toyota production system, had been nominated in the Best Change Management Programme category at the HR Excellence Awards in London.

Source: **www.scotsman.com/news/nhs-lothian-s-lean-vision-up-for-uk-award-1–1323263**

5.4 TEAMWORKING

We can now say that teamworking is virtually the 'default option' in job design today. Only if there are compelling reasons not to organise people in teams will alternatives be considered.

We can define a work group or team as:

A group of people collaborating in their professional work, or in a particular enterprise or task, who share common objectives and who need to work together to achieve them.

Tuckman (1965) studied the process of team development and identified four essential stages that all teams have to progress through if they are to be effective. He labelled these forming, storming, norming and performing:

- *Forming*, the first stage, begins when the members meet. This stage is typified by anxiety and formality as members learn what behaviour is expected of them and how they should undertake the task. There is usually a greater dependence on the team leader at this time. Members typically will be asking themselves whether they will be able to do the task and fit in with the rest of the team.
- *Storming* is the second stage. Here the formality of the forming stage is dispensed with. There is often conflict between members and with the leader. There may also be resistance to the demands of the team task.
- Group cohesion appears at the third stage, *norming*. The 'norms' of the team emerge – how it will behave and go about its task, how it will solve problems, etc. Mutual support and co-operation are evident and views can be openly expressed without conflict. A team identity starts to be built.
- When the norms have been established, the team can start to *perform* effectively.

All effective teams have to go through these four stages of development. Many of the processes in the forming, storming and norming stages happen at a non-verbal, barely conscious, level. Virtual teams – that is, those in which members operate at separate locations and use information technology for communication and co-ordination – have to go through the same development process as other teams if they are to be effective. It has been found that initial face-to-face meetings of the team greatly facilitate the development process – probably because the non-verbal and unconscious mechanisms seem to operate much more effectively face-to-face than when mediated by information technology. Geographical dispersion is no barrier to effective performance once a virtual team has reached the performing stage.

Tuckman and Jensen (1977) added a fifth stage to team development, which they termed 'adjourning', meaning the end of the team as an effective unit. This may happen explicitly, as with the disbanding of a project team when the team has successfully completed its remit, but it can happen informally as the team starts to disintegrate. It will often not be immediately obvious to those outside the team. Production and service teams that are designed to operate without any defined end-point are susceptible to drifting into adjournment without management realising.

5.4.1 TYPES OF TEAMS

Not all teams are the same in terms of their functions and how they work. *Production or service teams* tend to undertake a limited range of standard activities and be highly interchangeable in terms of team members: everyone can do each other's job. This requires a high degree of cross-training, but yields very high flexibility. Such teams can be self-managing.

Project teams on the other hand are typically composed of highly skilled experts who are therefore not interchangeable with each other, and the team may have a very wide range of activities to handle, which might include solving hitherto unknown and unexpected problems. A designated leader is usually required.

Top management teams may have as wide a range of activities to deal with as project teams but will probably have some degree of interchangeability.

There are many other types of teams. Examples include cross-functional or cross-departmental teams, quality circles, functional teams and problem-solving teams.

5.4.2 TEAM ROLES

After studying how management teams operated, Belbin (1981) identified a number of crucial roles that must be fulfilled by team members if the team is to be successful. Belbin's findings have been applied by many management writers to all teams, not just managerial ones. Belbin's work suggests that it is not sufficient to select effective teams solely on the basis of the functional skills of people.

Belbin labelled the eight roles he identified as being crucial to effective teamworking as: 'chairperson', 'company worker', 'completer-finisher', 'monitor-evaluator', 'plant', 'resource investigator', 'shaper' and 'team-worker'. These are explained below.

The 'chairperson' role helps control the team and encourages all the members to participate. This role is often carried out effectively by someone who is neither the cleverest nor most creative in the team. What is important is that the chairperson can identify team objectives clearly, can display a calm and confident manner, and stays in control.

The 'company worker' role helps the team to put proposals into practice. This requires self-discipline and the ability to organise. People who have a strong sense of duty and organisational loyalty, and who are dependable and predictable in their own behaviour, are well suited to this role.

The 'completer-finisher' role helps the team to finish the job and keeps a sense of urgency alive until it is done. This role needs someone who is good at the details of the problem or job in hand and is conscientious in seeing the task through to its end.

The 'monitor-evaluator' role enables the team to analyse problems and evaluate ideas and proposals. It requires the ability to make realistic and impartial judgements.

The 'plant' role encourages creative thinking within the team. It needs someone who is intelligent and perhaps unorthodox in their thinking – the good 'plant' can 'think the unthinkable'.

The 'resource investigator' function provides a link between the team and the rest of the organisation in order to obtain resources needed to complete the task. It needs someone who is extrovert and enthusiastic with good interpersonal social skills.

The 'shaper' role influences the way the team operates and is best performed by energetic and extrovert people who are not afraid to challenge the usual working norms and methods.

The 'team-worker' role helps support the individual team members and encourages team spirit and morale. This is best done by a 'people person' who can empathise with their fellow workers and who is good at reducing interpersonal friction and defusing conflicts.

People can take on more than one role each, so it is certainly possible to have effective teams of fewer than eight members, but as the descriptions given above suggest, personality traits seem to play a part in determining which roles individuals are best suited to undertake or most comfortable with.

? REFLECTIVE ACTIVITY 5.2

Consider your own behaviour in a team in which you have worked. Which of the Belbin team roles do you feel most comfortable with?

Why did these particular roles/this particular role suit you, do you think?

5.5 HRM IMPLICATIONS ARISING FROM TEAM-BASED WORKING

People have to be given the skills and knowledge they require to work effectively in the team – not only the technical skills to do the actual job, but the interpersonal skills required to work in a team, and also the presentational and communication skills necessary for the team to interface with other teams, with customers and with the rest of the organisation. The more autonomy the team has been granted, the higher the number, and the greater the complexity, of skills that are required.

Managers to whom autonomous teams are accountable will also require training to adapt to a supporting rather than a directing role in relation to the teams.

HRM DILEMMA 5.1

Teamworking: workers' liberation or management by stress?

Not everyone thinks teamworking is a good idea. Here is an extract from an article published by the *Socialist Worker*, a British Marxist newspaper. What do you think?

***Socialist worker* examines how modern management techniques are really about getting us to work harder and longer**

Bosses and neo-liberal ideologues tell us modern capitalism has changed our lives and the way that we work. According to them, the world of work has changed dramatically since the years of poverty, lack of control and constant work that characterised the lives of workers at the end of the nineteenth and early twentieth centuries.

But the world of work hasn't changed that much, as many workers could testify. How many of us have had to put up with human resource management? Workers have become used to 'key performance indicators', 'teamworking', 'appraisals' and a whole battery of measures that go under the rubric of 'flexibility' and 'modernisation'.

We all now own our 'own' jobs. In other words, we are blamed for every little thing that goes wrong.

We are flexible and we work in teams, meaning we do more work for less money. This means, of course, that we are 'empowered', or more likely, stressed out of our minds and completely exhausted. Getting people to be flexible and to work in teams is about far more than management finding new ways to annoy workers. The result will be as it always has been – longer hours, greater stress and job cuts.

'Modernisation' is what workers are told to accept. In reality there is nothing 'modern' about it. It is as old as capitalism. Its real meaning is the same as it always has been – 'You have to work harder and longer.'

Source: *Socialist Worker* 2035, 27 January 2007, **www.socialistworker.co.uk/art.php?id=10540**

5.6 ORGANISATIONAL DESIGN

In this section we look at the organisation of work at levels above that of the team.

Contemporary thinking is that there is no 'one right way' to organise a business or other form of institution. The big difficulty for managers in trying to organise work is that activities can usually be ordered in a number of different ways, each of which might seem plausible. For instance, activities might be organised around the different functions of the organisation: production, marketing, finance, sales, and so on. Or they might be arranged around the separate products, or by geographical location – the UK, Europe, North America, and so on. Large multi-product firms can be organised into separate divisions or strategic business units (SBUs). Some of these different ways of grouping work activities might be used within the same organisation, and even combined, as we will see in our discussion of the matrix structure in section 5.6.2. However, some general principles have been established.

5.6.1 BY FUNCTION OR BY PRODUCT?

We first consider the choice between organising by function or by product.

A functional structure can give some real advantages where the organisation is concentrated on a single product or service and where the rate of change is relatively slow:

- The management structure can be relatively simple and all major decisions can all be dealt with by a small top management team.
- The functional structure allows specialist expertise to be built up and can offer a good career path for specialists.
- The simple structure makes it easy to obtain economies of scale as production rises.

So a functional structure is often the best for small, single-product organisations which operate with relatively simple technology in markets where change and risk are predictable and manageable.

Organising activities around products usually becomes more effective than a functional structure as a firm diversifies into multiple products. This advantage increases as competitive or technological changes increase in rate. In these circumstances the product structure is definitely superior to the functional structure in speed of decision-making by top management, in knowledge of customers and markets, in communication between specialists and managers, and in product development. It is also more effective at developing future general managers.

5.6.2 THE MATRIX STRUCTURE: THE BEST OF BOTH WORLDS?

Experience has shown that it is possible, and often desirable, to combine aspects of both the functional and product organisation. Project teams which comprise experts from different functions and departments who are all working on the same task (for example developing a new product) show this. Project teams are of fixed duration, but when the arrangement is long term or permanent, it is called a *matrix structure*. The matrix structure is sometimes called 'the grid structure' when is applied over the whole of the organisation, as can be the case in knowledge-based industries.

In a matrix structure, functional specialists have two bosses: they report on project issues to the designated project manager but they are still under the overall authority of their functional managers (on whom their career progression might rely). Of course, this can lead to stresses and tensions when the demands of the managers conflict. One of the most important advantages of a matrix structure is that it helps to preserve flexibility as successful organisations grow. It can also help to encourage delegation, which assists both motivation and the development of managers.

There are some acknowledged problems with matrix structures. There is inevitable conflict between product and functional managers over priorities of resources, time and costs. Functional managers often fear that their authority will be undermined by matrix structures, whereas functional specialists have concerns about loss of their specialist identity and the possible threat to their career progression. Individual stress will be increased by the conflict of dual reporting and ambiguity over what is demanded of people in the system. It has been said that in a matrix structure conflict and stress is the price that has to be paid for adaptability and change. Administrative overheads often increase because of more complicated managerial hierarchies and more managerial time being spent on handling conflict.

A matrix structure can be advantageous if an organisation is diversified, if it operates in a market where technical complexity requires the use of many specialists, and if it faces high competitive pressures. Indeed, in those conditions a matrix structure will probably recognise and improve a situation that has emerged anyway.

5.6.3 DIVISIONALISATION

Most large and diversified companies now follow a divisionalised structure with separate divisions or strategic business units (SBUs) based on different product ranges or the geographical locations of customers. This offers several advantages to larger organisations:

- Each division can concentrate on its own particular market, so major decisions are taken nearer to the point of action and corporate management is freed for more strategic matters.
- Profit responsibility is delegated to divisions, allowing business activities to be evaluated separately.
- The decentralisation of decision-making and responsibility is likely to motivate middle-level general managers and provide them with earlier training in general management.

There are some potential problems with divisionalisation, of course:

- The best basis for creating divisions may not always be clear – as between product and geographical location, for example.
- There will be conflict between divisions over investment resources and share of central services.
- The idea of divisionalisation rests on the assumption that a firm can identify a number of separate self-contained areas of business. So the greater the interdependence of the various parts of the company, the harder it will be to make divisionalisation work effectively.
- Even where the original divisional design was appropriate initially, fast growth of a division may alter its characteristics.

> ### ? REFLECTIVE ACTIVITY 5.3
>
> The 'Bossless' Organisation?
>
> Valve, which describes itself as an 'entertainment and software technology' company, claims to have a completely flat organisational structure and to be a 'bossless' organisation.
>
> This is described in its new employee handbook, which is available at:
>
> **media.steampowered.com/apps/valve/Valve_Handbook_LowRes.pdf**
>
> Could your organisation be 'bossless'? If not, how many layers of hierarchy does it really need?

5.7 THE 'FLEXIBLE FIRM' AND HRM

As we will recall from Chapter 1, the Workplace Employment Relations Study (2004 WERS) found solid empirical evidence that many UK organisations operated a 'flexible organisation' with a core of key employees and a 'peripheral' workforce of other workers who enjoyed less secure and less attractive terms and conditions of employment.

'Core employees' are those who are crucial to the organisation's success. These are not just top managers – anyone with critical knowledge or skills should be in the core. Core employees have high market value. They will be well rewarded and receive good development and career opportunities. The idea of 'talent management' was created for this category of employees. The core is protected from short-term fluctuations in market demand by several peripheral shells of employees who, as we move out from the core, experience increasingly less attractive employment conditions and rewards. The outermost shell typically comprises temporary staff and low-skilled labour recruited on a casual basis from the local labour market, or perhaps migrant labour (Atkinson 1984) (see Figure 5.1).

The HRM content of the people management profile within the firm may drop rapidly from the core to the outer periphery. The people management applied to core employees will be HRM. These are the people for whom the 'war for talent' is waged. Those in shells close to the core will also probably enjoy the advantages of an HRM approach – many of them will become core employees in due course. But as we move further out from the core, the people management style will progressively resemble HRM less and less, employees receiving markedly fewer training and development opportunities, less secure employment and less attractive rewards. These people are more easily replaced from the local labour markets and figure much less in the 'war for talent'.

> ### ? REFLECTIVE ACTIVITY 5.4
>
> Does your employing organisation have the characteristics of a 'flexible firm'?
>
> If it does, what are the criteria for becoming a core employee?

5.7.1 A FINAL WORD ON ORGANISATIONAL STRUCTURE

Inappropriate organisational structure can be expected to hinder organisational performance. However, good structure by itself cannot guarantee success. We should think of organisational structure as being able to make a necessary but not in itself sufficient contribution to performance. The performance of an organisation is influenced by many factors. Structure cannot ensure that correct strategies are followed or correct decisions made. To quote A.P. Sloan, a former president of General Motors (Sloan 1967):

> An organisation [that is, structure] does not make decisions: its function is only to provide a framework, based upon established criteria, within which decisions can be fashioned in an orderly manner. Nor can structure compensate for lack of appropriate skills, the will to manage effectively, or the motivation to work together.

Figure 5.1 The flexible firm

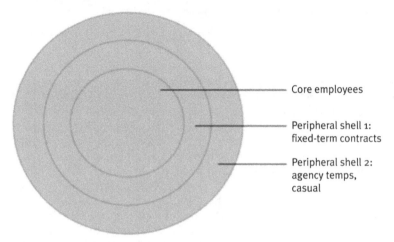

Source: adapted from Atkinson (1984)

5.8 THE SEARCH FOR FLEXIBILITY

Peter Drucker once remarked that until the time of the Industrial Revolution, 'only lunatics and criminals worked by the clock'. This may be something of an exaggeration, but it serves to remind us how industrialisation and the factory system has accustomed us to the idea of a 'normal working week' being something like 9 to 5, Monday to Friday. In fact, this 'normal working week' has been showing a steady reduction in the number of hours it entails since the first Industrial Revolution. The purpose of this section is to explore the alternative patterns of work that are available.

Employers pursue flexibility in working patterns for three main reasons:

- to minimise human resource costs in both the short and the long run
- to protect the core from short-term fluctuations in market demand
- in response to the demands of an increasingly diverse workforce in terms of both (1) minimum legal compliance, and (2) discretionary entitlement, surpassing the legal minimum, to attract and retain core employees.

In terms of economic efficiency, three forms of flexibility are of interest to employers:

- *functional flexibility*, by which employees can be redeployed quickly to new tasks and activities (for example multi-skilled craftsmen and teamworkers)
- *numerical flexibility*, enabling the organisation quickly to increase and decrease the numbers employed in response to market demand (for example temporary employment, part-time working, subcontracting) – see Figure 5.1
- *financial flexibility* – the establishing of pay systems that reinforce the requirement for flexibility (for example performance-related pay, pay for skills).

In addition to the need for compliance with equal opportunities legislation for all employees, employers are increasingly concerned in the 'war for talent' to be able to offer their core employees an employment package that not only is sufficiently attractive in financial terms but is able to meet their requirements in terms of flexibility.

And there is evidence that many employers are prepared to offer more flexible working arrangements for at least some of their employees. For example, according to the 2011 Workplace Employment Relations Study, 56% of UK workplaces offered reduced hours to some employees, while 34% offered flexitime, 30% working from home, 19% compressed hours, and 16% school term-time working (van Wanrooy *et al* 2013).

5.8.1 ANNUAL HOURS

Organisations typically establish permanent manning levels that will cope with normal demand. However, fluctuations in demand can result in inefficiencies in that there may be overmanning at times of low demand and undermanning, requiring the use of temporary workers or overtime, at times of peak demand. For many organisations, the demand for their goods or services fluctuates according to recognisable and predictable patterns, and in these cases the scheduling of employee hours according to annual hours should result in a better match between demand and hours actually worked in any period.

Annual hours arrangements are based on the principle that the number of hours that full-time employees must work is defined over a whole year rather than over a week or a month. Thus an average 38-hour week (with a total of five weeks' holiday per year) becomes 1,786 annual hours.

5.8.2 ALTERNATIVES TO PERMANENT FULL-TIME WORKING

Temporary working

The main purposes for employers in employing temporary workers are:

- to provide a more flexible alternative to full-time employees
- to cover for temporary peaks in demand
- to cover for holiday and sickness absence
- to protect the job security of core employees.

Most temporary workers are employed on short-term contracts of unspecified length or renewable from week to week. Typically, they receive the same basic pay and benefits as full-time workers but are usually excluded from fringe benefits.

Part-time working

Part-time working can cut down the need for overtime and/or unsocial hours payments to permanent staff and so be more cost-effective. It can lower unit labour costs where part-time workers' earnings are too low to incur employers' tax liabilities and where part-timers are ineligible for fringe benefits.

Job-sharing is where two or more employees share the responsibilities of one full-time position, with the salary and other benefits shared between them in proportion to the time each works. In principle any job could be shared in any way that was acceptable to the two parties involved and their employer, but the most common patterns are: split day, split week, or alternate weeks.

Home-working – information technology has significantly increased the scope for home-working by employees.

New forms of employment

We noted in Chapter 1 that new forms of employment have emerged to meet the need for increased flexibility by both employers and workers and that these are having a profound effect on the conventional one-to-one relationship between the employer and employee. These new forms include:

- *employee-sharing*, where an individual worker is jointly hired by a group of employers to meet the HR needs of various companies, resulting in permanent full-time employment for the worker
- *interim management*, in which highly skilled experts are hired temporarily for a specific project or to solve a specific problem, thereby integrating external management capacities in the work organisation
- *casual work*, where an employer is not obliged to provide work regularly to the employee but has the flexibility of calling them on demand
- *voucher-based work*, where the employment relationship is based on payment for services with a voucher purchased from an authorised organisation that covers both pay and social security contributions
- *portfolio work*, where a self-employed individual works for a large number of clients doing small-scale jobs for each.

Chapter 9 also looks at new forms of employment which utilise information and communication technology (ICT), such as 'crowdworking'.

?   REFLECTIVE ACTIVITY 5.5

What would you say are the implications for employees of the new forms of employment noted in section 5.8.2?

REFLECTIVE ACTIVITY 5.5 ANSWER GUIDANCE

Employee-sharing, job-sharing and interim management seem to offer beneficial working conditions, combining enhanced flexibility for workers with a good level of job security.

Voucher-based work entails some job insecurity, social and professional isolation and limited access to HR measures and career development, but offers workers the opportunity to work legally, better social protection and perhaps better pay.

Casual work is characterised by low income, job insecurity, poor social protection and little or no access to HR benefits. The high level of flexibility might benefit some workers, but most would prefer more continuity.

The forms that seem most likely to be beneficial to the labour market are employee-sharing, job-sharing and interim management, while casual work is likely to be the most disadvantageous. All of the new employment forms have the potential to aid labour market integration of specific groups of workers, but their job-creation potential is rather limited.

Most of these employment forms contribute to labour market innovation and make it more attractive to both employers and a wider range of potential workers. However, there is a danger of labour market segmentation, particularly from casual work and voucher-based work, if the result is a widespread acceptance of fragmented jobs that are inherently linked to low income and limited social protection.

These new forms of employment may be accelerating the divide within organisations between a core of high-value, permanent employees and others who enjoy significantly poorer employment rights and protection. In some of these new working relationships, the status of the worker as employee or self-employed contractor can be ambiguous.

KEY ISSUES

Work has to be to be organised in some way in order to (1) achieve the benefits of division of labour and specialisation, and (2) achieve the necessary synthesis of the outputs of that division. This is the basis of work and job design.

'Scientific management' represented the first systematic attempts at modern job design. The autonomous work group developed from attempts to humanise work while still achieving technical efficiencies. The Toyota production system of 'lean manufacture' is highly influential and it combines both teamwork and elements of Taylorism.

We understand quite a lot about how teams develop and the roles that are necessary for effective teamworking.

Employers pursue flexibility in working patterns to minimise human resource costs; to protect the core from short-term fluctuations in market demand; in response to the demands of an increasingly diverse workforce in terms of both (1) minimum legal compliance, and (2) discretionary entitlement, surpassing the legal minimum, to attract and retain core employees. The three forms of flexibility of most interest to employers are: functional flexibility, numerical flexibility and financial flexibility.

New forms of employment, especially those using information and communication technology, are intensifying the divide within organisations between a core of high-value, permanent employees and others who enjoy significantly poorer employment rights and protection.

CASE STUDY 5.3

KVADRAT

Kvadrat is an international company with more than 400 employees that produces fabrics for different customer groups (retail, hotels, furniture manufacturers, and so on). The company's headquarters is in Denmark, with beautiful surroundings that inspire creative design. There are 145 people employed in product development, marketing, finance, sales, HR, IT, logistics, customer service, sample and order expedition, and the quality department, all based at the headquarters. The products are manufactured in different European countries. Kvadrat's products are in the expensive price range.

Exercise

As an individual or group exercise, develop a short presentation for Kvadrat's top management team on how the principles of work design can assist the company to maintain its success on offering high-quality, high-price fabric designs.

CASE STUDY 5.1 ANSWER GUIDANCE

The story of Kvadrat is one of success and growth. The company develops new solutions and services using participatory meeting forms and having few organisational walls and ceilings. The company has a culture that is supportive of workplace innovation and their practices are developed and implemented in an incremental and experimental way. The company has won several prizes for being a great and healthy place to work. They ascribe the open culture to their strong market position.

The company regards workplace innovation as a way to ensure renewal and the ability to offer a service that customers will choose over others. In 2012 they introduced new multidisciplinary customer segment teams, where product developers, designers, customer service assistants, logisticians and representatives from the department of quality and environment work together across countries. The subsidiary companies take part in the teamwork as well. This teamwork practice provides the employees with a better understanding of the customers' needs, so they are able to provide better service. They are becoming better at sharing knowledge and are able to accommodate new demands. They have recently initiated partnerships with customers (in relation to corporate social responsibly and environmental issues, quality and logistics). Customers are less likely to switch to another supplier, because the company can offer them a much better product and targeted service. Teamwork, knowledge-sharing and employee initiative are seen as supportive of company success: 'It is simply what it takes to achieve our goals' (manager).

The customer segment teams are the latest addition to a longer tradition of sharing knowledge and supporting employee participation. The multidisciplinary teams are centred on specific customer segments (for example, hospitals, retail): 'We work directly on how to help the customer in the very best way.' The teams discuss their work organisation continuously and share knowledge and experiences. Other autonomous and semi-autonomous teamwork practices are used in the company as well. Teams in the order expedition department are distributing their work tasks at their daily morning meeting and proposing improvements to their work organisation.

The company's structure is characterised by having few organisational ceilings. It consists of: (1) a board of managers, (2) middle managers and (3) employees. Furthermore, there are few 'walls' as there are no strict lines of command.

The culture is focused on direct and informal dialogue: 'The "suggestion box" is dismissed. People propose changes directly to the management and their colleagues instead' (manager). The management group focuses on promoting trust by formulating performance scores and goals in co-operation with the employees.

The company has developed a meeting culture that supports dialogue and employee initiative. This example is from the workers in order expedition: 'We suggested during a morning meeting that we had to renew the procedure for customer claims. We proposed that in the future, the customer should be able to attach a photo to their claim. It was implemented widely in the business the following day' (employee).

The product development department conducts continual innovation meetings. The meetings are conducted with a very open agenda and focus on new ideas: 'We formulate all sorts of utopian and "crazy" ideas about how to organise our work. Afterwards, we work systematically on how to transform them into specific solutions.'

The company also seeks to inspire the employees to renew the products by inviting artists and arranging trips to art museums.

The general approach was to ensure participation from all (especially employees). The company focuses on making new workplace innovation practices a part of the culture – and the best way to do this is through employee involvement and engagement. New practices (such as the customer segment teams) were proposed by the management group. The managers quickly 'let go' of the process in order to enable employees to develop and implement the team structure in a way that they considered useful. Everybody took part in this process and they were focused on the fact that, although management was the instigator, it should be up to the employees to 'formulate the content in the concept'. It was therefore an incremental change. The employees are continuously testing new ideas and changing them along the way: 'You can always go back to the old ways.'

The company's future and employee influence in the workplace are considered a shared responsibility. Influence creates commitment and motivation in Kvadrat: 'If you have the opportunity to influence the process, you will be more committed' (employee). The company has a practice of conducting meetings that contribute to employees' ability to influence the work organisation.

The use of interdisciplinary customer segment teams makes it possible to approach the customer in new ways: 'It is the best way to respond to new demands in the market and to achieve our business goals' (manager). Workplace innovation practices are considered closely linked to the company's success. The manager stresses that an innovative culture, knowledge-sharing and autonomous, interdisciplinary teams give the company competitive advantage. Before 2000, the organisational model was more characterised by management control. The present model is characterised by autonomous and semi-autonomous teams and a 'flat' management structure.

Meeting practices enable managers and employees to create better work organisation – both internally in the department and across the company. It also supports incremental improvements. Employees can decide themselves how many meetings are needed and are therefore feeling 'in control'. It also makes it easier to get an overview of a company that is growing.

The point of introducing customer segment teams was to strengthen sales areas by bringing together different functions in multidisciplinary teams with a common focus. The employees describe this practice as highly motivating as well.

Interdisciplinary co-operation and knowledge-sharing give Kvadrat a competitive advantage, a greater understanding of the market and motivated employees.

Source: Eurofound (2015).

EXPLORE FURTHER

Armstrong, M. (2014) *Armstrong's Handbook of Human Resource Management Practice*. 13th edition. London: Kogan Page.

- Chapter 11, 'Work, organisation and job design'; Chapter 12, 'Organisational development'; Chapter 62, 'Organisational design toolkit'.

Boxall, P. and Purcell, J. (2006) *Strategy and Human Resource Management*. Basingstoke: Palgrave Macmillan.

- Chapter 5, 'Work systems and the changing priorities of production' – an account of how new forms of work organisation, stimulated by increased competition, have impacted on HRM.
- Chapter 6, 'Linking work systems and models of employment' – see pp133–5 for an interesting adaptation of Atkinson's model of the flexible firm.

Boxall, P., Purcell, J. and Wright, P. (eds) (2007) *The Oxford Handbook of Human Resource Management*. Oxford: Oxford University Press.

- Chapter 10, J. Cordery and S.K. Parker, 'Work organisation'.

Managing performance

INTRODUCTION

At one level, management is essentially concerned with the current performance of the organisation. Thus the primary aim of management studies, in all disciplines, has always been to help managers to harness employees' performance for the good of the organisation as a whole. At another level, management is also responsible for ensuring future performance, and so questions of performance and appraisal inevitably also involve issues of training and development. In the HRM paradigm performance management is frequently linked to the management of rewards. Reward management is discussed in the next chapter.

LEARNING OUTCOMES

On completion of this chapter you should:

- understand the principles of performance management
- appreciate the contribution that an effective performance management system can make in adding value to an organisation
- understand the components of performance management – namely, planning for, supporting and assessing performance, and how these components are related.

The 2011 Workplace Employment Relations Study (WERS) found that the trend of managers using performance appraisals for non-managerial staff had continued between 2004 and 2011. The percentage of workplaces formally appraising at least some non-managerial employees rose from 43% in 2004 to 70% in 2011 (van Wanrooy *et al* 2013).

The percentage of workplaces that directly linked pay to performance rose to 25% in 2011, for both the private and public sector, up from 17% and 11% respectively in 2004.

Although, as we will see in this chapter, there is more to performance management than just appraisal, the 2011 WERS provides strong empirical evidence that performance management is in widespread and increasing use in the UK.

Performance management has been defined as: 'a systematic process for improving individual, team and organizational performance' (Armstrong 2014, p331).

Performance management is a more comprehensive concept than simply performance-related pay or performance appraisal – although the latter is certainly an essential component of any performance management system. Performance management makes explicit reference to the organisation's mission, vision and values, and in a sense can be seen as almost a management philosophy rather than just a set of techniques.

Typical features of any performance management system are:

- There is a performance agreement between the individual employee and their manager, which sets out objectives but also development needs.
- Performance is continually monitored and assessed. High performance is reinforced with praise, recognition and the opportunity to take on more responsible work. Low performance is responded to by means of coaching and counselling. In both cases, management response is immediate rather than being deferred.
- In addition to monitoring and assessment, and to management response, there is a regular formal review of performance against objectives, and the setting of any new performance agreement.

Well-managed organisations pay close attention to recruitment and selection processes so that they increase the probability of recruiting individuals who possess the necessary attributes to become high-performers (see Chapter 2). However, we must always remember that no recruitment and selection process can be perfect, and that even the best-managed organisation occasionally employs someone who cannot perform well. We should also acknowledge that the possession of the attributes to do a job well is not in itself enough to ensure high performance.

If organisations are to be successful in maximising the performance of their employees, there are a number of things they must do:

- People need to know what is required of them.
- Their performance has to be assessed reliably and accurately.
- Causes of under-performance must be identified and understood.
- Training and development needs must be identified so that appropriate programmes can be implemented to meet these needs.
- Proper resources must be provided to allow individuals to fulfil the job requirements.

As well as all the above, many organisations now believe that in order to motivate employees to perform at a high level, the rewards the employees receive have to be linked to the assessment of their performance in the job.

The manager who is accountable for the performance of an employee clearly has a crucial role in all of the above, and this is what we focus on in the present chapter. However, the organisation as a whole derives great benefit from an effective performance management system.

6.1 THE CONTRIBUTION OF PERFORMANCE MANAGEMENT

Aguinis (2005) identified a number of advantages which effective performance management brings to an organisation:

- Motivation to perform is increased. Receiving feedback about one's performance increases the motivation for future performance, and recognition of successes provides the basis for continuing improvements.
- Self-esteem is increased. Receiving feedback about one's performance also fulfils a basic need to be appreciated and valued at work. This, in turn, is likely to increase employees' self-esteem.
- The job definition and criteria for job success are clarified.
- Managers gain insight about subordinates, which helps the manager build relationships with their staff. Also, supervisors gain a better understanding of each individual's contribution to the organisation. This can be useful for direct supervisors as well as for supervisors at one remove.
- Self-insight and development are enhanced. Participants in the system gain a better understanding of their strengths and weaknesses, which can help them better define future career paths.

- Employees become more competent. The performance of employees is improved. In addition, there is a solid foundation for developing and improving employees by establishing developmental plans.
- HR actions are likely to be fairer (and perceived as such) and appropriate. Performance management systems provide information which can be used for HR actions such as merit increases, promotions and transfers, as well as terminations. This leads to improved interpersonal relationships and enhanced supervisor–subordinate trust.
- There is better protection from lawsuits. Data collected through performance management systems can help document compliance with regulations (for example health and safety and equal opportunities legislation). When performance management systems are not in place, arbitrary performance evaluations are more likely; also, correct but unpopular evaluations cannot be defended easily.
- There is better and more timely differentiation between competent and poor performers. Supervisors are forced to address performance problems before they become too costly and cannot be remedied.
- Supervisors' views of performance are communicated more clearly. There is greater accountability in how managers discuss performance expectations and provide feedback. When managers possess these competencies, subordinates receive useful information about how their performance is seen by their supervisor.
- Organisational goals are made clear. The goals of the unit and the organisation are made clear, and the employee understands the link between what they do and organisational success.
- Organisational change is facilitated. Performance management systems can be a useful tool to drive organisational change. Performance management provides tools and motivation for individuals to change, which, in turn, helps drive organisational change.

6.2 THE COMPONENTS OF PERFORMANCE MANAGEMENT

We can think of effective performance management as comprising three distinct but related components:

- planning for performance
- supporting performance
- assessing performance.

6.2.1 PLANNING FOR PERFORMANCE

It is obvious that if a manager is made responsible for managing the performance of another employee, they must be thoroughly familiar with the task or job that the employee is undertaking. They must be able to tell whether the task or job has been done properly or not. In other words, the manager must know *the criteria for success or failure* in order to assess performance.

More specifically, we say that the manager must be aware of the knowledge, skills and abilities (KSAs) needed to do the job competently. 'Knowledge' here means having the information needed to perform the work. 'Skills' are attributes which are required. These usually have been gained by having done the work in the past. 'Ability' refers to having the physical, emotional, intellectual and psychological aptitudes to perform the work. It is a prime responsibility of the manager to ensure that the employee possesses the KSAs required and, if there are any deficiencies in them, to take steps to remedy them.

The KSAs and criteria for job success should be explicit in the relevant job description, which should summarise the duties and responsibilities – the KSAs – that are required, and the working conditions for the particular job or task.

As an illustration, see the job description in HRM in Action 6.1. This job description includes information about what tasks are performed (for example, 'Interview applicants to obtain information on work history, training, education, and job skills'). It also includes information about required knowledge (for example, of the organisation's principles and procedures for personnel recruitment, selection, training, compensation and benefits, employee relations and negotiation, and personnel information systems), skills (for example, 'active listening'), and abilities (for example, 'to communicate effectively').

HRM IN ACTION: PERSONNEL RECRUITER FOR TARTAN BANK

CASE STUDY 6.1

Job role: To seek out, interview, and screen applicants to fill existing and future job openings and promote career opportunities within Tartan Bank.

Reporting relationship: The post-holder will work as a member of a team of up to six HR specialists and will report directly to a human resources manager.

Work activities: The primary activities of the position are recruiting, interviewing, selecting, and hiring of employees in various parts of Tartan Bank. To do this the post-holder must communicate with, and provide information for, supervisors, co-workers and other peers, and in some cases, subordinates. They must be competent at gathering relevant information and establishing and maintaining interpersonal relationships with these fellow employees, and also be able to communicate effectively with people outside the organisations, such as recruitment agencies, media, customers, members of the public and industry agencies. On a personal level, the post-holder must be able to organise, plan and prioritise their own work, analyse information effectively and be capable in solving problems and making decisions. A very important part of the job is to ensure organisational compliance with both relevant legal/regulatory requirements and appropriate company policies on hiring staff.

Key tasks

Establish and maintain relationships with hiring managers to stay abreast of current and future hiring and business needs.

Interview applicants to obtain information on work history, training, education and job skills.

Maintain current knowledge of relevant employment legislation and policies.

Perform searches for qualified candidates according to relevant job criteria, using computer databases, networking, Internet recruiting resources, cold calls, media, recruiting firms, and employee referrals.

Prepare and maintain employment records.

Contact applicants to inform them of employment possibilities, consideration and selection.

Inform potential applicants about facilities, operations, benefits and job or career opportunities in organisations.

Screen and refer applicants to hiring personnel in the organisation, making hiring recommendations when appropriate.

Arrange for interviews and provide travel arrangements as necessary.

Advise managers and employees on staffing policies and procedures.

Required competencies

(i) Knowledge requirements

Administration and management: Knowledge of business and management principles involved in strategic planning, resource allocation, human resources modelling, leadership techniques, and co-ordination of people and resources.

Personnel and human resources: Knowledge of principles and procedures for personnel recruitment, selection, training, compensation and benefits, employee relations and negotiation, and personnel information systems.

English language: Knowledge of the structure and content of the English language, including the meaning and spelling of words, rules of composition, and grammar.

Clerical: Knowledge of administrative and clerical procedures and systems, such as word processing, managing files and records, designing forms, and other office procedures and terminology.

Communications and media: Knowledge of media production, communication and dissemination techniques and methods. This includes alternative ways to inform and entertain via written, oral and visual media.

Customer and personal service: Knowledge of principles and processes for providing customer and personal services. This includes customer needs assessment, meeting quality standards for services, and evaluation of customer satisfaction.

(ii) Skills requirements

Active listening: Giving full attention to what other people are saying, taking time to understand the points being made, asking questions as appropriate, and not interrupting at inappropriate times.

Reading comprehension: Understanding written sentences and paragraphs in work-related documents.

Speaking: Talking to others to convey information effectively.

Service orientation: Actively looking for ways to help people.

Time management: Managing their own time.

Writing: Communicating effectively in writing as appropriate for the needs of the audience.

Judgement and decision-making: Considering the relative costs and benefits of potential actions to choose the most appropriate one.

Critical thinking: Using logic and reasoning to identify the strengths and weaknesses of alternative solutions, conclusions or approaches to problems.

If a current job description is not available, it will be necessary to create one using the process of job analysis, which determines the key components of a particular job, including activities, tasks, products, services and processes. It will not normally be the responsibility of a general or line manager to undertake personally a job analysis or to produce a job description. Such tasks are typically undertaken by a job analyst or HR specialist, although the supervising manager will have a vital role in providing information.

For existing jobs, job analysis can be conducted using observation, standard questionnaires or interviews. Data may be collected from job incumbents (that is, those doing the job at present) and their supervisors. Alternatively, if the job is yet to be created, data can be gathered from the individual(s) responsible for creating the new position and from those who will supervise individuals in the new position.

Generic job descriptions can be obtained from the Occupational Informational Network (O*NET, **www.onetonline/org/find**). O*NET is a comprehensive database of worker attributes and job characteristics, and provides a common language for defining and describing occupations. The descriptions available via O*NET can serve as a foundation for a job description. O*NET descriptions can be easily adapted and changed to accommodate specific local characteristics.

Job descriptions are a prerequisite for any performance management system because they provide the criteria (that is, yardsticks) to be used in measuring performance. Criteria can correspond to behaviours (that is, how to perform) or to results (that is, what outcomes should result from performance).

In relation to our personnel recruiter example (HRM in Action 6.1), a behavioural criterion could involve the skill of interviewing job applicants. A supervisor could rate the extent to which the personnel recruiter effectively obtains information on work history, training, education and job skills.

In order to manage someone's performance, we need to be able to identify the results of their activities. To establish these we must be clear about the key accountabilities or broad areas of a job for which the employee is responsible. We also need to specify objectives we can understand as 'statements of important and measurable outcomes'. Finally, we need to establish performance standards. A performance standard provides a measure of how well employees have achieved each objective.

To summarise, planning for performance entails the supervising manager:

- knowing the knowledge, skills and abilities required on the part of the employee doing the job in question, and ensuring that the employee concerned possesses them; and
- knowing the key accountabilities of the job, the specific objectives that have to be achieved as part of each accountability, and the performance standards of each objective; and ensuring that the employee knows them also.

6.2.2 SUPPORTING PERFORMANCE

Managing the performance of other employees entails evaluating job performance in two complementary ways: first, by maintaining a more-or-less continuous awareness of how the employee is performing, and making suitable responses to this on a mainly informal basis; and second, by operating a formal performance appraisal system, which is documented and may be linked to performance-related pay and is typically part of the organisation's performance management system. The first is part of what we describe in this text as 'supporting performance', and is dealt with in the present section. The second covers what we term here 'assessing performance' and is described in section 6.2.3.

Both supporting and assessing the performance of others requires that the supervising manager is aware of the level of performance of those for whom they are held accountable. In assessing performance this will require documenting as part of the formal appraisal of performance (see section 6.2.3), but in supporting performance often this is unrecorded and is mainly a matter of observation and discussion on a day-to-day basis.

Because the organisation's goals may change over time, the supervising manager has to be able to update or revise initial objectives, standards, key accountabilities and competency areas as required without waiting for scheduled formal performance appraisal meetings.

Even the most capable and motivated individual can only do a good job if the organisation provides the resources that are required. These may be physical – the tools and equipment, hardware and software needed – but they may also be informational and/or human resources. It is the responsibility of the supervising manager to ensure that the employees obtain the resources they need to perform in their jobs as required.

Feedback on how an employee is performing in relation to their goals is essential to allow the employee both to understand clearly what is required and to let them know how the standard of their performance is perceived by the line manager or supervisor.

We also know from the study of organisational psychology that feedback on performance is essential to motivation, and in supporting performance a manager must regularly provide informal feedback on performance. Giving feedback allows the supervising manager to reinforce effective behaviours and progress towards goals, and conversely to discourage behaviours that are ineffective.

An employee's personal development plan is a vital part of any good performance management system because it specifies courses of action to be taken to improve performance.

6.2.3 ASSESSING PERFORMANCE

Here we are concerned with the formal appraisal of performance, which typically is based on a regular, periodic performance review. 'Performance appraisal' is the term usually given to the process of assessing individual performance in a formal, regular and systematic way.

Formal appraisal systems typically have the following characteristics:

- There is a set system with rules and guidelines which must be followed. For example, the intervals between appraisals will be specified (for example, six or 12 months), as will be the person(s) who are to conduct the appraisal.
- Traditionally, the appraiser is the direct supervisor or line manager, although it is now common for organisations to involve self-assessment from the appraisee and also input from other players such as peers, subordinates and customers (including 'internal customers') to give what is termed '360-degree' appraisal. Even with 360-degree appraisal, however, the input of the direct supervisor is still usually the most important single factor.
- The main intention of performance appraisal is to provide the organisation with a comprehensive assessment of all relevant aspects of performance. The information collected is recorded, usually in the form of a written report, or in the ratings of individual aspects of performance.
- The basis of the typical formal performance appraisal system is a review of past performance – that is, in the period since the previous formal appraisal.
- There will be feedback to the appraisee on their performance, usually by means of an interview but confirmed in writing. The interview will typically include a discussion not only of past performance but also of what might be done to improve performance in the future.

Although we are concerned here with the responsibilities of the manager, the employee who is being managed has certain important responsibilities that are worth bearing in mind. The employee should be committed to achieving the agreed goals and objectives and must be willing to communicate with managers about their performance and to supply any information required. They must also be ready to receive feedback on performance constructively. Of course, all this can be reinforced by training, and the manager must always be clear about the respective responsibilities of both supervisor and employee in the assessment of performance.

Most authorities caution that it is important to distinguish the use of appraisal for training and development purposes on the one hand from its use for rewards (including promotion) on the other, on the grounds that self-interest can corrupt the process of appraisal when tangible rewards are at stake (see HRM Dilemma 6.1).

The process of formal appraisal has the following elements:

- self-appraisal by the employee of their performance against agreed goals and objectives
- appraisal by the employee's supervisor/manager of the employee's performance against agreed goals and objectives
- appraisal by others of the employee's performance against agreed goals and objectives (for example, 360-degree appraisal)
- a regular periodic performance review interview following the above three appraisals at which the appraisals are discussed by the supervisor/manager with the employee

- a formal written report on the performance review interview signed by the supervisor/manager and the employee
- a development plan incorporated within the formal written report.

Formal appraisal relies on a record – usually known as an 'appraisal form' – being kept of the assessment of an employee's performance. Effective appraisal forms should be simple, relevant, clear and comprehensive.

Where a rating of performance is included in the appraisal, the organisation must be aware of the potential for raters to over- or under-rate performance. Mis-rating may occur intentionally or unintentionally. Managers may deliberately over-rate an employee's performance to avoid confrontation or as a result of favouritism. A manager might over-rate all of the employees for whom they are accountable in order to improve the perception of their own performance as a manager. Or a manager may consciously under-rate an employee out of spite or as a result of favouritism towards one or more other employees in the same team. Where peer assessment is operated, groups of peers might be motivated to over-rate each other.

Unintentional rating errors can occur because of the psychological complexity of the task. Psychologists have identified the phenomenon of the 'halo effect', whereby one attribute of the person being appraised obscures other aspects and unconsciously leads the appraiser to distort the overall assessment of the person's performance. The halo effect may operate either to increase or decrease rating wrongly. For example, a halo effect may occur when the appraisee and the appraiser share a common background, such as going to the same school or coming from the same town. In such instances the halo effect would probably lead to over-rating. However, significant dissimilarities may trigger a negative halo effect – for example, if the appraiser and appraisee belong to different cultural, national or ethnic groups which have traditional conflicts with each other – and in such cases under-rating would be the probable outcome.

Another source of error or bias is what is termed 'central tendency', which is where raters avoid the extremes of the scale and rate most or all employees at the mid-point, regardless of their actual performance. They may perhaps do this to avoid making difficult or controversial decisions about the performance of any particular employee. Some authorities recommend the use of an even number of points on the rating scale to avoid this. Others reject this solution on two grounds: (1) eliminating a precise mid-point does not in itself prevent the same sort of bias occurring – a biased rater would simply tend to rate everyone at the first available point above the central area (that is, the third point on a four-point scale or the fourth on a six-point one); and (2) there will be some instances where an employee's performance truly lies at the mid-point between the extremes of the scale.

Another solution sometimes recommended to avoid rating errors is to have a policy whereby everyone's performance is rated as 'acceptable' unless there are good reasons which can be documented to justify a higher or lower rating. This has the advantage of requiring raters to furnish proof of exceptional performance, whether good or bad. Critics suggest that this results in few people being rated as other than acceptable performers and can result in the appraisal system being rather too much of a blunt instrument.

Both intentional and unintentional distortion in performance ratings can be minimised by providing raters with appropriate training.

Teams are ever-present in modern workplaces; indeed, it would be difficult to find an organisation without some type of work done by teams. So including team performance as part of the performance management system is a natural extension of a system that focuses on individual performance only. The general principles we have discussed above still apply. However, teams differ on the basis of the tasks they perform (from routine to non-routine) and on membership configuration (from static to dynamic).

HRM DILEMMA 6.1

Should pay be linked to appraisal of performance?

It seems obvious that if people know that assessment of their performance will impact on their rewards, they will have an incentive to enhance their accounts of their own performance. '360-degree' appraisal may go some way to reducing this possibility, but even then peers may conspire tacitly to over-rate each other.

This is why standard advice to managers from social psychologists is never to link rewards directly to performance assessment.

On the other hand, one senior manager told the present author that when his firm started to link rewards to performance explicitly, 'At least then everyone wanted their regular performance appraisal interview. Before that, both employees and managers gave it very low priority and HR were always tearing their hair out trying to get people to do them.'

 REFLECTIVE ACTIVITY 6.1

Local authority seeks to raise standards after Khyra Ishaq case

Six social workers have been sacked from Birmingham City Council for failing to meet performance standards, it has been revealed.

Colin Tucker, Director of Children's Services at the Council, claimed the dismissed staff showed 'no sign whatsoever' of meeting expected levels of competence.

Tucker – who was brought in to head up the department after it was severely criticised by Ofsted – told the BBC that the staff in question were not doing their jobs properly

He said: 'There is a clear indication we are serious about our standards. We are not appointing some staff, and as well as that, we have dismissed six staff in the last year. They did not adhere to standards and expectations that we laid down. They showed no sign whatsoever that they were keen to do so, so we dismissed them.'

Birmingham social services were censured over the death of seven-year-old Khyra Ishaq, who died from starvation in May 2008, despite being known to social workers. The child's mother and stepfather were thereafter jailed for manslaughter, and the city council is currently conducting a serious review of the case.

While the recent sackings were not said to be directly linked to the Ishaq case, eight other children known to social services have died in the city in the past three years. Tucker said he was aware of 'one situation where a child died of neglect' in Birmingham in the past seven months.

Tucker also revealed that 120 vacant posts had been filled with agency staff, but that he was seeking to reduce this to between 40 and 50, filling the remaining roles through training and the recruitment of permanent workers. The department currently employs 750 social workers overall.

Source: Michelle Stevens, *People Management* Online, 19 March 2010.

Point for reflection

This is a particularly tragic case but it raises the question: just how can/should you measure the performance of social workers?

PERFORMANCE MANAGEMENT AT MID-SCOTLAND DISTRICT COUNCIL

CASE STUDY 6.2

Mid-Scotland District Council provides local government services for a population of approximately 500,000 people. One of these services is the provision of libraries for the general public under the management of the Council's Leisure and Communities Department. The department also provides three other main services: community learning and development; parks, sports and leisure; and development and support (which provides financial support for independent leisure and arts groups within the district).

The Council's Strategic Plan for 2016–20 states that:

> Library services provision will be enhanced throughout Mid-Scotland and a target has been set to increase readers' use of the library facilities by an average 5% overall per annum and with a specific target of 10% for young people (14 to 18).

This is the only reference to the Library Service in the Strategic Plan.

The Leisure and Communities Department has the following statements of vision and mission, although there are no specific statements for the library service.

Our Vision is:

We believe in the right of everyone to:

- be heard
- become an active, informed citizen
- develop their knowledge, skills and critical awareness
- influence and achieve change
- realise their potential.

Our Mission is to:

- encourage greater access, participation and creative expression through the promotion of a wide range of lifelong learning opportunities
- promote social, educational, cultural and recreational opportunities which

build self-confidence and raise aspirations
- assist in the creation of sustainable, healthier communities, which people feel they belong to and have a sense of pride in
- improve quality of life in the city through the delivery of quality services
- contribute to the continuing development of Mid-Scotland as a vibrant cultural, leisure and visitor destination.

Three of the key positions within the library service are those of senior librarian, librarian and library technician. Job descriptions for each post are given below.

Senior librarian

Job role: To administer libraries and perform related professional library services within the council's public library service.

Responsibilities include:

- administering a library
- managing one or more teams of up to 12 staff, comprising librarians and library technicians
- selecting, acquiring, cataloguing, classifying, circulating and maintaining library materials
- furnishing reference, bibliographical and readers' advisory services
- performing in-depth, strategic research, synthesising, analysing, editing and filtering information
- setting up and working with databases and information systems to catalogue and access information.

Reporting relationship: Senior librarians report directly to the director of library services.

Key tasks:

Manage a library team comprising librarian and library technicians, including supervising personnel activities, budgeting and planning.

Assist the director of library services in creating and implementing a library strategy.

Assist in the professional development of librarians and librarian technicians.

Search standard reference materials, including online sources and the Internet, to answer patrons' reference questions.

Analyse patrons' requests to determine needed information, and assist in furnishing or locating that information.

Teach library patrons to search for information using databases.

Keep records of circulation and materials.

Check books in and out of the library.

Explain the use of library facilities, resources, equipment and services, and provide information about library policies.

Review and evaluate resource materials such as book reviews and catalogues, in order to select and order print, audiovisual and electronic resources.

Code, classify and catalogue books, publications, films, audiovisual aids and other library materials based on subject matter or standard library classification systems.

Locate unusual or unique information in response to specific requests.

Post-holders must be educated to bachelor's degree level and hold a professional qualification in librarianship, and will be expected to have a minimum of five years' professional experience as a librarian or in a similar position.

Librarian

Job role: To provide professional library services and to assist in administering libraries, within the council's public library service.

Responsibilities include:

- selecting, acquiring, cataloguing, classifying, circulating and maintaining library materials
- furnishing reference, bibliographical and readers' advisory services

- performing in-depth, strategic research, synthesising, analysing, editing and filtering information
- setting up and working with databases and information systems to catalogue and access information.

Reporting relationship: Librarians work in library teams which comprise a number of librarians and library technicians, and they report directly to a senior librarian.

Key tasks:

Assist the senior librarian in managing a library team comprising librarians and library technicians. This may include supervising personnel activities and helping with budgeting and planning,

Assist the senior librarian in the development of librarian technicians.

Search standard reference materials, including online sources and the Internet, to answer patrons' reference questions.

Analyse patrons' requests to determine needed information, and assist in furnishing or locating that information.

Teach library patrons to search for information using databases.

Keep records of circulation and materials.

Check books in and out of the library.

Explain the use of library facilities, resources, equipment and services, and provide information about library policies.

Review and evaluate resource material, such as book reviews and catalogues, in order to select and order print, audiovisual and electronic resources.

Code, classify and catalogue books, publications, films, audiovisual aids and other library materials based on subject matter or standard library classification systems.

Locate unusual or unique information in response to specific requests.

Applicants must be educated to bachelor's degree level and hold a professional qualification in librarianship, and will be expected to have a minimum of two years' professional experience as a librarian or in a similar position.

Library technician

Job role: To assist librarians by helping readers in the use of library catalogues, databases and indexes to locate books and other materials; and by answering questions that require only brief consultation of standard reference. To compile records; sort and shelve books; remove or repair damaged books; register patrons; and check materials in and out of the circulation process. To replace materials in shelving area (stacks) or files.

Reporting relationship: Library technicians work in library teams which comprise a number of technicians and librarians. All library team members report directly to a senior librarian, who heads the team.

Key tasks:

Reserve, circulate, renew and discharge books and other materials.

Enter and update patrons' records on computers.

Provide assistance for teachers and students by locating materials and helping to complete special projects.

Answer routine reference inquiries, and refer patrons needing further assistance to librarians.

Guide patrons in finding and using library resources, including reference materials, audiovisual equipment, computers and electronic resources.

Sort books, publications and other items according to procedure and return them to shelves, files or other designated storage areas.

Deliver and retrieve items throughout the library by hand or using pushcart.

Post-holders should be educated to high school level with qualification suitable for entrance to college/university bachelor degree programmes.

Questions

Your services as an HR consultant have been engaged by Mid-Scotland District Council to assist the director of library services in improving the performance management of her staff.

1   The director of library services has announced that she wishes to pursue a results-oriented approach to performance management within the library service. What recommendations would you make on measuring results and behaviours for (1) senior librarians, (2) librarians, and (3) library technicians?

2   At his last performance review meeting with Sheila, the senior librarian, Bill – one of the library technicians – admitted that his job performance was suffering because he had not really got to grips with new digital technology. Bill is the designated visual arts (VA) technician and his main job for many years has been to look after the library's extensive collection of photographic slides and other images of artworks. Local students and schoolteachers are the main users of this facility, and many have been complaining that they cannot use the visual resources of the library because they cannot access images in digital form. Feedback from Bill's co-workers also indicates that a number of the younger members of staff have found him a bit unco-operative and 'difficult to work with'. Older team members who have worked with Bill for a number of years are less critical, but when asked directly by Sheila they admit that Bill is 'not a team player'. When Sheila discussed this with Bill, he replied that he had been the VA Technician for 20 years, 'long before we had these teams', and that he was used to working on his own. He admitted that he found working in a team difficult and did not really know how to handle it.

On the basis of the above, what would you recommend for Bill's personal development plan?

1 Measuring results and behaviours

In measuring performance when pursuing a results approach to performance management, the first step is to identify accountabilities, which are the particular areas in which an individual is expected to focus.

Examples of appropriate objectives might be:

- *Senior librarian*: effective and efficient administration of their library.
- *Librarian*: provision of professional library service to patrons.
- *Library technician*: provision of support to patrons.

Once all key accountabilities are identified, the second step is to set objectives for each accountability. These should be: specific and clear; challenging; agreed; significant; prioritised; bound by time; achievable; fully communicated; flexible; and limited in number.

For example, one of the objectives for the senior librarian could be *to increase book borrowing by the 14 to 16 age group*.

Similarly, appropriate objectives can be set for the librarians and library technicians from their job descriptions.

The third step is to determine performance standards. Good standards are: related to the position; concrete, specific and measurable; practical to measure; meaningful; realistic and achievable; and reviewed regularly.

For example, the performance standards for the objective specified above for the senior librarian could be to increase book borrowing by the 14 to 16 age group *by 5% in the following 12 months without increasing costs*.

Again, performance standards for the objectives that will have been offered for librarians and library technicians can be outlined in a similar fashion.

2 Bill's personal development plan

Personal development plans form a key component of a performance management system because they specify courses of action to be taken to improve performance. A good development plan allows employees to fully address two major objectives:

- to do better in the future
- to avoid performance problems faced in the past.

The two main problems with Bill's current job performance, and on which development should focus, are clearly his present deficiencies in (1) working with new technology, familiarity with which would enable him to replace the outmoded slides with electronically stored images of artworks which library users now desire; and (2) teamworking skills, which, given the nature and functions of the library, will probably be in the context of service teams but might also include project teams.

Development plans should include a description of the specific development objectives and of the specific steps to be taken to achieve them. A good plan therefore includes information on: the development objectives; how the new skills or knowledge will be acquired; a time-line regarding the acquisition of the new skills or knowledge; and standards and measures that will be used to assess whether the objectives have indeed been achieved.

Sheila and Bill should agree specific learning and development objectives for both technology and teamworking skills, and these should take into account the needs of both the individual and the organisation.

As direct supervisor, Sheila has a key role in helping Bill define the scope of the development plan and in explaining the relationship between the development objectives and strategic priorities for the library and the council. Sheila will also have direct responsibility for checking on Bill's progress towards achieving the agreed learning and development objectives, and for providing resources so that Bill will be able to engage in the appropriate activities. Supervisors must reinforce an employee's accomplishments towards completing a development plan so that the employee remains motivated. Supervisors themselves must be motivated to perform all these functions in support of their employees' development plans, and so Sheila's own performance review by the director of library services should include reference to Bill's ongoing development (and that of the rest of her staff in the library).

The reader may wish to refer back to Chapter 3 in considering Bill's development needs and how these may be met.

KEY ISSUES

Managing the performance of others is a continuous process. At the level of the individual manager (as opposed to the organisation), it comprises three closely related components or sub-competencies: (1) planning for performance, (2) supporting performance, and (3) assessing performance. Each of the three sub-competencies plays an important role. If any one of these is implemented poorly, the entire process of managing performance suffers.

Job description's provide vital information needed to manage performance, particularly the criteria for job success and failure, whether these are measured in terms of behaviour or in terms of results.

Performance management is really a management philosophy rather than just a set of techniques. It is a more comprehensive concept than simply performance-related pay or performance appraisal, and uses goals, measurement, feedback and recognition as a means of motivating people to achieve.

EXPLORE FURTHER

Armstrong, M. (2014) *Armstrong's Handbook of Human Resource Management Practice*. 13th edition. London: Kogan Page.

- Chapter 25, 'Performance management'.
- Chapter 68, 'Performance management toolkit'.

Boxall, P., Purcell, J. and Wright, P. (eds) (2007) *The Oxford Handbook of Human Resource Management*. Oxford: Oxford University Press.

- Chapter 18, G.P. Latham, L.M. Sulsky and H. MacDonald, 'Performance management'.

Torrington, D., Hall, L., Taylor, S. and Atkinson C. (2014) *Human Resource Management*. 9th edition. London/Englewood Cliffs, NJ: FT/Prentice-Hall.

- Chapter 10, 'Employee performance management'.
- Chapter 28, 'The appraisal interview'.

Wilkinson, A., Redman, T., Snell, S.A. and Bacon, N. (2010) *Sage Handbook of Human Resource Management*. London: Sage.

- Chapter 12, M. Brown and V.S. Lim, 'Understanding performance management and appraisal: supervisory and employee perspectives'.

CHAPTER 7

Managing rewards

'It's not money that brings happiness, it's lots of money' (Russian proverb, cited by Guthrie 2007).

INTRODUCTION

Rewards, both financial and other, are of obvious importance to employees and employers. One of the central changes which HRM has brought about in management thinking is that it is no longer enough for employers to think in terms of the old common-law principle of 'a fair day's pay for a fair day's work'. Employee commitment and motivation are so important in today's competitive, knowledge-based world that rewards have to be actively managed to secure the maximum utilisation of human assets, and to attract, motivate and retain core employees. HRM has introduced the term 'reward management' to replace simple 'wage and salary administration'.

LEARNING OUTCOMES

On completion of this chapter you should:
- have an appreciation of the main types of payment systems, including performance-related pay
- understand non-pay benefits
- appreciate the concept of reward management
- understand the principles of job evaluation.

Probably the single most significant change in reward management in the UK in the last 30 years has been the extension of performance-related pay beyond the shop floor to white-collar and professional staff, who traditionally were paid straightforward salaries.

Both employees and employers are always concerned about issues of reward and performance. So far as rewards are concerned, employees are most concerned about perceived fairness. Employers seek control and minimisation of costs combined with capacity to offer attractive packages to core staff. These objectives are not incompatible with an HRM viewpoint from management: performance-related pay, at least in principle, should allow reward and motivation for the employee and cost control at the same time.

7.1 PAY SYSTEMS

In considering the payment system for any part of their workforce, management will normally seek one that they believe will give the greatest degree of cost and supervisory control, and provide the best incentive for employees.

There is no perfect payment system for any situation, and no payment system will continue to operate satisfactorily indefinitely. Anomalies will develop over time and employees will come to regard bonuses as entitlements to be consolidated into basic pay.

7.2 MONEY MATTERS

Despite some interpretations of motivation theory that seem to play down money as a motivating factor at work, most organisations behave as if they believe that money certainly does motivate people. Even Frederick Herzberg – usually viewed as the leading advocate of the view that money is not a motivator – is reported as having admitted that 'It sure as hell helps me sort out my priorities!' (Child 1984, p188). Most people appear to be interested in making money if they have the opportunity to do so. This would seem to apply just as much to those who are fortunate enough to have jobs which are already high in financial and intrinsic rewards as to those who face genuine hardship. For example, hospital consultants and dentists working for the NHS in the UK are often keen to increase their earnings by taking private patients, and the remuneration of top executives in industry and commerce regularly causes scandals in both the USA and the UK because many seem to reward themselves excessively. Pay and fringe benefits remain central features in contracts of employment and are always prominent issues in collective bargaining.

The value that individuals put on pay compared with other rewards can vary according to personal circumstances, over which management have no control. An employee's domestic situation may dictate the extent to which they would be willing to trade off pay against other benefits, for example.

Pay is expressed in monetary terms, which makes it easy to calculate. This gives a clear scale of measurement and a link to measures of performance or output. It also means that it can be easily costed.

Until relatively recently, the management of pay in Britain tended to focus narrowly on the issues of pay and job performance. However, in the twenty-first century, 'reward management' is seen as an integral part of HRM, with an interest in wider motivational issues of attraction, retention, employee expectations, skill development, and the reinforcement of organisational culture and business strategy. We should always remember that rewards can include pay and non-monetary benefits.

7.2.1 FAIRNESS

Any pay system will fail if it is perceived to be unfair by the employees.

Fairness of pay is a comparative concept, not an absolute one, and it may vary from society to society and workplace to workplace. It is concerned with the relationship between the pay of different individuals and different groups, and it reflects perceptions of esteem and self-esteem. People tend to take comparisons, as we might expect, more seriously with those physically and socially closer, rather than with those who are distant. Convention seems to be the usual basis for accepting the fairness of a pay differential, and so changes in the status quo always provoke most anxieties about unfairness (Wootton 1955).

Collective bargaining, by which management and trade unions jointly agree pay rates, usually reinforces the perception of fairness because the use of traditional comparisons provides both employers and trade unions with a basis that is seen to be reasonable.

7.3 TYPES OF PAYMENT SYSTEM

Payment systems may be classified broadly as either:

- *payment by time* schemes, in which the amount of pay awarded is principally determined by the time spent at work – for example an hourly rate or a monthly salary

or

- *performance-related pay* (PRP) or 'incentive pay schemes', in which some element of the total pay is variable. Two types of PRP system are popular:
  - ○ *payment by results* (PBR), in which the variable element is determined by some objective measure of the work done or its value
  - ○ *merit-based systems*, in which the variable element is related to an assessment of overall job performance by a supervisor or manager.

The 2011 WERS survey found that 41% of UK workplaces had incentive pay schemes, a slight increase since the previous survey in 2004. These were still more popular in the private sector than in the public, and there were still significant variations from industry to industry (van Wanrooy *et al* 2013).

In the HRM approach, pay policy is based on three principles which move away from earlier perceptions of simply 'a fair day's pay for a fair day's work':

- Pay policy should reflect and support the business objectives and strategies of the firm.
- Pay should be part of a wider human resources strategy.
- Pay policy and practices should help reinforce the dominant culture of the organisation.

7.4 NON-PAY BENEFITS

'Non-pay benefits', which are also called 'fringe benefits' or 'employee benefits', are elements of remuneration that are additional to cash pay.

The main objectives of offering employees non-pay benefits are:

- to ensure that a competitive total remuneration package is provided to attract, retain and motivate staff
- to increase the employees' commitment to the organisation
- to take advantage of tax-efficient methods of rewarding employees (that is, where the employer can reduce its tax liability by offering some benefit instead of cash).

7.4.1 PRINCIPAL TYPES OF NON-PAY BENEFITS

The main types of non-pay benefits are:

- *pension schemes*, generally regarded by employees as the most important employee benefit
- *personal security*, which includes: extra-statutory sick pay; death in service benefits; personal accident cover; medical insurance; health screening; permanent health insurance (long-term disability cover); business travel insurance; and career counselling (outplacement service)
- *financial assistance*, which includes: company loans, season ticket (travel loans); house purchase assistance; relocation assistance; discounts; and fees to professional bodies
- *personal needs*, which includes: holidays; compassionate leave; extra-statutory maternity leave and pay; paternity pay; child care; career breaks; counselling; fitness and recreational facilities; and other forms of leave
- *company car and petrol*
- *other (tangible) benefits*, such as: subsidised meals; clothing allowance; telephone costs; and credit card facilities
- *intangible benefits*, such as: job satisfaction; status; power; recognition of achievement; training opportunities; career progression; good working conditions; recognition of the need to balance work and family responsibilities; and flexibility.

Note that all *tangible* non-pay benefits have a cash value: they can be costed and a cash equivalent could be offered.

> **?   REFLECTIVE ACTIVITY 7.1**
>
> Outline the key elements of the following occupations (you may want to review the principles of job design from Chapter 5). Design a rewards package for the following jobs:
>
> - surgeon
> - architect
> - university teacher
> - software engineer.

REFLECTIVE ACTIVITY 7.1 ANSWER GUIDANCE

You may want to refer to the job descriptions available at: **www.onetonline.org** (bearing in mind the North American context of these).

Each of these occupations might be expected to feature high intangible benefits. What place, if any, did these have in your proposed rewards packages?

7.5 PUTTING IT ALL TOGETHER: THE 'CAFETERIA' APPROACH TO MANAGING REWARDS

This allows employees a degree of choice in their total remuneration package – for example, by permitting them to take fewer fringe benefits and more pay, or vice versa. The total overall value of their compensation remains the same whatever choices they make. This allows individuals to tailor their rewards to their particular needs and, importantly, allows them to alter their rewards as their needs change. For example, a working mother might choose to reduce her superannuation contributions in favour of more take-home pay for a number of years, whereas a middle-aged employee might wish to increase his superannuation payment to improve his eventual retirement package.

Typically, a cafeteria system features a core package of benefits topped up by a percentage of gross pay available for additional components. The principle advantages of cafeteria systems are:

- employee satisfaction
- the communication of the real costs of benefits to employees and employers
- the identification of the popularity of various benefits.

The disadvantages are:

- the complexity of costing out non-pay benefits
- potentially greater administrative costs
- potentially considerable tax complications for employees.

OPINION: THE UNPREDICTABLE DIGITAL AGE CALLS FOR A FRESH APPROACH TO REWARD MANAGEMENT

When designing reward packages, organisations must focus on their future needs rather than what's worked in the past, says Duncan Brown.

The answer I receive from most organisations when asking why they have their particular set of pay and reward arrangements in operation is a history lesson. They explain what happened in the past, rather than what they need in the future. But in this uncertain, digital age, reward needs to reconnect with the types of flexible jobs people are doing today and regain its place as a central part of the way people are managed.

As the authors of the recently published third edition of *Reward Management** point out, the disputes and debates that have occurred since the previous version was published five years ago mean 'the days when you could simply reuse many of the previous chapters are over'.

In that time we have seen a real decline in average earnings and the continued escalation in executive rewards, serious questioning of the whole concept of 'total reward', 'performance management' and performance-related pay, and incessant tax and pension changes.

Authors Stephen Perkins *et al* explain how the ambitious and aggressive performance-driven strategies of the so-called 'new pay' advocates of the 1990s have, in the face of continuing uncertainty and difficulties experienced in changing pay systems, been replaced by 'leave it alone', 'let's wait and see what the chancellor does in the budget' and a generic 'me too' approach, in areas such as flexible benefits.

A few weeks ago I read another new book on this subject by a friend and former colleague, Daniel Hibbert: *Thunder Cloud: Managing reward in a digital age*. He could hardly have picked a better title for his book, given the current warnings and uncertainty. And as he points out, the current situation with regards to reward management 'is becoming untenable in a rapidly changing digital age'.

It is a fundamental dilemma facing almost all HR directors at the moment, with their strategies for business impact. We know from research that successfully changing organisations and improving people's performance takes multi-faceted and long-term approaches, but how can you ever pursue these in the face of such massive uncertainties and intense pressure to achieve short-term returns and quick fixes?

Both publications give us some clues as to answers in the area of rewards. Hibbert, for example, uses Karl Popper's philosophy to highlight how many HR functions treat rewards as 'clocks' – complex, interrelated engineered designs, of cascaded objective-setting systems, points-based job evaluation and formula-driven incentive plans.

Both books illustrate that we need to treat rewards cautiously, like our current weather or the British electorate, as Popper's 'clouds' (Hibbert) or Burrell and Morgan's 'open systems' (Perkins *et al*), as 'parts of a vast evolving ecosystem (in which) it is very difficult to predict how they will behave'.

Rather than just surveying supposedly rational economic and pay markets, HR functions need to consider corporate philosophies and cultures, and employees' attitudes and values, think about fairness rather than formulas and intrinsic, rather than just extrinsic, rewards. And in particular we need to get much better at communicating reward and managing employee expectations about it, embracing new concepts such as employee financial well-being.

As Winston Churchill once said: 'Plans are of little importance, but planning is essential.' From one of our greatest leaders, and at a time when we really do need effective political and organisational leadership, this is tremendous advice for how employers and HR functions should be managing their approaches to reward in the uncertain months and years ahead.

Dr Duncan Brown is head of HR consulting at the Institute for Employment Studies

Source: Duncan Brown, *People Management* 25 July 2016.

* Perkins, S.J., White, G. and Jones, S. (2016) *Reward Management: Alternatives, consequences and contexts,* 3rd edition. London: CIPD.

7.6 JOB EVALUATION

As Rosabeth Moss Kanter has put it, the basis for determining pay is changing 'from position to performance, from status to contribution' (Kanter 1988).

This would seem to be inevitable for organisations operating in increasingly uncertain and competitive markets. In fact, we should expect employees' pay to be determined by the market worth of their skills, knowledge and experience, and their actual performance in the job. Increasingly, these factors are becoming important in the UK, but the fact remains that many employers feel the need for some method of establishing the relative internal value of jobs. There are two main reasons for this:

- If a hierarchy of jobs can be determined in as independent and objective a manner as possible, decisions about actual grades – and so, pay rates – should be more consistent and defensible.
- In many countries, equal-value pay legislation decrees that women are entitled to equal pay with men (and vice versa) where the work is of equal value in terms of demands made in areas such as effort, skill and decisions. In Britain the case of *Bromley v H&J Quick Ltd* [1998] IRLR 249, CA established that a job evaluation scheme can only provide a defence in an equal-value claim if it is analytical in nature. This implies that it should be a points scheme based on factor comparisons (see section 7.6.2). So employers who feel that they may be vulnerable to equal-value claims are easily persuaded that such schemes are essential. Above all, Article 119 of the Treaty of Rome provides that member states of the EU shall maintain the application of the principle that men and women should receive equal pay for equal work.

Whereas under UK law the burden of proof lies on an applicant to show that on the balance of probabilities they are not receiving equal pay, a decision of the European Court in *Handels- og Kontorfunktionaerernes Forbund i Danmark v Dansk Arbejdsgiverforening* (the 'Danfoss case') indicates that if a pay system manifestly produces inequalities of pay between the sexes, the burden of proof lies with the employers to show that the criteria used which produce these inequalities are not discriminatory.

7.6.1 THE JOB EVALUATION PROCESS

A job evaluation scheme has to be carried out with a view to evaluating jobs in terms of demands made of a worker under various headings such as effort, skill, decision-making, and so on, so as to lead to a fair comparison with a comparator's job. This is termed the 'analytical' approach and is to be preferred to the 'felt-fair' or 'whole-job' approach.

There are some general points to note:

- Job evaluation is intended to determine the relative positions of jobs within a hierarchy. It is a comparative process which determines grades but *not* actual rates of pay. These must be established by some other mechanism.

- Job evaluation is normally conducted by a panel on the basis of information obtained by means of job analysis. It is a systematic but not infallible process.
- The performance of individuals in the jobs being evaluated should play no part in the evaluation process: it is the job, not the job-holder, that is being evaluated. This important general principle is easily applied in most situations but it should be noted that in complex, specialist jobs it can be more difficult to separate individuals' performance from their job requirements since, as jobs become more complicated and innovative, they are more likely to become constructed around the personal strengths and capabilities of the job-holder. This can be the case with, for example, highly specialised technical jobs or senior managerial ones.
- Job analysis provides the raw material for job evaluation.

7.6.2 JOB EVALUATION SYSTEMS

The three conventional categories of job evaluation are:

- job ranking
- job classification
- points-factor schemes.

Job ranking

The most simple form of job evaluation, job ranking is non-analytical in that it considers the job as a whole, and does not attempt to assess different aspects of the job separately. Job ranking determines the relative value of jobs in a hierarchy by placing them in rank order according to the worth of each job as established by job analysis.

The advantages of job ranking are that it is simple to undertake, easily understood and relatively inexpensive.

The disadvantages are that: (1) there are no defined standards for judging relative values and this can lead to inconsistencies; (2) it can be difficult to establish ranking order between broadly similar jobs – the technique of paired comparisons is sometimes used to alleviate both these problems; and (3) it does not equate to a defence in 'equal value' cases.

Job classification

Job classification is a non-analytical technique in which the grades to be used are first defined, and then jobs are allocated to grades by comparing the job description (produced by job analysis) with the grade definitions.

The advantages of job classification are that it is simple to introduce and use, and that the grade definitions provide some standards for judgement.

The disadvantages are that: (1) grade definitions are usually so general that they are not terribly helpful in assessing borderline cases; (2) it is not very applicable to senior or complex jobs; and (3) it does not equate to a defence in 'equal value' cases.

Points-factor schemes

Points-factor schemes comprise an analytical technique in which jobs are compared in terms of a number of separately defining characteristics or 'factors' – for example skill, knowledge, decision-making, and so on. It is assumed that all factors are present in most if not all jobs. Each factor is weighted to reflect its relative importance. A range of points is allocated to each factor, and this range is divided into 'degrees' or levels. Evaluation is based on an analysis of the job in terms of the factors. Decisions are made on the level at which the factor applies to the job. The points for each factor are added to give a total points score.

When designing a typical points-factor scheme, the following checklist is helpful:

- Select factors and decide on the number of levels required. This is typically anything between three and 12 factors, which may be grouped under three headings – input, processes and output.
- Allocate points to levels and weights to factors.
- Select benchmark jobs (some authorities recommend as many as 20–25% of the jobs under review).
- Analyse benchmark jobs.
- Rank jobs according to points values.
- Determine the number of job grades and define them in terms of points.
- Allocate jobs according to points values.

The advantages of points-factor schemes are that their greater detail gives better descriptions of jobs, helps to achieve more consistent results, increases perceptions of fairness and often helps to achieve a greater consensus on grading between management and trade union/staff association representatives; and that they *can* provide a defence in 'equal value' cases.

The disadvantages are that they are complex and expensive to install and maintain, and that they can give a spurious impression of 'scientific' accuracy. Moreover, some critics argue that important skills – such as judgement – cannot in any case be properly evaluated by analytical means.

7.6.3 CRITICISMS OF CONVENTIONAL JOB EVALUATION SCHEMES

There have been some criticisms of job evaluation schemes, notably to the effect that:

- They measure the wrong things: the idea that the focus should be on measuring the job, not the job-holder, runs counter to the way work is increasingly organised. More and more functions and businesses are subject to rapid change and depend on the ability of groups of employees to apply their skills in a flexible way. The established systems fail to measure what is important in the contribution of these 'knowledge workers' (IDS 1991).
- Job evaluation has a place in modern management but it must be used flexibly, not bureaucratically: 'Job evaluation used to be about control of uniformity. It cannot and should not fulfil that role any more. What it can contribute is help in the management of diversity in the kind of organisations and structures that we are now learning to live with' (Armstrong and Murlis 1998).

 JOB EVALUATION IN SCOTTISH SOFTRONICS PLC

CASE STUDY 7.2

Background information

Scottish Softronics is a small, high-tech engineering firm located in a greenfield site in the Scottish central belt, which specialises in providing complex electronic/mechanical engineering products that interface with state-of-the-art software engineering. Its major clients are leading software producers in the financial services industry. It has grown in size rapidly in the last few years after creating a number of new product lines. The firm prides itself on its reputation for

being a well-managed, technologically competent, high-quality supplier. The firm recently won its first Queen's Award for Exports. Trade unions are not recognised by the firm, but management acknowledge the importance of employee relations and there is a staff association which employees are encouraged to join and with which management regularly consult over pay and main conditions of employment.

Concerns about equal pay issues in the industry, combined with more general worries that the pay/grading structure is becoming unwieldy as a result of rapid growth and fast-changing work practices, have prompted the managing director to ask the HR director to brief him on the advisability of using job evaluation in the firm.

The HR director responded with a confidential memorandum, the contents of which may be summarised as follows:

Job evaluation (JE) is widely used in British industry, partly – as the MD perceived – to protect employers against 'equal value' claims from employees at tribunals.

JE has a tendency to become bureaucratic and to encourage a multiplicity of rigid grades. Such developments would not be helpful to Scottish Softronics, which has invested considerable time, effort and expense in introducing flexible work practices on the shop floor and lower management. If JE is to be introduced, every effort should be made to avoid these potential difficulties.

JE should not be used to set the actual pay rates for each grade, but rather to set the general structure.

Scottish Softronics has recently introduced performance-related pay (PRP) for all employees. The company would have to ensure that any JE scheme it adopted would not interfere with PRP. The HR director added that through his membership of the CIPD, he was acquainted with several organisations which shared Scottish Softronics' general business philosophy and which appeared to be able to combine JE and PRP successfully. The HR director's recommendation was that JE should be adopted.

If this was accepted, a small steering committee should be formed, consisting of seven working members – four from management and three nominated from the staff association. The HR director would chair the committee and report to the MD on progress.

The MD responded that the board accepted the HR director's recommendation, and he instructed the director to proceed.

The job evaluation exercise

Scottish Softronics employs approximately 400 people, of whom just over 300 are shop-floor staff.

At the first meeting of the steering committee it was agreed that there should be no more than four general grades: associate (that is, shop floor), senior associate, administration, and management. An inspection of the payroll and personnel records revealed that there were something like 80 different jobs. The HR director indicated that although he would expect to see that number reduced, he was not too concerned about job titles or the number of jobs in total, so long as the proposed system of four grades could be made to work.

At two further meetings of the committee, ten existing jobs were selected as benchmarks. A list of ten factors was drawn up: skill, effort, job complexity, responsibility, diplomacy, job conditions, supervision received, contact, dexterity, training.

Questions

Consider the ten factors listed above:

1   Would you make any changes to them?

2   Would you weight any of them – and if you would, how?

CASE STUDY 7.2 ANSWER GUIDANCE

Resolution and outcomes

The original factors were provisionally weighted in points terms. The benchmark jobs were then analysed and scored by the committee. From this process it was concluded that some factors overlapped and others were hard to define clearly. The factors were redesigned working on the basis of four generic factors: skill, effort, responsibility and job conditions. The factors were then reweighted.

Generic factors	Job factors	Points range	Weighting
SKILL	Education	1–5	3
	Experience	1–5	3
	Initiative	1–5	3
EFFORT	Physical demands	1–5	1
	Mental demands	1–5	3
RESPONSIBILITY	Process/equipment demands	1–5	1
	Material/product demands	1–5	1
	Responsibility for the work of others	1–5	3
	Responsibility for the safety of others	1–5	3
JOB CONDITIONS	Working conditions	1–5	1
	Unavoidable hazards	1–5	2

The benchmark jobs were then re-evaluated. The committee agreed that the results gave an acceptable grading structure and that the process should be applied to the remaining jobs in the firm.

?   REFLECTIVE ACTIVITY 7.2

Outline a reward system for:

- casual agricultural workers employed seasonally to pick fruit
- skilled electricians employed on maintenance duties in a power station
- university lecturers.

REFLECTIVE ACTIVITY 7.2 ANSWER GUIDANCE

We might recommend that for casual agricultural workers a simple piece-rate system by weight of fruit gathered (provided the quality was maintained – for example by means of inspection at the point of weighing) might be both the most motivating and fairest in terms of workers' perceptions. It would also give the employer the tightest control of pay costs.

The situation is more difficult in respect of both skilled electricians and university lecturers. In both cases, clear criteria for job performance would have to be established – for example, for the electricians, the number of inspections carried out in a given period and/or the average number of breakdowns/emergencies dealt with in a representative period; for the lecturers, some specified combination of teaching, research and administration. In both cases, additional objectives might be agreed, opening up the possibility of additional pay for skills/competence.

KEY ISSUES

Rewards have to be actively managed to secure the maximum utilisation of human assets, and to attract, motivate and retain core employees. Despite some interpretations of motivational theory, we cannot ignore the importance of money in rewards packages. Payment systems may be based on time, or may be variable where an element of total pay is dependent on some measure of output or an assessment of overall performance.

A 'cafeteria system' of rewards allows employees the flexibility, within limits, to decide the particular make-up of their total rewards package, and gives them scope to alter it as their personal needs and requirements change. This can be very attractive to core employees, but such schemes are administratively complex.

Job evaluation is in some ways a bureaucratic throwback to the days of traditional personnel management, but because only an analytical job evaluation scheme can provide an employer with a legal defence in 'equal value/pay' cases, its importance is actually growing in the twenty-first century.

EXPLORE FURTHER

Armstrong, M. (2014) *Armstrong's Handbook of Human Resource Management Practice*. 13th edition. London: Kogan Page.

- Chapters 26, 'Reward management: strategy and systems'.
- Chapter 27, 'The practice of reward management'.
- Chapter 28, 'Managing rewards for special groups'.
- Chapter 69, 'Strategic reward toolkit'.

CIPD. (2015a) *Reward Management*. Annual survey report. London: Chartered Institute of Personnel and Development.

CIPD. (2015b) *Show me the Money! The behavioural science of reward*. Research report. London: Chartered Institute of Personnel and Development.

Boxall, P., Purcell, J. and Wright, P. (eds) (2007) *The Oxford Handbook of Human Resource Management*. Oxford: Oxford University Press.

- Chapter 17, J.P. Guthrie, 'Remuneration: pay effects at work'.

Torrington, D., Hall, L., Taylor, S. and Atkinson C. (2014) *Human Resource Management*. 9th edition. London/Englewood Cliffs, NJ: FT/Prentice-Hall.

- Chapter 21, 'Setting pay'.
- Chapter 22, 'Incentives'.

Wilkinson, A., Redman, T., Snell, S.A. and Bacon, N. (2010) *Sage Handbook of Human Resource Management*. London: Sage.

- Chapter 13, B. Gerhart, 'Compensation'.

CHAPTER 8

The global context of HRM: international and comparative HRM

INTRODUCTION

There are two aspects to the global context of HRM, which are termed, respectively, international HRM (IHRM) and comparative HRM (CHRM):

1 IHRM focuses on the degree to which multinational companies can or should practise uniform HRM policies and practices in all the countries in which they operate.
2 CHRM is concerned with the degree to which HRM as practised in different countries (for example, USA, China and India) shows general similarities or difference.

LEARNING OUTCOMES

On completion of this chapter you should:

- be able to appreciate the different approaches to HRM that may be possible in multinational companies (MNCs)
- know about Hofstede's concept of dimensions of culture and what these can tell us about managing people in the interface between national and organisational culture
- be aware of some of the grounds for criticism of Hofstede's work
- understand something of the complexity inherent in selecting, preparing and supporting personnel for expatriate assignments
- have some appreciation of the idea of comparative HRM
- have some understanding of the convergence–divergence debate in comparative HRM.

The cultural background to HRM as an approach to managing people is, as we have seen in this text, predominantly North American. It has been largely through the agency of multinational companies that HRM practices have spread internationally. However, not all the world shares all features of North American work culture. It is more individualistic and more achievement-oriented than most other countries (Hofstede 1980), and this is reflected in employment practices and employee relations legislation in the USA.

But it can also be said that, for instance, the EU is unique in having its members committed to an international level of legislation which affects the employer–employee relationship, and in the context of HRM, Europe can be distinguished from the USA in a number of other important ways. Western Europe is still a relatively heavily unionised continent. Although unions have lost members in most European countries, recognition by employers remains high, as does trade union influence, even if there are some significant differences in this among the various European nations.

The high Western European levels of educational and vocational training and government support for the labour market are quite different from those in America. Patterns of ownership are also different.

The newly developing markets in Eastern Europe, even those within the EU, are still significantly different from those in Western Europe in many respects.

Then there is Japan and the 'tiger economies' of the Pacific Rim, and of course the emerging new economic superpowers of China and India. Each of these countries has unique features of culture, employment law and regulation of the labour market. The global economy is enormously diverse.

Clearly, the idea of 'international HRM' is a huge subject. We will focus in this chapter on one important aspect of it: how operating in different countries affects the HRM of the companies concerned – that is, MNCs. CHRM is discussed later in the chapter.

Armstrong (2009, p151) defined IHRM as:

the process of managing people across international boundaries by multinational companies. It involves worldwide management of people, not just the management of expatriates.

8.1 APPROACHES TO IHRM

A widely used typology of the approaches which an MNC can take to its subsidiaries in other countries is that devised by Perlmutter (1969). This identified four different approaches:

- *the ethnocentric approach*, in which the MNC simply transfers the HR practices and policies used in the home country to foreign subsidiaries: expatriates from the home country manage the foreign subsidiaries and the MNC
- *the polycentric approach*, where each subsidiary can develop its own HR policies appropriate to its circumstances: local managers are hired to manage HRM activities
- *the regiocentric approach*, in which for a given regional grouping of subsidiaries (for example Europe, Asia, or the Americas) HR policies are co-ordinated within the region, but may vary from region to region: subsidiaries may be staffed by managers from any of the countries within the region
- *the geocentric approach*, in which the firm views itself as a single international business rather than one with a home base and a number of foreign subsidiaries. HR policies are developed to meet the global goals of the enterprise. HRM and other activities are managed by the individuals judged to be most appropriate without regard for their own nationality – so a Dutch manager might handle HRM in a British plant, and vice versa.

Many factors may influence the IHRM approach taken by a particular MNC. These include national politics and legislation, managerial culture, educational and technological development in the host and subsidiary countries, production technology and the nature of the product, the organisational lifecycle, and national cultural differences.

When asked by researchers to identify the most important global pressures on IHRM (Roberts *et al* 1998), senior HR managers in MNCs nominated:

- getting the right knowledge, skills and competencies to where they were needed globally
- disseminating knowledge and innovation effectively throughout the organisation
- identifying and developing talent globally.

8.2 NATIONAL CULTURES: THE WORK OF HOFSTEDE

Geert Hofstede (1980/2001) researched the interface between company and national culture. In the 1970s with colleagues at the University of Limburg in the Netherlands, he surveyed IBM employees' attitudes in over 70 countries. This work took into account responses of over 110,000 questionnaires. A total of 20 different language versions of the questionnaire had to be made.

It was assumed that national cultural differences found within the company would reflect those existing within the countries at large. The survey was repeated after four years and found reliable results, supporting the conclusion that valid cultural differences had been found.

Hofstede initially identified four basic dimensions of the differences between national cultures, and thereafter positioned each of the cultures on a scale from high to low on each of the four dimensions, giving each culture a distinctive profile.

The initial four dimensions were:

- power-distance
- uncertainty avoidance
- individualism/collectivism
- masculinity/femininity.

The *power-distance* dimension measures how close or how distant subordinates feel from their superiors, and is an index of power inequality in a culture. In high-inequality cultures (for example India or France), where people are respectful of traditional authority, it is unlikely that employees will be expected, or will wish, to challenge their superiors in the workplace. The management style is more likely to be autocratic or paternal. Organisations will usually be hierarchical and decision-making will be centralised.

In low-inequality cultures (for example Israel, Australia), employees will feel able to voice disagreement with their managers and will not see this as disrespectful. Employees will expect to be consulted by their managers when major decisions affecting their jobs and careers are to be made. The management style is therefore more likely to be participative or consultative, and the organisational structure will tend to be flat and flexible. Networks and self-managed teams are more likely to flourish in low-inequality/high-equality cultures.

The *uncertainty-avoidance* dimension shows how easily the culture copes with innovation and change and can tolerate ambiguity. In strong uncertainty-avoidance cultures, such as Japan and Greece, people feel the need for clarity and order, and risk-taking is not pursued or encouraged. Employees are attracted to long-term careers with the same company. In a weak uncertainty-avoidance culture – for example Denmark and Hong Kong – uncertainty is more easily accepted. A pragmatic view is taken of the need to change, or occasionally break, company rules. Employees do not seek or expect the long and stable employment patterns typical in the high uncertainty-avoidance countries and are more likely to be entrepreneurial in their behaviour. Organisations are more likely to be decentralised and a higher degree of empowerment granted to employees.

The *individualism/collectivism* dimension shows the degree to which the culture encourages individual as opposed to collective concerns. In an individualist culture such as the USA or the UK, the emphasis is on personal initiative and achievement. It is also accepted that everyone has a right to a private life and opinion. In a more collectivist culture such as Iran or Peru, there are tighter social frameworks and people are seen more as members of extended families or clans, which protect them in exchange for loyalty. Careers are pursued to increase standing in the family by being able to help other members of it. In collectivist cultures, the aim is to be a good member, whereas in individualist ones it is to be a good leader (Pugh and Hickson 1995).

In individualist cultures the relationship is contractual – that is, employees offer their labour for commensurate pay during their working hours. Most employees, especially non-managerial and non-professional ones, will not expect to work beyond the normal hours of work without being paid overtime, and they will not expect their relationship with their employing organisations to overlap with social or private lives. In collectivist cultures, by contrast, the employee–workplace relationship is emotional as well as contractual and the boundary between private and professional spheres of life in many instances is blurred. The superior is not just a manager but could also be a father or mother figure to seek advice from on private issues, such as the need for a loan to buy a house or get married. Most employees are prepared to work well beyond the official working hours if required, without expecting additional pay. In addition to the pay in exchange for labour as stated in the formal employment contract, it is understood that the workplace looks after employees' total well-being in return for loyalty and commitment (Tayeb 2008).

The *masculinity/femininity* dimension is not about discrimination or liberation in gender terms. It refers to the value placed on traditionally male or female values as conventionally understood in most Western cultures. 'Masculine' cultures such as Japan, Italy and Australia value competitiveness, assertiveness, ambition, and the accumulation of wealth and material possessions, whether pursued by males or females. 'Feminine' cultures such as the Netherlands and Sweden place more value on relationships and quality of life, and service rather than ambition is valued. 'Anglo' cultures such as the USA and the UK are moderately 'masculine'. The terminology is somewhat offensive or embarrassing to many readers of Hofstede's work and this dimension is often renamed 'quantity of life versus quality of life' in the secondary literature.

Hofstede later developed a fifth dimension of culture – that of long-term versus short-term orientation. This describes the 'time horizon' of a society. China, Japan and the Asian 'tiger' countries scored very highly on this dimension; most Western countries scored rather low, and many less developed countries scored very low (Hofstede 2001).

Culture not only influences an MNC's overall approach to IHRM, it has a potential impact on every HR function.

 HRM IN ACTION

CASE STUDY 8.1

Pugh and Hickson (1995) used Hofstede's framework to analyse the use of *management by objectives* (MbO) in an MNC with subsidiaries in Germany and France.

American companies pioneered the use of MbO for the performance appraisal of managers, and it has been claimed that this technique has had more success there than in many other countries. Hofstede's analysis of culture may give an answer.

MbO requires that:

- the subordinate is sufficiently independent to negotiate meaningfully with the boss (that is, low power-distance)

- both are willing to take some risks – the boss in delegating power, the subordinate in accepting some responsibility (low uncertainty avoidance)
- the subordinate is personally willing to 'have a go' and try to make their mark (high individualism)
- both regard high performance and results as important (high masculinity).

Germany's work culture has low power-distance, which is appropriate for MbO, but is high on uncertainty avoidance, which suggests a lack of willingness to take the risks and tolerate the ambiguity needed to accept 'stretch' goals. France has high power-distance and high

> uncertainty avoidance, suggesting that MbO may be highly inappropriate there as a means of managerial performance appraisal. In fact, research indicates that in Germany MbO can be successful but takes a more participative approach than in the USA, reducing the uncertainty. In France, MbO has never really been popular.

8.2.1 CRITICISMS OF HOFSTEDE'S WORK

Hofstede's studies initiated a stream of research exploring the relationship between national cultural diversity and management practices (De Ceri 2007, p511). Hofstede's work has been widely applied in international management, but it has also generated significant debate and criticism, both of his conceptualisation of culture and his labelling of the dimensions. His methodology has also been questioned, notably his data collection and the generalisability of his findings (for example, Chiang 2005). According to De Ceri (2007, p512), Gerhart and Fang's (2005) re-analysis of Hofstede's results has reinforced such criticism, at least in some academic circles.

Notwithstanding these criticisms of Hofstede's work, the question of national culture has enduring importance for both international management research and practice, and a number of researchers have attempted to discover other cultural dimensions. The Global Leadership and Organizational Behavior Effectiveness (GLOBE) project collected data over seven years from 18,000 middle managers in 62 countries (House *et al* 2004). The managers were compared on nine cultural dimensions: performance orientation, future orientation, assertiveness, uncertainty avoidance, power-distance, institutional collectivism, family collectivism, gender egalitarianism, and human orientation. The influence of Hofstede's work on the GLOBE project is evident. The GLOBE research has implications for many managerial areas, including communication preferences and management style (De Ceri 2007, Javidan and House 2001).

While these cross-cultural studies have contributed greatly to our knowledge and understanding of cultural diversity and its relationship to management practice, other researchers have questioned the emphasis they place on national culture. Cultural diversity can be observed not only at national level but also at regional or within-national levels. Can we really talk about one single culture for the USA or China or India (Husted 2003)?

8.3 INTERNATIONAL TALENT MANAGEMENT

The 2009 CIPD *Learning and Talent Development* survey (CIPD 2010a) produced the following findings in respect of international organisations.

Learning and talent development were seen as a key driver for the international aspects of the business by almost two-thirds (64%) of international organisations. Almost six in ten (57%) also saw it as key to have trained expatriate and local staff in international locations. However, only a third of international organisations (34%) carried out specific learning and talent development with managers who have international responsibilities.

These specific interventions included coaching and mentoring methods for eight in ten (83%) of those organisations carrying it out, training on-the-job for three-quarters (74%), and classroom courses and instruction for seven in ten (72%).

To nurture talent, most international organisations used company-wide talent management programmes for high-potentials (55%), coaching and mentoring to help international staff move into key roles (38%), and experienced expatriate staff to mentor and develop local talent (23%).

In order to meet business objectives in two years' time, international organisations considered that their expatriate staff needed to develop management and leadership skills (42%). However, four in ten (40%) international organisations also believed that their expatriate staff needed to develop inter-cultural skills to help raise awareness of other cultures.

Although only just over a third (36%) currently had programmes to equip their staff in foreign languages training, three in ten (29%) international organisations said their staff required training in English, a quarter (23%) in French, two in ten (18%) in Spanish, and a sixth (17%) in German. For these last three languages, an understanding of technical terms and a conversational level was the most important, whereas fluency in English training was a need for three-quarters of such employers (73%).

8.4 IHRM AND THE SELECTION PROCESS: SELECTING EXPATRIATES

The most common forms of international assignments are (Scullion and Collings 2006):

- short-term or contractual assignments, typically between 3 and 12 months in duration; temporary projects or troubleshooting assignments
- traditional expatriate long-term assignments, usually from one to five years, in which the expatriate has a clearly defined role in the host organisation
- rotational assignments – regular short assignments abroad alternating with home leave: for example oil rig engineers
- international commuter assignments, for which the family remains at home while the employee commutes to a foreign workplace on, for example, a weekly or fortnightly basis
- frequent-flyer assignments, where the employee undertakes frequent and varied short-term international assignments but does not relocate from the home base
- virtual assignments: staff manage international employees via technology from their usual home workplace.

The management of expatriate employees is a particularly challenging task in IHRM, and the failure rate of expatriate assignments is high. Scullion (1995) found that UK MNCs experienced lower failure rates than did US ones because UK managers tended to have a more international outlook than did US ones. UK firms valued international experience more highly, and they tended to have more effective HR policies on expatriation, especially in relation to the selection of personnel for expatriate projects.

Research has shown that there are identifiable attributes which contribute to the success or failure of expatriate employees:

- personality traits – the ability to tolerate ambiguity; behavioural flexibility; the ability to be non-judgemental; the level of cultural empathy and ethnocentrism; interpersonal skills (Mendenhall and Oddou 1985, Tung 1986)
- motivational state – belief in the mission; the congruence of the assignment with the career path; interest in overseas experience; interest in the host-country culture; a willingness to learn new behaviour patterns and attitudes
- family situation – the willingness of a partner to live overseas; the adaptability and supportiveness of the partner; the stability of the relationship with the partner
- language skills – an ability to quickly learn the host-country language; a facility also in non-verbal communication.

8.5 EXPATRIATE RE-ENTRY

The task of effectively repatriating employees after foreign assignments is often initially overlooked by organisations and, indeed, by expatriates themselves and their families (IDS 2010).

Many returning expatriates leave their firms within a year of returning home, often finding returning home a greater culture shock than moving abroad.

The problems associated with re-entry adjustment can be divided into those related to general cultural readjustment and those dealing specifically with readjustment to the job.

8.5.1 GENERAL CULTURAL READJUSTMENT

Re-entry often brings a feeling of cultural and social loss. The international assignment may have presented an exciting and fulfilling experience for the employee and their partner, together with a considerably higher standard of living – possibly including the provision of servants and a desirable social life. Children may experience difficulties in readjusting to school. There may be unexpected financial difficulties in reverting to domestic salary levels. All these can result in marital strain.

8.5.2 JOB READJUSTMENT

Returning expatriates often find that their 'home office' has not planned for their return and they typically feel isolated from changes that have occurred during their foreign assignment. They may feel that they have fallen behind with new technology, and they may feel that they have missed promotion opportunities. Very often the expatriate enjoyed a higher level of authority and responsibility while on the foreign assignment and may find it difficult to accept their former, less responsible, role. (It is a particularly difficult transition to make.) All these difficulties mean that many returning expatriates are vulnerable to feelings of demotivation and may be more likely to accept employment offers from other organisations.

> ## ? REFLECTIVE ACTIVITY 8.1
>
> Defend or refute this statement:
>
> *It is not a good idea to send female managers to countries that have a very 'masculine' work culture (in Hofstede's terms).*

REFLECTIVE ACTIVITY 8.1 ANSWER GUIDANCE

It is acknowledged that there are special issues regarding female expatriates, but clichés must be examined rather than taken at face value.

In most Western countries, women are under-represented as managerial expatriates. Although women represent around 50% of middle management talent in US companies, they represent only 14% of expatriate managers sent abroad (Dessler 2005).

Some male managers assume that women do not want to work abroad, are reluctant to move their families, or cannot persuade their spouses or partners to move because they are the main breadwinners. In fact, all of these assumptions are false (Tyler 2001). Women managers do want international assignments, are not less inclined than male managers to move their families abroad, and their male partners are not necessarily the family's main breadwinner.

In selecting individuals for foreign positions, it seems most rational to look for the kinds of attributes associated with success in foreign assignments, regardless of the sex of the candidate (Napier and Tully 2002, Fischlmayr 2002, Mayrhofer and Scullion 2002).

CASE STUDY 8.2

HRM IN ACTION: NO PLACE LIKE HOME

The way some relocation specialists talk, you'd think taking a job overseas was simply a question of booking a man with a van.

But the real issues behind moving abroad these days are psychological, spiritual and cultural. More people are thinking twice about uprooting themselves for an overseas job, even though it may be an astute career step.

Take Carrie, who works for an insurance company in Cheltenham and lives with her IT consultant husband Chris and six-year-old son Jed. If her employer asked her to go to Cairo for two years, Chris's business would suffer and Jed would be wrenched away from his school. The expatriate life wouldn't appeal since they belong to a community of friends in Cheltenham. International schools? The local ones are among the best in the country. Carrie's worried about uprooting her family, terrorism and the unpopularity of the British in the Middle East since the Iraqi invasion. What if she stays at home and visits Cairo regularly? Saying no wouldn't be the end of her career, simply a personal statement about work–life balance. This isn't just psychological, spiritual and cultural – it's personal too.

Source: *People Management*, 27 July 2006.

? REFLECTIVE ACTIVITY 8.2

By what criteria would you judge the success of an expatriate re-entry?

REFLECTIVE ACTIVITY 8.2 ANSWER GUIDANCE

There are six criteria that should be met before a re-entry can be judged successful. The returning expatriates should:

- perform at a level and quality expected by their managers
- exhibit a reasonable level of job satisfaction with the new position
- be able to use the skills developed during the foreign assignment
- be able to maintain a career progression comparable with cohorts who did not go abroad
- remain (or at least intend to remain) with the employer for a reasonable period of time after returning
- avoid dysfunctional levels of stress during re-entry.

The main factors that affect successful re-entry are:

- the similarity of the international and domestic assignments
- the amount of change in the home organisation
- the nature and personality of the expatriate
- the support available to the returning expatriate
- the career planning system of the organisation.

HRM IN ACTION: SEND THE RIGHT PEOPLE TO THE RIGHT PLACES

CASE STUDY 8.3

A failure to take into account different business cultures, and ways of working, when arranging overseas assignments is costing international organisations dear.

Sending senior business executives abroad is an expensive undertaking. Yet research suggests that around 40% of those who take on an expatriate assignment fail, at a cost to their employer of two to four times their annual salary. So what causes this surprisingly high failure rate?

The Global Personality Inventory (GPI) contains data gathered by Personnel Decisions International (PDI) from more than 12,000 managers and executives who have gone through its leadership screening process across the globe. It suggests that the chief cause of the high failure rate for expatriate assignments is the inability of managers to appreciate differences between their own business cultures and foreign work environments. In other words, troubles often arise because of personality-based perceptions rather than substantive business issues.

According to the GPI data, 'agreeableness' and emotional balance accounted for 85% of differences between managers and executives working across countries. That is, the tendency to seek group harmony versus fostering individuality, or to have quick and deep emotional reactions to events rather than muted emotional responses. Problems arise when an individual's own attributes in these areas don't match those of the culture where they are sent. A leader who favours individuality will rub up the wrong way co-workers in a

country where group needs traditionally take precedence. Likewise, an even-keeled leader in a culture where emotional expression is the norm risks being seen as cold and unfeeling.

By matching individuals' personality traits in these two key areas to the cultural norms of the countries to which they are being assigned, businesses can achieve greater success than by relying on 'gut instinct'. For example, tackling business problems as a team is common practice in the UK, while working solo is the norm in China. The French most closely match their colleagues in Mexico in business leadership style, placing strong emphasis on individuality. By contrast, Japanese executives are more in tune with their colleagues in Saudi Arabia, both nationalities placing strong emphasis on maintaining group harmony.

PDI then grouped together similar cultures and drew up a shortlist of the most valuable managerial skills for potential expatriates. The top six on this list were the ability to act with integrity, to champion change, to build relationships, to demonstrate adaptability, to use sound judgement, and to coach and develop others. The two with most significant between-country differences were the ability to act with integrity and to champion change.

The lesson for HR, as well as leaders working across borders, is obvious. Smart businesses will take cultural similarities and differences into account when working across the globe.

Source: *People Management*, 13 July 2006.

8.6 COMPARATIVE HRM: CONVERGENCE AND DIVERGENCE

The 'convergence–divergence' debate in comparative HRM asks to what extent HRM systems of developing countries are converging or diverging with respect to those in the developed world.

HRM researchers have examined whether Western-derived, global, standardised HR policies and practices can be successfully implemented in the context of developing countries. They have also tried to identify unique aspects of indigenous HRM policies and practices. The evidence suggests that managerial attitudes, values, behaviours and efficacy all differ across national cultures (see for example the GLOBE studies noted in section 8.2.1).

The term 'soft convergence' has been coined to describe the 'partial impact' of globalisation of HRM policies and practices (Warner 2002). This is typified by the implementation by multinational companies (MNCs) of globally standardised HRM policies and practices but allowing for local adjustments. Under globalisation, international trade and finance places pressure on firms to standardise practices and policies to seek competitive advantage. But this standardisation is necessarily moderated by the inescapable local variations in factors such as demography, geography, economics, legal and political systems, and national culture.

The recognition of this has brought many commentators to the conclusion that 'soft convergence' is the most that realistically can be expected and that the notion of total or 'hard' convergence of HRM is a chimera (Budwhar and Debra 2010).

8.7 TRUST AND LEADERSHIP

Delegation of power and responsibility is essential to the Western HRM model. How does national culture affect this?

One of the major factors that influences the extent to which managers are willing to delegate power and authority to their subordinates is whether they can trust them (Tayeb 1988, 2008). First, are they technically capable of making decisions on their own, and do they possess the requisite knowledge and competence? Second, will they put the company's interests before theirs? The level of trust in other people's good intentions varies widely between cultures, dependent on such factors as the extent of corruption prevalent in public bureaucracies and in private companies as well.

If a culture is such that the people are in general honest, with a traditionally good work ethic, and the society possesses an educated workforce, managers will be able to trust them to make decisions on their own. In cultures characterised by corruption or by low levels of skills and competence and a poor work ethic, to protect their own interests and those of their company managers are likely to delegate decision-making authority only to a few trusted employees and by preference to members of their own clan, their relatives or friends.

8.7.1 PREFERENCE FOR CERTAIN LEADERSHIP BEHAVIOURS

People in cultures which have low tolerance for ambiguity and risk-taking tend to prefer major decisions affecting the community to be taken by their leaders as 'benevolent autocrats', whereas in cultures with a higher tolerance for ambiguity people usually prefer to participate in decision-making or at least to have their leaders take their views into account when making decisions on their behalf.

The preference for leadership models is reflected within organisations. For instance, in cultures with a preference for benevolent autocratic leaders, managers may well be looked up to as 'father figures' who usually know best. In cultures with a preference for a participative consultative model, the manager is seen as another team member who contributes to the discussions the same as anyone else.

A comparison between Japanese and British leadership styles (Tayeb 1994b) also showed that there are some behaviours that are associated with a high employee-oriented behaviour by respondents in one country but which are perceived quite differently by people in another country.

The Japanese see it as high employee-oriented behaviour when a supervisor or manager:

- spends more time at work than official work hours
- expects to discuss an employee's personal difficulties with other team members in the employee's absence
- talks with the subordinates frequently about progress in relation to a work schedule
- spends some time with the subordinates socially
- spends time with subordinates discussing their career plans
- evaluates performance on the work of the group as a whole
- meets the group frequently for social or recreational purposes, and
- consults the subordinates when substantially new work procedures are being discussed.

British employees see a supervisor as showing high employee-oriented behaviour when they:

- frequently use or demonstrate how to use any of the equipment used by the group
- make it possible for subordinates to put forward suggestions for work improvement
- discuss with the group if they believe that there is a substantial problem in the group's work procedures, and
- may be addressed by first name.

For a supervisor to discuss a subordinate's personal difficulties behind their back with other group members was very definitely regarded by the British (unlike the Japanese) as anything but high employee-oriented behaviour. The British considered such an act an invasion of personal privacy and unacceptable.

These findings reflect the cultural characteristics of the countries. Strong features of British culture are the willingness to take account of other people's opinions, consultation and participation, a love of privacy and 'minding their own business', and individualism. The Japanese, in contrast, do not seem to mind their superiors' discussing their personal affairs with others in their absence, which is consistent with a more collectivist culture.

Tayeb's findings are reinforced by a major study of relationship between societal culture and organisational behaviour, namely the Global Leadership and Organizational Behavior Effectiveness (GLOBE) studies, already noted in section 8.2.1. (See Dorfman *et al* 2012 for a summary of the GLOBE project, and further information on GLOBE can be found at: **www.uvic.ca/gustavson/globe/index.php**)

The GLOBE project studied (amongst other things) leadership styles and culturally different ideas of the characteristics of outstanding leaders. It found that some aspects of leadership are culturally dependent, while charismatic and team-oriented leadership are universally desirable styles.

Six leadership styles were identified, as follows:

- *the charismatic/value-based style*, which stressed high standards, decisiveness, and innovation; sought to inspire people around a vision; created a passion among them to perform; and did so by holding on to core values
- *the team-oriented style* instilled pride, loyalty, and collaboration among organisational members; and highly valued team cohesiveness and a common purpose or goals
- *the participative style* encouraged input from others in decision-making and implementation; and emphasised delegation and equality
- *the humane style* stressed compassion and generosity; it was patient, supportive, and concerned with the well-being of others
- *the self-protective style* emphasised procedural, status-conscious, and 'face-saving' behaviours; and focused on the safety and security of the individual and the group
- *the autonomous style* was characterised by an independent, individualistic and self-centric approach to leadership.

The first two styles, charismatic/value-based and team-oriented style, were seen in all cultures as contributing to outstanding leadership. However, there was significant cultural variation regarding the other four styles. In some cultures, they were seen as good and effective styles, while other cultures saw them as hindering outstanding leadership.

The GLOBE study also found that certain leader characteristics such as ambition, enthusiasm, formality, taking a logical approach, and being a risk-taker are valued very differently around the world.

But there were also some leader characteristics that are universally endorsed across all societies in the GLOBE study. People in all societies want their leaders to be trustworthy, just, honest and decisive. However, how these traits are expressed and enacted can be significantly different from society to society. For example, for a leader to be described as decisive in the US, they are expected to make quick and approximate decisions. In contrast, in France or Germany, being decisive tends to mean a more deliberate and precise approach to decision-making.

The reader will see the obvious implications for the adoption of HRM policies and practices.

HRM IN ACTION: THE DEVELOPMENT OF HRM IN CHINA

CASE STUDY 8.4

HRM functions and practices have been adopted by different types of Chinese companies (Zhang 2012) and it has been argued that, as the market economy in China developed, the companies that successfully adopted Western HRM (such as Lenovo, Formosa Plastics, Haier and Huawei Technology) performed better than their competitors which did not (Zhang *et al* 2009).

Not only did these companies benefit from modern knowledge and experience in managing people, the adoption of HRM functions and practices helped them mitigate some disadvantages accruing from the traditional Chinese culture, for example, the prevalence of guanxi networks in Chinese culture – that is, networks of mutual social obligations which, while giving stability and providing social capital, often resulted in unqualified employees being recruited or promoted because of their personal connections with influential managers in companies. Competency-based selection and performance-based reward systems from Western HRM could overcome this, at least to some extent.

However, even Chinese companies that adopted HRM practices still typically followed a 'logic of collaboration' derived from Chinese traditional values and/or socialism (Zhang 2012), which held that

interpersonal co-operation and harmonious relationships lead to good outcomes. Before 1978, this supported practices such as lifelong employment, inflexibility and fixed wage systems, all of which depressed efficiency and employee incentives. During the following period of economic reform, many Chinese companies abandoned those practices, at least in extreme form, and espoused a 'logic of competition' and individual responsibility. However, observers think it is doubtful whether Chinese companies will abandon the logic of collaboration completely because it is deeply rooted in Chinese culture. So, although Chinese companies are typically enthusiastic in learning HRM principles and practices from Western countries, they are cautious in applying them (Zhang *et al* 2009). For example, where companies implement job/position evaluation systems, they still manage the income gap between different ranks carefully. It has been reported that the income gap between top managers and common employees in Chinese state-owned companies tends to be a multiple of only around 12 (compared with, in some extreme cases, several hundred in some large, for-profit, Western companies) and within-grade performance-related incentives are limited by Western standards in order to preserve interpersonal co-operation among employees (Zhang 2012).

The future of HRM in China will be influenced by many factors, but one important aspect will be the effect of rising labour costs. For several decades China has capitalised on its competitive labour costs, but its comparative advantage in that area is diminishing as these costs rise, reflecting its growing prosperity (Cai 2010). The increasing labour costs will force China to seek new ways of continuing economic growth. Like its Western competitor countries, economic success in the future will depend on encouraging creative, innovative, knowledge-based industries and services. But again there would seem to be cultural barriers – since Chinese traditional culture emphasises hierarchy and obedience, which in the West are thought to be inconsistent with the sort of risk-taking necessary for innovation.

But as Warner (2009) has pointed out, although the Chinese people have experienced great economic change, they have never given up their most important cultural characteristic, the ability to manage paradoxes (Warner 2009).

GLOBAL TALENT MOBILITY

CASE STUDY 8.5

Mobility, in the increasingly borderless world of multinational firms, can help to address talent shortages and close skills gaps that persist even in the face of pervasively high levels of unemployment. Talent mobility also has the potential to fuel economic growth, while enhancing workers' lives.

Mercer carried out a study of international talent mobility, in partnership with the World Economic Forum, which was unveiled in January 2012 at the forum's annual meeting at Davos in Switzerland. Mercer surveyed practitioners and experts in 45 countries, supplementing this with in-depth interviews in more than 100 business, government and academic entities.

The study found that the mobility efforts of most private organisations remained anchored to narrow concerns over expatriate assignments and leadership development, while public sector actions often reflect similarly parochial concerns. Over 40% of the organisations surveyed moved 5% or less of their employees each year, and fewer than half said that they selected international assignees well. Overall, workforce mobility in the developed world has hardly increased over the previous 20 years. The study identified four key issues that impede talent mobility:

- widespread unemployability owing to lack of basic employment skills, particularly among people in disadvantaged communities;
- critical gaps between the skills employees possess and those that businesses need;
- information gaps that make it difficult for labour markets to match workers to jobs effectively;
- constraints such as minimum wage rates and visa restrictions, which prevent labour markets from balancing supply and demand by adjusting wages or the number of workers available.

Source: *People Management*, April 2012.

? REFLECTIVE ACTIVITY 8.3

Outline some solutions to the problems that face global talent mobility.

The main conclusion of the Mercer study (Case Study 8.1), which was entitled *Talent Mobility Good Practices: Collaboration at the core of driving economic growth*, was that collaborative approaches to talent mobility are the most effective in addressing labour market failures and creating jobs.

For example, the UK-based corporate communications firm Taylor Bennett worked with external partners both to address the problem of employability and to increase the ethnic diversity of its industry's talent pool. The resulting intervention, 'The Taylor Bennett Foundation PR training and internship programme', was a ten-week, full-time training course, promoted through the employability unit of the University of East London and other universities that have a high proportion of ethnic minority students.

Similarly, the European Commission's Department of Employment, Social Affairs and Inclusion addressed the issues of high levels of youth unemployment in the EU and the difficulty of moving workers across member states by creating the 'Your first EURES job' programme. This has led EU countries to collaborate in policy-making and in the design of programmes intended to mobilise young workers, including job-abroad schemes within the EU, a microfinance facility to support young entrepreneurs, and a 'Youth on the Move' website to provide information for young people about studying, training or working abroad.

In the US, meanwhile, the Department of Labor launched a 'mySkills myFuture' website as an electronic tool enabling previously employed jobseekers to match their skills with those needed in other occupations.

Levels of collaboration

The study demonstrated that collaboration among multiple stakeholders was central to successful efforts to surmount impediments to talent mobility. In fact, actions by any organisation acting alone were unlikely to have much effect. The broader the co-operation, the more likely interventions were to address the four sources of market inefficiency or failure. The research identified four levels of collaboration in relation to talent mobility which, in its broadest sense, refers to the movement of workers within or across organisations, industries or countries, as well as across occupations or skill sets.

- **Level 1: collaboration within the organisation** – this level of collaboration across functions, units and geographies was often critical in designing and implementing talent mobility practices that encourage economic growth. These practices helped to develop staff, close information gaps, and better balance internal supply and demand. Examples included forecasting the supply and demand of critical talent; career and leadership development focusing on building critical skills; and promoting internal mobility across business units and jobs.

A practical example from the survey was that of COM DEV, a Canada-based space equipment manufacturer, which established consistent mobility guidelines to review all international assignments. Similarly, global luxury goods producer LVMH implemented cross-divisional talent exchange meetings at global and regional levels to improve the succession planning process by promoting internal mobility across its divisions and brands.

- **Level 2: collaboration across organisations within a country** – when they cannot solve talent issues on their own, leading organisations went beyond their own walls to collaborate with others to source and develop talent locally.

Examples include: seconding employees to other organisations; partnerships between companies, governments or educators on training, developing and deploying talent; and public sector initiatives on sharing information on labour supply and to facilitate immigration. The Taylor Bennett programme cited previously was a good example of both this level of collaboration and of the next one.

- **Level 3: collaboration on an industry or regional level** – this included public–private partnerships designed to foster talent mobility and skill development. For example, local businesses taking part in the University of the West of England's International Talent Scheme offered work experience to overseas students studying in the UK.
- **Level 4: collaboration on a global or multi-stakeholder level** – this involved sectors, governments, international organisations and academia working closely together to solve complex talent mobility issues, often across several countries and regions. For example, private companies could develop innovative talent sourcing and development strategies by working closely with educational institutions, governments and NGOs in multiple countries.

The study also found international development initiatives in the area of skills development and trade agreements between countries. The EC programme cited previously was an example, as was the Japan International Cooperation Agency's programme to send volunteers to developing countries to provide technical assistance and bring valuable experience of those countries back to Japanese corporations.

One of the case studies from the Mercer study, Walmart, is shown below.

Walmart looks to emerging markets

The world's largest retailer, Wal-Mart Stores, Inc (known as Walmart) developed innovative partnerships with government, educational institutions and NGOs to develop talent to support its growth ambitions in emerging markets.

Preparing for massive growth in India, Walmart entered the Indian market in 2009, establishing seven stores in three years. With a current workforce of about 8,000, the company's Indian joint venture, Bharti Walmart, expected this number to soar to 60,000 employees over the following five years. India has the largest youth population in the world, according to the UN, with close to 200 million people between the ages of 15 and 24. Yet significant skills deficits among this population hamper not only the employment prospects of many individuals but also the economic growth prospects of the country as a whole.

In Brazil, Walmart's accelerated growth over the past decade and created a large demand for talent in the retail sector. In 2010 alone, nearly 2.5 million formal positions were created. As Brazil's third largest retailer, with 87,000 employees, Walmart added 10,000 jobs in 2010. Given Brazil's large pool of young adults, 18% of whom are unemployed, it might be thought that the talent exists to fill these new jobs, but many of Brazil's young adults lack the education, work skills, and professional, personal and social development to access the labour market.

In both India and Brazil, Walmart's strategy was to increase the pool of qualified talent. So, before opening its first store, Bharti Walmart began discussions with the chief minister of the State of Punjab about training young people. The state was eager to prepare a large cross-section of its young people for productive careers in the growing retail sector. At the same time, Bharti Walmart wanted to help develop a pipeline of talent ready to step into positions in retail. Over the previous three years, nearly 8,000 students had been certified through Bharti Walmart training centres, and some 2,900 had been placed in formal jobs, including almost 500 in Walmart stores.

In 2010, Walmart Brazil launched a 'social retail school' to teach high school students the behavioural and technical skills they needed to become employable in the retail sector. Offering a programme similar to the one in India, the school accepted young adults from low-income families, and in its first year trained approximately 1,000 young people, 83% of whom have been placed in jobs. Another 1,740 students participated in 2011.

Walmart HR leaders learned from these initiatives that the multi-stakeholder approach to sourcing and developing talent had significant advantages over a unilateral approach. Rather than simply competing with other retailers for workers who already have the skills it needs (and so pushing up labour costs for the whole sector), or bearing all the costs of recruiting and training talent on its own, Walmart is helping to increase the overall supply of skilled talent in the market.

Source: *People Management*, 24 April 2012.

KEY ISSUES

There are two aspects to the global context of HRM: IHRM, which focuses on the degree to which multinational companies practise uniform HRM policies globally; and CHRM, which is concerned with the degree to which HRM as practised in different countries (for example the USA, China and India) shows general similarities or difference.

National cultures differ significantly, and, not surprisingly, this affects the implementation of HRM. The GLOBE project studied leadership styles in different cultures and found that some aspects of leadership are culturally dependent but charismatic and team-oriented leadership are universally desirable styles.

EXPLORE FURTHER

Armstrong, M. (2014) *Armstrong's Handbook of Human Resource Management Practice*. 13th edition. London: Kogan Page.

- Chapters 37–39, 'International HRM'.

Boxall, P., Purcell, J. and Wright, P. (eds) (2007) *The Oxford Handbook of Human Resource Management*. Oxford: Oxford University Press.

- Chapter 24, W.N. Cooke, 'Multinational companies and global human resource management'.
- Chapter 25, H. De Cieri, 'Transnational firms and cultural diversity'.

Boxall, P. and Purcell, J. (2006) *Strategy and Human Resource Management*. Basingstoke: Palgrave Macmillan.

- Chapter 10, 'Corporate human resource management in the global economy'.

CHAPTER 9

Contemporary issues and future trends

INTRODUCTION

This chapters deals with a number of issues which affect HRM but which do not merit a full chapter in a text such as this. Many of these themes cut across the main HRM functions of resourcing, learning and development, and employee relations. Some, such as new forms of employment and HR analytics, may have a profound effect on HRM in the future.

LEARNING OBJECTIVES

On completion of this chapter you should have some understanding of the following topics and their implications for HRM:

- high-involvement or high-performance work practices (HWPW)
- HR analytics
- leadership
- change management
- new forms of employment based on information and communication technology (ICT)
- corporate social responsibility
- ethics.

9.1 HIGH-INVOLVEMENT OR HIGH-PERFORMANCE WORK PRACTICES

The UK Workplace Employment Relations Studies (WERS) identified increasing interest in the UK in 'high-performance', 'high-commitment' or 'high-involvement' work organisation and practices. The trend was confirmed in the latest WERS, that of 2011 (van Wanrooy *et al* 2013). The authors note (pp166–7) that:

> For some time employment relations commentators and practitioners have been occupied with the idea of managerial practices that increase employees' involvement not only in their jobs but the wider workplace The concept, widely defined, encompasses discussion of 'high involvement management' (HIM) and somewhat more recently 'employee engagement' (see MacLeod and Clarke 2009, Rayton *et al* 2012).

A study funded by the UK government Department of Trade and Industry (DTI) and conducted in association with the CIPD, *High-Performance Work Strategies: Linking strategy and skills to performance outcomes* (DTI/CIPD 2005), established 'good practice' in a range of 'high-performance work practices' (HPWPs), these being defined as:

- a set of complementary work practices covering three broad areas or 'bundles' of practices covering:
- high employee involvement practices – for example self-directed teams, quality circles and sharing/access to company information
- human resource practices – for example sophisticated recruitment processes, performance appraisals, work redesign and mentoring
- reward and commitment practices – for example various financial rewards, family-friendly policies, job rotation and flexi-hours.

The importance of high-performance working for organisational performance was confirmed in the international context by an earlier joint study from the International Federation of Training and Development Organizations (IFTDO) – of which the CIPD in the UK is a member – and the International Labour Organization (ILO). This examined high-performance working in nine organisations around the world (ILO/IFTDO 2000).

High-performance working was understood to be associated with:

the achievement of high levels of performance, profitability and customer satisfaction by enhancing skills and engaging the enthusiasm of employees.

The report also cited an Organization for Economic Co-operation and Development (OECD) definition of the characteristics of HPW organisations as:

flatter non-hierarchical structures, moving away from reliance on management control, teamworking, autonomous working based on trust, communication and involvement. Workers are seen as being more highly skilled and having the intellectual resources to engage in lifelong learning and master new skills and behaviours.

The report concluded:

Increasing evidence is becoming available about the connections between people management and development and 'the bottom line'. Researchers have identified three ways in which this occurs: through the use of best HR practice; getting the right 'fit' between business strategy and HR practices; and using specific 'bundles' of practices, varied according to organisational context. The case studies used in the ILO/IFTDO research show significant evidence of the use of all these approaches. They bear witness to the search by organisations for an alignment between practices and outcomes and active searching for examples of good practice.

The report thus also illustrates how HRM now had a global relevance beyond the US/UK industrial cultures in which it first developed:

It is the business strategy that gives the high-performance working practices their dynamism and provides the framework against which performance can be evaluated and improved.

Wood *et al* (2013) took the definition of Belt and Giles (2009, pii) as 'a general approach to managing organisations that aims to stimulate more effective employee involvement and commitment to achieve high levels of performance'.

These authors found that HPWPs cover a range of areas, including work organisation, employment relations, management and leadership, and organisational development. They include skill and knowledge acquisition, employee involvement and motivational practices. They involve enriched job design, teamwork, functional flexibility, idea-capturing, training and development, information-sharing and appraisal, performance-related pay and equal opportunities policies. The most commonly used HPWPs were discretion (87%), variety (87%), team briefings (79%) and access to flexible working (78%).

The authors concluded that the research evidence suggested that the adoption of HPWPs is linked to improved organisational performance, and are most effective when they are used together as a synergistic set, sometimes referred to as 'high performance work systems'.

The question of HPWPs has obvious implications for HRM across a number of areas: recruitment, performance management, job design, and learning and development.

9.2 HR ANALYTICS

Basic descriptive HR data on subjects such as employee absence, annual leave, turnover, training, and so on, have of course long been collected by effective HR departments, but, as the term implies, human resource analytics (HRA) involves more than simple description. It uses modern statistical and computing techniques to analyse the HR data in a multivariate way which allows insight into more complex areas such as leadership capability and employee engagement. It enables trend analysis and the modelling of future HR requirements in a way not possible previously (CIPD 2016d).

There is great potential here for HRM to demonstrate how it adds value to the organisation. Evidence-based HR and HRA have become increasingly important (Boudreau and Ramstad 2007, Gibbons and Woock 2007), and, as Ulrich and Dulebohn put it:

Without rigorously tracking HR investments and outcomes, HR decisions and priorities remain whims not science (2015, pp202–3).

One implication of HRA is the need for HR managers, and those other managers who are using the outcome of the analyses, to acquire the necessary competencies in statistics and computing to be able to assess the outputs appropriately. The implications for learning and development should be recognised. This may be a challenge, but a worthwhile one. Ulrich and Dulebohn state:

With HRA, line managers and HR professionals can better justify, prioritise and improve HR investments. While many HR decisions require insight and judgement, improved HR metrics help HR to *move towards professional respectability* and decision-making rigour (2015, pp202–3, emphasis added).

9.3 HRM AND LEADERSHIP

We saw in Chapter 1 that Ulrich and Brockbank (2005) regarded leadership as a key role for HR, by which they meant not only leadership of the HR function but contributing to and supporting organisational leadership as whole. Strategy and change management are two areas where HR can be expected to contribute to the leadership function.

Leadership can be defined as:

the capacity to influence people, by means of personal attributes and/or behaviours, to achieve a common goal (CIPD 2016f).

Some authorities clearly differentiate the two concepts of management and leadership (for example Kotter 1999) – 'management' being understood to relate to what managers do under stable organisational and business conditions, and 'leadership' describing what organisations require when undergoing transformation or when operating in dynamic conditions. On this view, leaders and managers make different contributions – 'leaders have followers and managers have subordinates' (Kotter 1999). The leader is someone who develops vision and drives new initiatives; the manager is someone who monitors progress towards objectives to achieve order and reliability.

Of course, this view has never precluded the two roles from being undertaken by the same individual, but the crucial point is that they require distinct sets of skills, with the implication that one might be a competent manager without being a competent leader, or vice versa. Mintzberg (1973) suggested that in practice the distinction between effective leadership and effective management is blurred: effective managers require at least some leadership qualities.

Whetton and Cameron (2005, p16) state that:

the recent research is clear that such distinctions between leadership and management, which may have been appropriate in previous decades, are no longer useful. . . . Managers cannot be successful without being leaders, and leaders cannot be successful without being managers.

This is the view endorsed in this text.

The 'classical' school of management theory defined a manager's work in terms of planning, organising, co-ordinating, commanding and controlling (Fayol 1950). Mintzberg (1973) famously disputed whether managers actually behaved like that, although arguably he missed the point: a normative statement of the primary functions or obligations of management is not necessarily supposed to be a description of observable behaviour. Successful managers must somehow make and implement plans, however hectic their work schedule, and whether or not it is done in a calm, reflective manner or in a busy, disjointed fashion. They have to organise activities, people and knowledge effectively, even if it is often done by informal communication such as face-to-face encounters, phone or email, rather than by formal written statements or pronouncements; by influence, rather than by direct command.

This is not to say that the classic description of managerial work is adequate for the twenty-first century. Contemporary managers certainly have to plan, organise, co-ordinate, and ultimately be accountable for the activities and achievements of other people. But these functions are often done 'at arms' length', especially in the increasingly common cases of the self-directed team and the empowered worker. In modern organisations, managers might explicitly command people relatively rarely, although they have to be able to do so when necessary, and they sometimes may have to veto some proposals from staff. They will certainly always be concerned with influencing and motivating their people, and they need to be able to be directive when required.

Control of activities, people (including teams) and knowledge ultimately rests with designated managers – but the whole thrust of work organisation and job design over the last two decades has been to move power and decision-making down the organisation to the teams and individual workers who actually perform the tasks concerned. All organisations still necessarily exercise power and control over their employees, and this is done through the management structure, but the boundaries of control and authority are typically moved further from the individual worker or team than was previously the case, giving them a higher (although ultimately still limited) degree of power and discretion.

Consequently, there have been significant differences in the emphasis given to leadership and influence. These were always both present in work, since no organisation can operate solely on the basis of direct, formal and explicit commands for all activities, but they are much more important in the era of the knowledge worker and the self-directed and empowered team. Twenty-first-century economies require far fewer of the sort of semi-skilled and unskilled jobs that were the staple of industrialised economies until the last quarter of the twentieth century. The 'scientific management' of Taylor and others which developed to design and control such tasks was predicated on the manager's always knowing more than the worker (which is one reason why skilled workers in particular so resented its application). In the twenty-first century it is understood that it is knowledge that ultimately gives an organisation sustained competitive advantage, and twenty-first-century managers have to be able to lead and influence workers who often have more expert knowledge and skill at their own jobs than they do. So managers often have to play the role of 'coach' to empowered teams or workers, rather than that of supervisor, but even in those circumstances there are situations where workers and teams have to be directed – for example dealing with crises, or with major technological or cultural change.

As a general rule, the more skilled and knowledgeable the workers are, the less directive will be the style of the effective manager. But the reality is that managers have to possess a range of management styles from highly directive to a supportive, coaching approach. Also, it is worth noting in this context that the empirical evidence suggests that although there have certainly been important changes in the traditional employment relationship between managers and workers, in practice there have been limits to the extent of empowerment given to workers, at least in the UK (Gallie *et al* 1998, pp1–27): the genuinely self-managing team is comparatively rare.

Another important dimension of the manager's job that was not recognised in the classical school's description of managerial work is the role of manager as developer of others. Peter Drucker clearly stated some fifty years ago that a key characteristic of managerial work is that it simultaneously operates in the here and now by ensuring efficient and effective current activities, and in the future – trying to ensure that the organisation and its people *will* perform efficiently and effectively (hence the need for corporate strategy). A direct consequence of that proposition is that senior managers had the responsibility to develop junior managers who reported to them, to 'grow the stock of managerial talent' for the future (Drucker 1955). Nowadays, many organisations go further than this and expect managers to support the training and development of all who report to them, whether managers or non-managers. So effective managers have to be able to support their people, both in the short and in the long term.

Thus a range of management styles is required of the twenty-first-century manager. Goleman (2000) has used the analogy of the clubs in a golf professional's bag: all golf professionals need to be competent in the use of each club, and have the knowledge and experience to know which is the right one to use in any particular situation.

9.3.1 THEORIES OF LEADERSHIP

Research into leadership can be categorised into three broad approaches: (1) the trait approach, (2) the behavioural (or 'style') approach and (3) the situational approach.

The *trait approach* assumes that successful leaders possess certain attributes or traits such as physical characteristics, intellectual abilities, certain personality features and interpersonal skills which distinguished them from ordinary people. This approach implies that the basis of successful leadership is personality and perhaps genetics.

The *behavioural approach* seeks appropriate behaviour patterns or styles in which managers and other leaders could be trained. Two major research programmes, the Michigan and Ohio studies, underpinned the investigations into leadership style.

The *situational approach* suggest that different situations may require different management styles.

Each of these three approaches sheds light on the complex issue of leadership, though none provides a definitive description. The approach taken in this text recognises the contribution of each of these perspectives but is influenced in particular by the situational school. This approach is based on the assumptions that:

- Certain styles of leadership are more effective in some circumstances than others.
- Although the ultimate effectiveness of any particular individual's leadership ability may be constrained by genetic or other more-or-less permanent factors deriving from their

personality and psychological make-up, *all individuals can improve their effectiveness in leading and influencing others.*

- No single style is intrinsically 'right' or 'wrong': different situations need different styles of leadership and influencing.
- An effective leader selects the appropriate style for the particular situation.

Although few of us could ever be a Steve Jobs or a Winston Churchill or a Martin Luther King, all of us can improve our leadership and influencing skills, and learn how and when to use these to the best effect.

9.3.2 LEADING AND INFLUENCING OTHERS: THE BASES OF POWER AND INFLUENCE

The processes of power are pervasive, complex, and often disguised in our society (French and Raven 1959, p259).

A manager has five principal 'bases of power' in exerting influence on others, each of which forms the perceptions held by the others. These bases are: (1) *reward power*, which rests on the others' perception that the manager has the ability to apply or intercede in rewards for them; (2) *coercive power*, from the perception that the manager has the ability to apply or intercede in punishments for them; (3) *legitimate power*, based on the perception by the others that the manager has a legitimate right to their authority over them; (4) *referent power*, founded on the others' admiration for and wish to identify with the manager as a person; and finally (5) *expert power*, based on the perception that the manager has some special knowledge which the others need or can benefit from.

Successful managers often exert more than one type of power at the same time. For example, a charismatic business leader like Steve Jobs possessed legitimate power as head of Apple and reward and coercive power over his subordinate colleagues and employees, but he also enjoyed referent power because of his astounding business success, which most people would love to emulate, and expert power as one of the men who changed the world of computing.

These considerations bring us back to the question of *leadership style*. Goleman (2000) has argued for six leadership styles: coercive, authoritative, affiliative, democratic, pace-setting, and coaching. These are based on the author's previous work on 'emotional intelligence'. The styles can be thought of as occupying positions on a continuum of leadership and influencing styles from directive through to coaching.

Choice of leadership style depends in part on the beliefs and attitudes of the manager. Some managers feel uncomfortable with highly authoritarian styles; they tend to ask employees to participate in leadership activities. Others feel that they are responsible for issuing orders to those whom they supervise. Managers who are confident in their leadership abilities will feel more confident in conferring with employees.

9.3.3 TRANSFORMATIONAL CHARISMATIC LEADERS

Section 9.3.2 deals with leadership as a largely rational, transactional process. Some leaders rely on charismatic qualities they are perceived to possess (that is, referent power as discussed above). Such leaders can bring about transformational change, radically altering the structure and strategy of the organisation. However, charismatic leadership is highly risky. It relies on those being led acting as uncritical followers and is ultimately irrational. It can achieve great success – or destructive failure.

9.3.4 IMPLICATIONS FOR HRM

Apart from line management leadership issues within the HR department itself, which is no different from leadership in other functions, the main implications of leadership for

HRM is in the fields of recruitment, performance management and learning and development: enabling the organisation continually to acquire and develop the leadership capabilities it needs.

9.3.5 ENCOURAGING EMPLOYEE ENGAGEMENT AND INCREASED DISCRETIONARY EFFORT

The CIPD Profession for the Future 'stresses the need for leadership in the HR profession as organisations increasingly realise the value of their people, but have not yet developed sustainable approaches to fostering productive, win-win relationships between the business and its workforce' (CIPD 2016f). HR practitioners are encouraged to act as 'provocateurs', encouraging innovative ways of doing business or new areas of strategic focus.

? REFLECTIVE ACTIVITY 9.1

1 Think about a situation in which you influenced another person towards a goal (work or other). What type(s) of power or influence did you exert?

2 Think about a situation in which you were influenced towards a goal (work or other) by another person. What type(s) of power or influence did they exert?

9.4 HRM AND CHANGE MANAGEMENT

We noted in Chapter 1 that Ulrich and Brockbank (2005) specified as one of their key roles for HRM that of 'strategic partner', which in addition to business strategy had an emphasis on transformation and cultural change. Also, we saw that Torrington *et al* (2014) identified change management objectives as central to people management.

'The only constant is change' has become a cliché, but reflects the acknowledgement now that the competitive global economy and continuous increasing technological advances are realities. Physical resources are relatively easy to change; human ones are much more challenging. HRM is often tasked with taking the lead and co-ordinating change across the organisation.

Organisations face change for many reasons, such as: dealing with global economic market changes; changes in technology; changes in strategy; the need to acquire new organisation behaviours and skills; mergers and acquisitions; customer pressure; or changes in government legislation and regulation.

Kurt Lewin famously summed up change management as a three-stage process of 'unfreezing, changing and re-freezing': a simple formula capable of endless elaboration but essentially true.

Managers have to be able to introduce and lead change and ensure organisational objectives are met, while maintaining the commitment of their employees through and after the change. While change management programmes can fail for many reasons, including lack of strategic and project planning, lack of communication or inadequate leadership, one factor which managers of change must always face is resistance to change.

Given its organisation-wide presence, HRM has a crucial role to play in supporting the change process by ensuring management and employee 'voice' are both heard throughout the process, and also in learning and development initiatives which help the organisation to acquire the skills needed both for the actual change process itself and in order to flourish in the new situation envisaged by the change.

9.5 NEW FORMS OF EMPLOYMENT UTILISING INFORMATION AND COMMUNICATION TECHNOLOGY (ICT)

We commented in Chapter 1 that societal and economic developments, such as the need for increased flexibility by both employers and workers, have resulted in the emergence of new forms of employment across Europe. Some of these were noted in Chapter 5.

The use of information and communication technology is also having a profound effect on the traditional one-to-one relationship between the employer and employee. Such developments are typically characterised by unconventional work patterns and places of work, or by the irregular provision of work. Three particularly important examples of ICT-based employment are:

- *ICT-based mobile work*, where employees can do their job from any place at any time, supported by modern technologies
- *crowd employment*, where an online platform matches employers and workers, often with large tasks being split up and divided among a 'virtual cloud of workers'; see for example Amazon Mechanical Turk (www.mturk.com/mturk/welcome)
- *collaborative employment*, where freelancers, the self-employed or micro-enterprises co-operate in some way to overcome limitations of size and professional isolation.

These new employment forms have a wide range of implications for working conditions and the labour market and consequent implications for the HRM function.

? REFLECTIVE ACTIVITY 9.2

What would you say are the implications of these new forms of ICT-based employment for employees?

REFLECTIVE ACTIVITY 9.2 ANSWER GUIDANCE

ICT-based mobile work offers some flexibility, autonomy and empowerment, but also incurs the danger of work intensification, increased stress levels and working time, and blurring of the boundaries between work and private life. It may also outsource traditional employer responsibilities, such as health and safety protection, to workers.

For freelancers and the self-employed, crowd employment and collaborative employment may enrich work content through diversification.

 HRM IN ACTION: LEADERSHIP IN A CREATIVE INDUSTRY

CASE STUDY 9.1

Opinion: Five lessons the film industry can teach us about creative leadership

Business leaders can learn fresh approaches from the directors who inspire and lead teams of thousands, writes Linda Aspey

At the international Sheffield Doc/Fest 2016 last month, a member of the audience asked me: what lessons can we learn from the film industry about

creative leadership? I've been pondering the answer ever since.

The festival heard from filmmakers such as Sir David Attenborough, Joanna Lumley and Michael Moore, and screened hundreds of new documentaries from around the world. These films were made by people who are leaders in their own way: from the group of neighbours protesting about the destruction of their local woodland, to the international pioneers showing the effects of climate change on global security.

It was fascinating to think about the creative journeys these filmmakers had been on, from inception through to outcome. And it made me wonder – what could leaders from other industries learn from their endeavours?

Production companies and network channels run like any other business, with a core of staff and the normal administrative functions. Yet the making of a film is a very different beast – sometimes involving thousands of people, many of whom are specialist freelancers who haven't necessarily worked together before. The type of leadership needed is quite different from that of the operational leader.

So what attributes of leadership can we learn from them?

1 The ability to empower

This is distinct from the skill of delegation; these leaders create conditions in which creativity can happen. As one producer said to me: 'It's paradoxical. I have to make sure the whole thing works and yet I can't interfere. The closer I get, the less creative they become. If they start to do something just to please me, we've lost the essence.'

2 Giving balanced, considered, constructive and appreciative feedback

The leader of creatives knows they give a little bit (or a lot) of themselves every time they work. It's always personal. This can be advantageous, as creatives are typically deeply engaged – but disadvantageous, as they can veer from arrogance to vulnerability. Telling a director that their film isn't good is akin to saying their child

is ugly! These leaders must draw on a range of influencing skills and tactics to manage performance.

3 Using instinct and experience – and taking risks

As one senior commissioner said: 'Without your instinct you're nothing. Of course you consult with others, but when you come across a really strong pitch you just know it, and it's then you bring your experience to bear. It's like a first date; if you over-analyse it, you let doubts dominate your thinking.' Creative leaders know that if some of their ideas don't fail, they're probably not risking enough.

4 Staying sanguine

In the film and TV industry, there's a much closer proximity to audiences than in many other sectors. Ratings can make overnight decisions that are worth millions. Keep a flagging movie going or pull it early? Sack the presenter and try someone new? The industry gets feedback like no other – which requires nerves of steel, the ability to know when it's time to stop and a leader who can quell anxieties sufficiently so that people can recover quickly, 'pick themselves up, brush themselves off, and start all over again'.

5 Embracing diversity

Creative leaders draw different skills, perspectives, experiences and voices to each and every production. They bring together surprising groups of people to create surprising content. They must therefore nurture an environment where all voices are valued and matter deeply, because without them there is no disruption and – most importantly of all – no innovation.

Source: *People Management*, 19 July 2016.

9.6 CORPORATE SOCIAL RESPONSIBILITY

There is no single, universally accepted definition of corporate social responsibility (CSR), also often termed simply corporate responsibility (CR), but that of McWilliams and Siegel (2001, p117) is as good as any to start with:

CR [comprises] actions that appear to further some social good, beyond the interests of the firm and that which is required by law.

The CIPD (2015a, p1) offers a more extensive definition:

Corporate responsibility (CR), also known as corporate social responsibility (CSR) or business sustainability, addresses the ethics of an organisation's activities and how it operates in a way that is viable over the long term. . . . At the CIPD, we use the term corporate responsibility to include financial as well as social and environmental responsibility.

Contemporary concerns about companies' activities beyond merely keeping to the letter of the law and making profits stem from debates in the USA in the 1960s and 1970s about firms' social responsibilities. These debates opened the way to thinking about multiple interests or stakeholders, not just shareholders or owners.

The idea of multiple interests emerged strongly in the UK in the mid-1990s with the notion of a 'stakeholder economy'. This was partly in reaction to economic policies which had been widely acknowledged to have worked, at least in narrow terms of economic success, but, in the view of many, only at an unacceptable social cost. Yet despite this, by the early 2000s the interest in a stakeholder society had rather diminished in the UK. Ironically, this was at least partly due to the fact that those European economies in which a social agenda had been more explicit than in the UK were perceived to be performing less well economically than those following the 'Anglo-Saxon' model (Eurofound 2003).

However, notorious cases of company scandal such as Enron, and spectacularly mismanaged environmental disasters – such as the 2010 BP 'Deepwater Horizon' oil spill in the Gulf of Mexico, and more recently the 2015 Volkswagen diesel emissions scandal – have kept the notion of CR on social and managerial agendas. This has increased demands from customers, employees, statutory bodies and the general public for detailed information about whether companies are meeting acceptable standards.

We can see from the above why CR should be of general strategic interest to an organisation – but what has CR to do with HRM?

The most obvious role that the HR function has to play in shaping and embedding CR strategy is in ensuring fair employment practices. But even on aspects of CR that don't primarily link to employment and people management (for example, environmental sustainability), HR plays a central role in making sure CR is embedded in organisational practice and isn't simply 'window-dressing' (CIPD 2015a).

 HRM DILEMMA 9.1

Should *everyone* have a say?

Are there limits to how far we should extend stakeholding?

In one academic study it was found that although commitment-based HRM systems did generally have a positive impact on corporate performance, this could be constrained by corporate governance regimes which privileged 'remote' stakeholders, such as institutional shareholders in large PLCs or the Treasury in public sector organisations (Konzelmann *et al* 2006).

Yet these parties would seem to be legitimate stakeholders.

9.7 ETHICS AND HRM

The CIPD Code of Professional Conduct for HR practitioners makes the standard declaration expected from a professional body:

> In the public interest and in the pursuit of its objectives, the Chartered Institute of Personnel and Development is committed to the highest possible standards of professional conduct and competency. To this end members:
>
> - are required to exercise integrity, honesty, diligence and appropriate behaviour in all their business, professional and related personal activities
> - must act within the law and must not encourage, assist or act in collusion with employees, employers or others who may be engaged in unlawful conduct.

But, in a residual echo of the welfare role of traditional personnel management, HRM is often expected to be something of a guardian of organisational ethics, and to act as a guarantor of organisational fairness and justice for all employees.

'While HRM does need to support commercial outcomes ... it also exists to serve organisational needs for social legitimacy' (Boxall *et al* 2007). This means something more than just ensuring compliance with legal protection for employees with respect to health and safety at work and against discrimination in employment.

9.8 FUTURE TRENDS IN HUMAN RESOURCE MANAGEMENT

The CIPD research report *From Best to Good Practice HR: Developing principles for the profession* (CIPD 2015g) identified the following trends which would impact on the world of work and on the HR profession:

1   *Increasing use of technology* will accelerate the range and complexity of tasks which are subjected to automation. This will be accompanied by an increased demand for jobs requiring high-level cognitive skills, that is, there will be fewer, but more highly skilled jobs. It will also increase cross-discipline and cross-sector collaboration and lead to greater discretion over where and how people work. These changes will challenge traditional employment models and increase the risk of disengagement of remote and dispersed employees.
    Technology will also enable more open access to organisational data, which offers benefits in terms of transparency but with dangers to trust regarding organisations' use of personal data.
    The implications for HRM from the above include: the necessity for innovative job and organisational design to exploit the new opportunities accruing from technology; multiskilling and retraining of employees to combat skills' obsolescence; and greater emphasis on trust and responsibility towards employees.

2   *Increasing workforce diversity*, which will bring greater cultural diversity to the workplace and also greater demands for flexibility in employment – HRM will require more flexible approaches to the attraction, retention, motivation and development of talent.

3   *Increasing diversity in working patterns and types of employment contracts* – the two-tiered flexible firm model discussed in Chapter 5, with the core of permanent staff supported and protected by peripheral shells of part-time workers, contractors, freelancers, and so on, will continue to spread. There will also be fragmentation of organisations into collaborative networks of contingent workers. HR will have the task of helping to change organisational cultures to support flexible management processes and to manage the inequalities between the various categories of workers. They will also have the ethical responsibility of giving a voice to the non-core, less empowered, contingent workforce.

4   *Continuing and increasing economic globalisation* leading to the relocation of work, driven by local labour costs – this, combined with larger international movements of

people, might be expected to lead to a rise in social and workplace conflicts. HR will need to harmonise HR policies and practices in organisations which operate in different countries and support dialogue between different parties to avoid or manage conflict.

5   *Industrial changes* driven by consumer demand for high value-added products and 24/7 services – this in turn will increase demand for more highly skilled and educated workforces. As a consequence, HR will need to focus on managing knowledge capital rather than traditional labour. These changes will drive performance management systems that reward 'softer' aspects of service delivery. They will also reinforce the need for continuous updating of workforce knowledge and skills.

6   *Individualism* – employees will demand a better work–life balance in their employment relationships. Highly skilled people will seek individualised rather than collectivised contracts of employment. Customers/clients will also expect flexible responses from service providers and will show little customer loyalty in increasingly competitive markets. HR will need to support individualised rather than collectivised employment relations.

7   *Increasing social responsibility* – there will be pressure on organisations to pursue ecologically sustainable business models and technologies. Organisations will take care to manage their reputations to attract customers and talent. Implications for HR include a focus on employee brand, communications and ethics.

8   *A rise in educational standards and opportunities* to equip populations to compete globally, together with a greater emphasis on individual development, lifelong learning and reskilling – HR will need to provide talent development and ensure workplace support for learning, coaching and mentoring.

9.9 TO CONCLUDE

As in the first edition of this text, we can do no better to conclude our study of HRM than by quoting again the words of Linda Holbeche (Holbeche 2007, pp10–11) that:

> building organisational capability is HR's heartland...

and that HR managers:

> can help make capitalism human...

and by suggesting that her last phrase should be applicable to all managers.

EXPLORE FURTHER

Department for Business, Innovation and Skills. (2012) *Leadership and Management in the UK: the key to sustainable growth: a summary of the evidence for the value of investing in leadership and management development.* London: Department for Business, Innovation and Skills.

Gold, J., Thorpe, R. and Mumford, A. (2010) *Leadership and Management Development.* 5th edition. London: Chartered Institute of Personnel and Development.

Holbeche, L. (2010) *HR Leadership.* Oxford: Butterworth Heinemann.

Ulrich, D., Younger, J., Brockbank, W. and Ulrich, M.D. (2013) The state of the HR profession. *Human Resource Management.* Vol 52, No 3. pp457–71.

The Society for Human Resource Management. (2015) *Five Key Trends from SHRM's Special Expertise Panels.* Alexandria, VA: SHRM Foundation.

References

ADLER, P.S., GOLDOFTAS, B. and LEVINE, D.I. (1997) Ergonomics, employee involvement and the Toyota production system: a case study of NUMMI's 1993 model introduction. *Industrial and Labor Relations Review*. Vol 50, No 3. pp416–37.

ADVISORY, CONCILIATION AND ARBITRATION SERVICE. (2011) *The future of workplace relations – an ACAS view*. London: Acas. Available at: www.acas.org.uk.

ADVISORY, CONCILIATION AND ARBITRATION SERVICE. (2014) *MacLeod and Clarke's concept of employee engagement: an analysis based on the Workplace Employment Relations Study*. London: Acas.

AGUINIS, H. (2005) *Performance management*. Edinburgh: Edinburgh Business School.

AITKEN, H.G.J. (1960) *Taylorism at Watertown Arsenal*. Cambridge, MA: Harvard University Press.

ALFES, K., TRUSS, C., SOANE, E., REES, C. and GATENBY, M. (2010) *Creating an engaged workforce*. London: CIPD.

ARGYRIS, C. and SCHÖN, D.A. (1978) *Organizational learning*. Reading, MA: Addison-Wesley.

ARMSTRONG, M. (2009) *Armstrong's handbook of human resource management practice*. 11th edition. London: Kogan Page.

ARMSTRONG, M. (2014) *Armstrong's handbook of human resource management practice*. 13th edition. London: Kogan Page.

ARMSTRONG, M. and MURLIS, H. (1998) *Reward management*. 4th edition. London: IPM/Kogan Page.

ASHBY, W.R. (1940) Adaptiveness and equilibrium. *Journal of Mental Science*. Vol 86. pp478–83.

ATKINSON, J. (1984) Manpower strategies for flexible organizations. *Personnel Management*. August. pp28–31.

BARNEY, B. (1991) Firm resources and sustained competitive advantage. *Journal of Management*. Vol 17, No 1. pp99–120.

BEER, M., SPECTOR, B., LAWRENCE, P.R., MILLS, D. and WALTON, R.E. (1984) *Managing human assets*. New York: Free Press.

BELBIN, M. (1981) *Management teams: why they succeed or fail*. London: Heinemann.

BELT, V. and GILES, L. (2009) *High performance working: a synthesis of key literature*. Evidence Report 4. Wath upon Dearne: UK Commission for Employment and Skills.

BIRDI, K., CLEGG, C., PATTERSON, M., ROBINSON, A., STRIDE, C.B. and WALL, T. D. (2008). The impact of human resource and operational management practices on company productivity: a longitudinal study. *Personnel Psychology*. Vol 61, No 3. pp467–501.

BOUDREAU, J.W. and RAMSTAD, P.M. (2007) *Beyond HR: the new science of human capital.* Boston: Harvard Business Review Press.

BOXALL, P. and PURCELL, J. (2006) *Strategy and human resource management.* Basingstoke: Palgrave Macmillan.

BOXALL, P., PURCELL, J. and WRIGHT, P. (2007) *The Oxford handbook of human resource management.* Oxford: Oxford University Press.

BOYATZIS, R.E. (1982) *The competent manager: a model for effective performance.* London: Wiley.

BRAVERMAN, H. (1974) *Labour and monopoly capitalism: the degradation of work in the twentieth century.* New York: Monthly Review Press.

BUCHANAN, D. (1994) Principles and practice in work design. In Sissons, D. (ed) *Personnel management: a comprehensive guide to theory and practice in Britain.* Oxford: Blackwell.

BUDHWAR, P.S. and DEBRA, Y.A. (2010) Human resource management in developing countries. In Wilkinson, A., Redman, T., Snell, S.A. and Bacon, N. (eds) *Sage handbook of human resource management,* pp393–406. London: Sage.

CAI, F. (2010) Demographic transition, demographic dividend, and Lewis turning point in China. *China Economic Journal.* Vol 3, No 2. pp107–19.

CALDWELL, R. and STOREY, J. (2007) The HR function: integration or fragmentation? In Storey, J. (ed.) *Human resource management: a critical text.* 3rd edition. London: Thomson Learning.

CHIANG, F. (2005) A critical examination of Hofstede's thesis and its application to international reward management. *International Journal of Human Resource Management.* Vol 16. pp1545–63.

CHILD, J. (1984) *Organisation: a guide to problems and practice.* 2nd edition. London: Paul Chapman.

CIPD. (2005) *What is employee relations?* London: Chartered Institute of Personnel and Development. Also available online at: cipd.co.uk/subjects/empreltns/comconslt/empvoice

CIPD. (2006) *Learning and development.* Survey report. London: Chartered Institute of Personnel and Development. Also available online at: cipd.co.uk/onlineinfodocuments

CIPD. (2009) *Corporate and social responsibility.* Factsheet. London: Chartered Institute of Personnel and Development. Available online at: cipd.co.uk/onlineinfodocuments

CIPD. (2010a) *Learning and talent development.* Survey report. London: Chartered Institute of Personnel and Development. Also available online at: cipd.co.uk/surveys

CIPD. (2010b) *Diversity in the workplace.* Factsheet. London: Chartered Institute of Personnel and Development. Available online at: cipd.co.uk/onlineinfodocuments

CIPD. (2012) *Managing employee relations in difficult times.* Research report. London: Chartered Institute of Personnel and Development. Also available online at: cipd.co.uk/onlineinfodocuments

CIPD. (2013) *International resourcing and recruitment*. Factsheet. London: Chartered Institute of Personnel and Development. Also available online at: cipd.co.uk/onlineinfodocuments

CIPD. (2014) *Management development*. Factsheet. London: Chartered Institute of Personnel and Development. Available online at: cipd.co.uk/onlineinfodocuments

CIPD. (2015a) *Corporate responsibility*. Factsheet. London: Chartered Institute of Personnel and Development. Available online at: cipd.co.uk/onlineinfodocuments

CIPD. (2015b) *Talent management: an overview*. Factsheet. London: Chartered Institute of Personnel and Development. Available online at: cipd.co.uk/onlineinfodocuments

CIPD. (2015c) *Learning and development*. Annual survey report. London: Chartered Institute of Personnel and Development. Also available online at: cipd.co.uk/surveys

CIPD. (2015d) *Competence and competency frameworks*. Factsheet. London: Chartered Institute of Personnel and Development. Available online at: cipd.co.uk/onlineinfodocuments

CIPD. (2015e) *Resourcing and talent planning*. Survey report. London: Chartered Institute of Personnel and Development. Also available online at: cipd.co.uk/onlineinfodocuments

CIPD. (2015f) *Selection methods*. Factsheet. London: Chartered Institute of Personnel and Development. Available online at: cipd.co.uk/onlineinfodocuments

CIPD. (2015g) *From best to good practice HR: developing principles for the profession*. Research report. London: Chartered Institute of Personnel and Development. Also available online at: cipd.co.uk/onlineinfodocuments

CIPD. (2016a) *Employer brand*. Factsheet. London: Chartered Institute of Personnel and Development. Available online at: cipd.co.uk/onlineinfodocuments

CIPD. (2016b), *Employee engagement*. Factsheet. London: Chartered Institute of Personnel and Development. Available online at: cipd.co.uk/onlineinfodocuments

CIPD. (2016c) *Employee voice*. Factsheet. London: Chartered Institute of Personnel and Development. Available online at: cipd.co.uk/onlineinfodocuments

CIPD. (2016d) *HR analytics*. Factsheet. London: Chartered Institute of Personnel and Development. Available online at: cipd.co.uk/onlineinfodocuments

CIPD. (2016e) *Human capital*. Factsheet, July 2016. London: Chartered Institute of Personnel and Development. Available online at: cipd.co.uk/onlineinfodocuments

CIPD. (2016f) *Leadership*. Factsheet. London: Chartered Institute of Personnel and Development. Available online at: cipd.co.uk/onlineinfodocuments

CIPD. (n.d.) *Professional framework for the future* [PFF]. Chartered Institute of Personnel and Development. Available online at: cipd.co.uk/pff

COFFIELD, F., MOSELEY, D., HALL, E. and ECCLESTONE, K. (2004) *Should we be using learning styles? What research has to say to practice*. London: Learning and Skills Research Centre.

CULLY, M., WOODLAND, S., O'REILLY, A. and DIX, G. (1999) *Britain at work: as depicted by the 1998 Workplace Employee Relations Study*. London: Routledge.

DE CERI, H. (2007) Transnational firms and cultural diversity. In Boxall, P., Purcell, J. and Wright, P. (eds) *The Oxford handbook of human resource management*. Oxford: Oxford University Press.

DEPARTMENT OF TRADE AND INDUSTRY and CIPD. (2005) *High-performance work practices: linking strategy and skills to performance outcomes*. London: HMSO. Also available online at: www.dti.gov.uk

DEPARTMENT OF TRADE AND INDUSTRY and DEPARTMENT FOR EDUCATION AND EMPLOYMENT. (1997) *Partnerships at work*. London: HMSO.

DESSLER, G. (2005) *Human resource management*. 10th (International) edition. Englewood Cliffs, NJ: Prentice-Hall.

DORFMAN, P., MANSOUR, J., HANGES, P., DASTMALCHIAN, A. and HOUSE, R. (2012). GLOBE: A twenty year journey in to the intriguing world of culture and leadership, *Journal of World Business*. Vol 47. pp504–18.

DRUCKER, P. (1990) *Managing the non-profit organization*. New York: HarperCollins.

DRUCKER, P. (1993) *Post-capitalist society*. Oxford: Butterworth-Heinemann.

DRUCKER, P.F. (1955) *The practice of management*. London: Heinemann.

EMERY, F.E. (1963) *Some hypotheses about the ways in which tasks may be more effectively put together to make jobs*. London: Tavistock Institute of Human.

EUROFOUND. (2003) *Corporate and social responsibility*. London: European Foundation for the Improvement of Living and Working Conditions.

EUROFOUND. (2005) *Industrial relations in the airline industry*. 28 September. Dublin: European Foundation for the Improvement of Living and Working Conditions.

EUROFOUND. (2010) *European company survey 2009*. London: European Foundation for the Improvement of Living and Working Conditions.

EUROFOUND. (2010a) *Representativeness of the European social partner organisations: civil aviation*. Dublin: European Foundation for the Improvement of Living and Working Conditions.

EUROFOUND. (2015) *3rd European company survey*. London: European Foundation for the Improvement of Living and Working Conditions.

FAYOL, H. (1916/1950) *Administration industrielle et générale*. Paris: Dunod.

FISCHLMAYR, I. (2002) Female self-perception as a barrier to international careers? *International Journal of Human Resource Management*. Vol 13, No 5. pp773–83.

FOX, A. (1966) *Royal Commission: trade unions and employers' associations research papers 3: industrial sociology and industrial relations*. London: HMSO.

FRENCH, J. and RAVEN, B. (1959) The bases of social power. In Cartwright, D. (ed) *Studies in social power*. Ann Arbor, MI: Institute of Social Research, University of Michigan.

GALLIE, D., WHITE, M., CHENG, Y. and TOMLINSON, M. (1998) *Restructuring the employment relationship*. Oxford: Clarendon Press.

GERHART, B. and FANG, M. (2005) National culture and human resource management: assumptions and evidence. *International Journal of Human Resource Management.* Vol 16. pp971–86.

GIBBONS, J. and WOOCK, C. (2007). Evidence-based human resources: a primer and summary of current literature. *The Conference Board*, Research Report E-0015.

GOLEMAN, D. (2000) Leadership that gets results. *Harvard Business Review.* March–April. pp78–90.

GUEST, D. (1987) Human resource management and industrial relations. *Journal of Management Studies.* Vol 24, No 5. pp503–21.

GUEST, D. (1996) *The state of the psychological contract in employment.* London: Institute of Personnel and Development.

GUTHRIE, J.P. (2007) Remuneration: pay effects at work. In Boxall, P., Purcell, J. and Wright, P. (eds) *The Oxford handbook of human resource management.* Oxford: Oxford University Press.

HACKMAN J.R. and OLDHAM, G.R. (1980). *Work redesign.* Reading MA: Addison-Wesley.

HALL, R. and WAILES, N. (2010) International and comparative human resource management. In Wilkinson, A., Redman, T., Snell, S.A. and Bacon, N. (eds) *Sage handbook of human resource management*, pp115–32. London: Sage.

HAMEL, G. and PRAHALAD, C.K. (1994) *Competing for the future.* Boston, MA: Harvard Business School Press.

HAMMARSTRÖM, O. and LANSBURY, R.D. (1991) The art of building a car: the Swedish experience re-examined. *New Technology, Work and Employment.* Vol 6, No 2. pp85–90.

HANDY, C., GORDON, C., GOW, I. and RANDLESOME, C. (1988) *Making managers.* London: Pitman.

HERSEY, P. and BLANCHARD, K.H. (1988) *The management of organizational behavior.* Englewood Cliffs, NJ: Prentice-Hall.

HERZBERG, F. (1966) *Work and the nature of man.* Cleveland, OH: World Publishing.

HERZBERG, F., MAUSNER, B. and SNYDERMAN, B. (1959). *The motivation to work.* Oxford: Wiley.

HOFSTEDE, G.H. (1980/2001) *Culture's consequences: international differences in work-related values.* Thousand Oaks, CA: Sage.

HOLBECHE, L. (2007) Building high performance – the key role for HR. *Impact: Quarterly Update on CIPD Policy and Research.* Vol 20. pp10–11.

HOLMAN, D., PAVLICA, K. and THORPE, R. (1997) Rethinking Kolb's theory of experiential learning: the contribution of social constructivism and activity theory. *Management Learning.* Vol 28. pp135–48.

HONEY, P. and MUMFORD, A. (1989) *A manual of learning opportunities.* Maidenhead: Peter Honey.

HOUSE, R.J., HANGES, P.J., JAVIDAN, M., DORFMAN, P.W. and GUPTA, V. (2004) *Culture, leadership and organizations: the GLOBE study of 62 societies.* Thousand Oaks, CA: Sage.

HOUSE, R.J., JAVIDAN, M. and DORFMAN, P. (2001). The GLOBE project. *Applied Psychology: An International Review.* Vol 50, No 4. pp489–505.

HUSELID, M. (1995) The impact of human resource management practices on turnover, productivity and corporate financial performance. *Academy of Management Journal.* Vol 38, No 3. pp635–72.

HUSTED, B.W. (2003) Globalization and cultural change in international business research. *Journal of International Management.* Vol 9. pp427–33.

ILO. (2015a) *International Labour Office, Labour Relations and Collective Bargaining.* Issue Brief No 1. Geneva: ILO.

ILO. (2015b) *International Labour Office, Labour Relations and Collective Bargaining.* Issue Brief No 3. Geneva: ILO.

INCOMES DATA SERVICES. (1991) *Guide to incentive payment schemes.* London: IDS.

INCOMES DATA SERVICES. (2010) *Employee mobility.* IDS Study 916. April. London: IDS.

INTERNATIONAL LABOUR ORGANIZATION and IFTDO. (2000) *Supporting workplace learning for high-performance working.* London/Geneva: ILO.

JAVIDAN, M. and HOUSE, R.J. (2001) Cultural acumen for the global manager: lessons from project GLOBE. *Organizational Dynamics.* Vol 29. pp289–305.

JORENS, Y., GILLIS, D., VALCKE, L. and DE CONINCK, J. (2015) *Atypical employment in aviation.* European Sectoral Social Dialogue Committee for Civil Aviation and European Commission.

KANTER, R. MOSS (1989) *When elephants learn to dance.* New York: Touchstone.

KATZ , H.C. and DARBISHIRE, O. (2001) Converging divergences: world changes in employment systems. *Industrial and Labour Relations Review.* Vol 54, No 3. pp681–716.

KEENAN, T. (2005) *Human resource management.* Edinburgh: Edinburgh Business School.

KENNEDY, G., BENSON, J. and McMILLAN, J. (1984) *Managing negotiations.* 2nd edition. London: Business Books.

KENNEY, M. and FLORIDA, R. (1993) *Beyond mass production: the Japanese system and its transfer to the U.S.* Oxford: Oxford University Press.

KIRKPATRICK, D.L. (1967) Evaluation of training. In Craig, R.L. and Bittel, L.R. (eds) *Training and development handbook.* New York: McGraw-Hill.

KOLB, D.A., RUBIN, I. and MCINTYRE, J.M. (1971) *Organizational psychology: an experiential approach.* Englewood Cliffs, NJ: Prentice Hall.

KONZELMANN, S., CONWAY, N., TRENBERTH, L. and WILKINSON, F. (2006) Corporate governance and human resource management. *British Journal of Industrial Relations*. Vol 44, No 3. pp541–67.

KOTTER, J. (1999) *John Kotter on what leaders really do*. Cambridge, MA: Harvard Business School Press.

LANDY, F.J. and CONTE, J.M. (2007) *Work in the twenty-first century: an introduction to industrial and organizational psychology*. 2nd edition. Oxford: Blackwell.

LEGGE, K. (1989) Human resource management: a critical analysis. In Storey, J. (ed) *New perspectives on human resource management*. London: Routledge.

LEGGE, K. (1995) *Human resource management: rhetorics and realities*. Basingstoke: Macmillan Business.

MACLEOD, D. and CLARKE, N. (2009) *Engaging for success: enhancing performance through employee engagement*. London: Department for Business, Innovation and Skills.

MANGHAM, I. and SILVER, M. (1986) *Management training: Context and practice*. Swindon: Economic and Social Research Council.

MASLOW, A. (1943) *A theory of human motivation*. New York: Harper.

MAYRHOFER, W. and SCULLION, H. (2002) Female expatriates in international business: evidence from the German clothing industry. *International Journal of Human Resource Management*. Vol 13, No 5. pp815–36.

MCKINLAY, A. and STARKEY, K. (1998) *Foucault, management and organization theory*. London: Sage.

MCWILLIAMS, A. and SIEGEL, D. (2001) Corporate social responsibility: a theory of the firm perspective. *Academy of Management Review*. Vol 26, No 1. pp117–27.

MEISTER, J. (1998) Ten steps to creating a corporate university. *Training and Development*. Vol 52. pp38–43.

MENDENHALL, M. and ODDOU, G. (1985) The dimensions of expatriate acculturation: a review. *Academy of Management Review*. Vol 10, No 1. pp39–47.

MILLWARD, N. (1994) *The new industrial relations*. Poole: Policy Studies Institute.

MINTZBERG, H. (1973) *The nature of managerial work*. New York: Harper & Row.

MUCHINSKY, P.M. (1986) Personnel selection methods. In Cooper, C.L. and Robertson, I.T. (eds) *International review of industrial and organisational psychology*. London: Wiley.

NAPIER, N. and TULLY, S. (2002) Experiences of woman professional managers abroad. *International Journal of Human Resource Management*. Vol 13, No 5. pp837–51.

NISBET, R.A. (1969) *Social change and history: aspects of the Western theory of development*. Oxford: Oxford University Press.

NONAKA, I. and TAKEUCHI, H. (1995) *The knowledge-creating company*. Oxford: Oxford University Press.

PARKER, S.K. and OHLY, S. (2010) Extending the reach of job design theory: going beyond the job characteristics model. In Wilkinson, A., Redman, T., Snell, S.A. and Bacon, N. (eds) *Sage handbook of human resource management*, pp269–85. London: Sage.

PEARN, M.A., KANDOLA, R.S., MOTTRAM, R.D. and PEARN KANDOLA ASSOCIATES. (1987) *Selection tests and sex bias*. Equal Opportunities Commission Research series. London: HMSO.

PEDLER, M., BURGOYNE, J. and BOYDELL, T. (1991) *The learning organisation*. Maidenhead: McGraw-Hill.

PERLMUTTER, H.V. (1969) The tortuous evolution of the multinational corporation. *Columbia Journal of World Business*. Vol 4. pp9–18.

PETERS, T. (1987) *Thriving on chaos: handbook for a management revolution*. London: Macmillan.

PFEFFER, J. (1994) *Competitive advantage through people*. Boston, MA: Harvard Business School Press.

PFEFFER, J. (1998) *The human equation: building profits by putting people first*. Boston, MA: Harvard Business School Press.

POLANYI, M. (1966) *The tacit dimension*. London: Routledge & Kegan Paul.

PORTER, M.E. (1980) *Competitive strategy: techniques for analyzing industries and competitors*. New York: Free Press.

PRAHALAD, C.K. and HAMEL, G. (1990) The core competence of the corporation. *Harvard Business Review*. Vol 68, May–June. pp79–91.

PUGH, D. and HICKSON, D.J. (1995) *Writers on organisations*. 5th edition. London: Penguin.

PURCELL, J. (2010) *Building employee engagement*. London: Acas.

RAYTON, B., DODGE, T. and D'ANALEZE, G. (2012) *The evidence: engagement task force 'nailing the evidence' workgroup*. London: Engaging for Success.

REYNOLDS, M. (1999) Critical reflection and management education: rehabilitating less hierarchical approaches. *Journal of Management Education*. Vol 23. pp537–55.

ROBERTS, K., KOSSEK, E. and OZEKI, C. (1998) Managing the global workforce: challenges and strategies. *Academy of Management Executive*. Vol 12, No 4. pp93–106.

ROBERTS, R. and KNYASTON, D. (2001) The rout of the stakeholders. *New Society*. 17 September.

ROETHLISBERGER, F.J. and DICKSON, W.J. (1939) *Management and the worker*. Cambridge, MA: Harvard University Press.

SCHMITT, N., GOODING, R.Z., NOE, R.A. and KIRSCH, M. (1984) Meta-analysis of validity studies published between 1964 and 1982, and the investigation of study characteristics. *Personnel Psychology*. Vol 37. pp407–22.

SCHULER, R. and JACKSON, S. (1987) Linking competitive strategies and human resource management practices. *Academy of Management Executive.* Vol 1, No 3. pp207–19.

SCULLION, H. (1995) International human resource management. In Storey, J. (ed) *Human resource management.* London: Routledge.

SCULLION, H. and COLLINGS, D.G. (2006) Alternative form of international assignments. In Scullion, H. and Collings. D.G. (eds) *Global staffing.* London: Routledge.

SENGE, P. (1990) *The fifth discipline: the age and practice of the learning organization.* New York: Doubleday.

SLOAN, A.P. (1967) *My years with General Motors.* London: Pan Books.

STOREY, J. (ed) (1989) *New perspectives in human resource management.* London: Routledge.

STOREY, J. (ed) (2001) *Human resource management: a critical text.* 2nd edition. London: Thomson Learning.

STOREY, J., EDWARDS, P. and SISSON, K. (1997) *Managers in the making: careers, development and control in corporate Britain and Japan.* London: Sage.

TAYEB, M.H. (1988) *Organizations and national culture: a comparative analysis.* London: Sage.

TAYEB, M.H. (1994a) National culture and organizations: methodology considered. *Organization Studies.* Vol 15, No 2. pp429–46.

TAYEB, M.H. (1994b) Japanese managers and British culture: a comparative case study. *International Journal of Human Resource Management.* Vol 5, No 1. pp145–66.

TAYEB, M.H. (1998) Transfer of HRM practices across cultures: an American company in Scotland. *International Journal of Human Resource Management.* Vol 9, No 2. pp332–58.

TAYEB, M.H. (2008) *Managing people in the global markets.* Edinburgh: Edinburgh Business School.

TAYLOR, F.W. (1911) *Principles of scientific management.* New York: Harper.

THOMPSON, P. and MCHUGH, D. (2002) *Work organisations: a critical introduction.* 3rd edition. Basingstoke: Palgrave Macmillan.

THOMSON, A., MABEY, C., STOREY, J., GRAY, C. and ILES, P. (2001) *Changing patterns of management development.* Oxford: Blackwell.

TORRINGTON, D., HALL, L., TAYLOR, S. and ATKINSON, C. (2014) *Human resource management.* 9th edition. London/Englewood Cliffs, NJ: FT/Prentice-Hall.

TRIST, E.A. and BAMFORTH, K.W. (1951) Some social and psychological consequences of the longwall method of coal-getting. *Human Relations.* Vol 4. pp3–38.

TUCKMAN, B.W. (1965) Development sequence in small groups. *Psychological Bulletin.* Vol 93, No 3. pp384–99.

TUCKMAN, B.W. and JENSEN, N. (1977) Stages of group development revisited. *Group and Organisation Studies*. Vol 2, No 3. pp419–27.

TUNG, R.L. (1986) Selection and training of personnel for overseas assignments. *Columbia Journal of World Business*. Vol 16, No 1. pp68–78.

TYLER, K. (2001) Don't fence her in. *HR Magazine*. Vol 46, No 3. pp69–77.

ULRICH, D. and BROCKBANK, W. (2005) *The HR value proposition*. Boston, MA: Harvard Business School Press.

ULRICH, D. and DULEBOHN, J.H. (2015) Are we there yet? What next for HR? *Human Resource Management Review*. Vol 25. pp188–204.

ULRICH, D. (1998) A new mandate for human resources. *Harvard Business Review*. January–February. pp124–34.

US DEPARTMENT OF LABOR. (1993) *High-performance work practices and work performance*. Washington, DC: US Government Printing Office.

VAN WANROOY, B., BEWLEY, H., BRYSON, A., FORTH, J., FREETH, S., STOKES, L. and WOOD, S. (2013) *Employment relations in the shadow of recession: findings from the 2011 Workplace Employment Relations Study*. Basingstoke: Palgrave Macmillan.

VINCE, R. (1998) Behind and beyond Kolb's learning cycle. *Journal of Management Education*. Vol 22. pp304–19.

WALL, T.D. and CLEGG, C. (1998) Job design. In Nicholson, N. (ed) *Blackwell's encyclopaedic dictionary of organizational behaviour*, pp265–8. Oxford: Blackwell.

WALTON, R.E. and MCKERSIE, R.B. (1965) *Behavioral theory of labour negotiations*. New York: McGraw-Hill.

WARNER, M. (2002) Globalization, labour markets and human resources in Asia-Pacific economies: an overview. *International Journal of Human Resource Management*. Vol 13, No 3. pp384–98.

WARNER, M. (2009) 'Making sense' of HRM in China: setting the scene. *International Journal of Human Resource Management*. Vol 20, No 11. pp2169–93.

WHETTON, D.R. and CAMERON, K.S. (2005) *Developing management skills*. 6th edition. Harlow/Englewood Cliffs, NJ: Pearson/Prentice-Hall.

WOOD, S. (2013) *Employment relations in the shadow of recession: findings from the 2011 Workplace Employment Relations Study*. Basingstoke: Palgrave Macmillan.

WOOD, S., BURRIDGE, M., GREEN, W., NOLTE, S. and RUDLOFF, D (2013) *High performance working in the employer skills surveys*. Evidence Report 71. London: UK Commission for Employment and Skills.

WOOTTON, B. (1955) *The social foundations of wages policy*. London: Allen & Unwin.

YOUNDT, M., SNELL, S., DEAN. J. and LEPACK, D. (1996) Human resource management, manufacturing strategy and firm performance. *Academy of Management Journal*. Vol 39, No 4. pp836–66.

ZHANG, M. (2012) The development of human resource management in China: an overview. *Human Resource Management Review*. Vol 22. pp161–4.

ZHANG, Y.Y., DOLAN, S. and ZHOU, Y. (2009) Management by values: a theoretical proposal for strategic human resource management in China. *Chinese Management Studies*. Vol 3, No 4. pp272–94.

Index

Models of Culture: Traditional Approaches

LEARNING OBJECTIVES

After reading this chapter you should be able to:

- identify and understand mainstream models purporting to explain cultural differences in diverse societies
- see how these models go on to explain differences at workplace level
- recognise commonalities between frameworks of culture and the development of thinking in this area
- evaluate the usefulness of mainstream models of cultural difference in explaining aspects of work organisations
- be aware of emerging alternative approaches to understanding culture (discussed in more detail in Chapter 4).

3.1 INTRODUCTION

In Chapter 2 we reviewed the nature of culture as a concept, noting its multifaceted nature and the ways in which its effects could be manifested at different levels. We now go on to look in more detail at some of the more popular and influential models which claim to both define the characteristics of culture and also classify and differentiate individual cultures and cultural groups or 'clusters'.

We have already noted that the field of cross-cultural management emerged relatively recently and one might reasonably conclude that it must, therefore, be in its infancy both in terms of its conceptual frameworks and scope of application to business operations. The non-global nature of most business activity prior to the late twentieth century meant that until that point cross-cultural study was mainly carried out by anthropologists, so the field of business and management studies was largely culture-free. However, in the period from 1980 to 2015, there has been a steep rise in interest in how culture affects processes and behaviour at work. There are, of course, good practical reasons underlying the increasing volume of academic contributions. Gerhart (2008a) posits that culture became a topical area because it is regarded as a constraint on management action. In other words, managers would need to be aware of culture and cultural difference in order to adapt their ideas and practices to local settings. Patel (2014) concludes that a changing role for managers, who were increasingly required to link with many agents within networks, had led to a need for cultural understanding of those agents and the ways in which managers connected with them. More specifically, Holden (2008) highlights growing awareness of a distinctive Japanese model of management as another springboard to a focus on cultural difference, noting that Japanese organisations would themselves stress differences between their own management systems when setting up operations elsewhere in the world. The desire to learn from (currently) successful competitor nations continues to be a spur to greater cross-cultural awareness. Gelfand et al (2007) characterise the cross-cultural study of similarities and differences in organisational behaviour as having a long past but short research history, identifying the 1980s as the key period when both managers and academics began to focus on culture in a rigorous way.

If cross-cultural management theory is in its infancy, it is, nonetheless, possible to identify a dominant paradigm – in other words, a mainstream approach – in cross-cultural management thinking in the period after 1980. This mainstream approach can be located within the etic perspective introduced in Chapter 1. While alternative models of culture have emerged and become increasingly influential (see Chapter 4), new mainstream work continues to be published. In 2014, for example, Minkov and Hofstede produced evidence replicating Hofstede's 1980 cultural dimensions in 25 European countries plus Israel. So in identifying and evaluating the mainstream etic approach we are looking at live as well as historical data.

This etic approach is essentially comparative, involving, firstly, the identification of core dimensions of culture and then plotting (or scoring) countries along these dimensions. A key point is that differences are relative rather than absolute. So the UK is more individualistic than China but one cannot characterise it as individualistic *per se*: it is only individualistic in comparison to China – and indeed many other countries. The majority of writers within this tradition perceive culture as primarily expressed through individuals' values, although there is some focus on the institutional level as well. Other etic models of culture stress the centrality of communication styles when understanding and classifying cultures. Jackson and Aycan (2006, p10), in summarising the development of cross-cultural management thinking, conclude that, 'cross cultural theory has developed strength in comparing nations [as the cultural unit of analysis] in terms of broad value dimensions'. These authors go on to look ahead to newer preoccupations such as cross-cultural interactions at work. We will explore these developing themes in Chapter 4, but at this point will examine in greater detail models within the etic frame of reference, which a number of writers suggest continues to dominate research in the field (Tsui et al 2007; Aycan et al 2014; Patel 2014).

In this chapter we will set out the major theories identified within the etic approach to cross-cultural management which, as indicated, has formed the mainstream view of the topic since 1980. We will not only summarise these models, but will also provide some brief evaluation of individual contributions to the cross-cultural management canon. This is necessary to ensure that these models are more than superficially understood and can also be applied in a thoughtful and feasible way. A deeper understanding can advance the academic debates, and at the same time, provide relevant insights for current or aspiring cross-cultural managers.

At the end of the chapter, we will pose some more general questions concerning the validity of the mainstream models of culture identified. These broader questions will be explored in greater detail in Chapter 4. For example, it is possible to overplay the impact of culture as an explanatory variable and so it is necessary to look at explanations of organisational structure and behaviour which *minimise* the influence of culture as an explanatory factor. While recognising and in many cases stressing the importance of culture as a key influence upon organisational life, the aim here is to balance this perspective by comparing the culture-specific approach with an alternative view emphasising similarities between organisations across the world and, in some cases, pointing to increasing *convergence* between them. The true value of a cross-cultural perspective can only be ascertained if it is held up to critical scrutiny against competing approaches. I contend that *culture matters*, but do not assume that this view should be unchallenged or held to be self-evidently true, as is the case in other writings in this field.

We now go on to examine commonalities in thinking in the cross-cultural management mainstream literature by taking a 'time-tunnel' approach, beginning with a summary of one recent study in the field and, via an examination of its academic roots, travelling back to refocus on some classic models of culture and their potential role in understanding aspects of work organisations.

3.2 PROJECT GLOBE: TRACING THE BLOODLINE

Project GLOBE is a large-scale contemporary research programme which explores the relationship between national (or societal) culture, organisational culture and leadership within organisations (Chokar et al 2013). In one introduction to their study the principal authors (House et al 2001, p492) note that, 'The meta-goal of GLOBE is to develop an empirically based theory to describe, understand and predict the impact of specific cultural variables on leadership and organisational processes and the effectiveness of these processes.' The precise findings and significance of this study are reviewed more fully in Chapter 7. At this stage we examine the theoretical underpinnings of the programme, and in particular the earlier academic influences which frame the approach taken in Project GLOBE. These are explicitly stated by the GLOBE researchers who have sought to apply insights obtained from existing models to a particular area of study – in this case, leadership.

The GLOBE researchers in approaching their study were concerned to identify *dimensions* of culture (in their case, both societal and organisational) in order to identify intra-cultural similarities and inter-cultural differences. We have already recorded in Chapter 2 the need, when engaged in cross-cultural study or management, to identify differences which are meaningful and consistent. In this way one can develop models of culture which focus on the core elements of the concept and do not deal with spurious or insignificant aspects. This preoccupation has been shared by all of the major contributors to this area since the 1950s.

In Project GLOBE the following nine dimensions of culture were identified. These are listed together with a summary of characteristics or, as the GLOBE authors refer to them, culture construct definitions.

- *Power distance* – This refers to the extent to which an identified group expect that power will be distributed relatively equally or unequally. Furthermore, in GLOBE the researchers also examined whether individuals agreed with existing power relations or wished things to be different.
- *Uncertainty avoidance* – In this dimension the focus is on the extent to which group members welcome unusual events and uncertainty as opposed to seeking to avoid such situations and circumstances.
- *Collectivism I* – This dimension differs from the previous two in that here the emphasis is on actual practice rather than the preferences of individuals – specifically, the degree to which a society or work organisation enables and encourages collective rewards and collective action.
- *Collectivism II* – This refers to the extent to which an individual is bonded with, and is loyal to, a sub-societal group – for example, a family or work organisation.
- *Gender egalitarianism* – In this dimension the focus is on how far males and females are treated relatively equally in a society or workplace setting, and whether gender-based role differences are comparatively insignificant.
- *Assertiveness* – Here the researchers sought to identify the prevalence and acceptability of assertive behaviour on the part of individuals within a particular society.

- *Future orientation* – The focus in this category is on the extent to which individuals plan and generally consider future implications of their actions.
- *Performance orientation* – This dimension examines the incidence of cues and outcomes within organisations or the wider society which are intended to encourage ongoing high performance.
- *Humane orientation* – If societies or organisations elicit and reinforce qualities of kindness, generosity and altruism, they score highly on this final dimension.

Readers who have already been introduced to the cross-cultural business literature may recognise a number of these dimensions, and it is interesting to record that this major contemporary research project very evidently has many of its academic roots in earlier work. It is possible, after more than 30 years of work in this area, to discern an emerging consensus on the question of which dimensions of culture are significant in terms of their impact at workplace level. Power distance (PD) and uncertainty avoidance (UA) are taken from the work of Geert Hofstede, and both gender egalitarianism and assertiveness are adaptations of Hofstede's masculinity/femininity dimension, while his individualism/collectivism bipolar scale emerges in the GLOBE study as collectivism I and II. The GLOBE authors also acknowledge another source (House et al 1999, p16) as follows: 'Collectively, the nine dimensions reflect not only the dimensions of Hofstede's theory but also David McClelland's theories of national economic development (McClelland 1961) and human motivation (McClelland 1985). The humanism, PD and performance orientation of cultures, when measured with operant [behavioural] indicators, are conceptually analogous to the affiliative, power and achievement motives in McClelland's implicit motivation theory. We believe that the nine core GLOBE dimensions reflect important aspects of the human condition.'

In summary, the GLOBE study marks the reappearance of pre-existing dimensions of culture, which point to some measure of acceptance in locating those aspects of culture which most significantly affect policies and practices within organisations. The GLOBE research programme also adopts a theoretical framework which partly draws on previous work in the area. Again, we can see how particular themes emerge from pioneer research into the impact of culture on organisations and are then expanded on and/or applied to specific areas of organisational activity.

Selected parts of the conceptual model developed by the GLOBE researchers (see House et al 2001) are set out below. A full listing of the 13 elements which make up the model is provided in Chapter 7.

- Societal cultural values and practices affect what actors (in this case, leaders) do.
- Societal cultural values and practices affect organisational culture and practices.
- Relationships between strategic organisational contingencies and organisational form, culture and practices are moderated by cultural forces.

All of the insights listed here can be viewed within the context of developing knowledge in the cross-cultural field, and again the earlier work of Hofstede can be seen as an important influence. The notion that societal-level cultural norms affect behaviour through individuals' socialisation into their own culture was put forward by Hofstede (1980) in his oft-quoted conception of national culture as the collective programming of the mind, which, he concluded, would characterise the members of one culture and hence differentiate them from others.

With regard to the second point addressing the impact of societal culture at the organisational level, the GLOBE model again follows on from a line of researchers, including Hofstede, who concluded that individuals bring their 'collective programming' into organisations, thereby influencing them. However, it should also be noted that organisations are frequently viewed, within these frameworks, as microcosms of society, so organisational culture – as a mini-version of societal culture – may in turn affect individuals within them.

The third point taken from the GLOBE model deals with the relationship between 'strategic contingencies' and culture as explanatory factors. In claiming that culture will moderate the effect of contingent factors (such as size of organisation, technologies employed and the relative volatility of the market within which the organisation operates) on organisational arrangements, the GLOBE project reinforces earlier findings, namely, that culture can itself be seen as a contingent factor, albeit an important one. We can see this line of reasoning in Hofstede's approach in his choice of one organisation (IBM) as the main focus for his study. Here we have an organisation which should be largely similar across the world in that its technologies and, more generally, its *raison d'être* as expressed by its organisational or corporate culture, were uniform. The important differences uncovered by Hofstede are, it is argued, due to the impact of national or societal culture. This is in effect an earlier manifestation of GLOBE's 'modified contingencies' approach.

It can, finally, be seen that Project GLOBE draws upon a tradition common in cross-cultural studies in this area, of identifying clusters of societies. Gupta et al (2002) identified ten clusters arising from the GLOBE findings, positing that particular societies could be grouped together along particular measures of similarity, which then enabled them to be differentiated from other clusters. The full list of ten country clusters is again detailed in Chapter 7. At this point for illustrative purposes we identify two: the Southern Asian cluster and the Anglo cluster. Countries grouped within these clusters are listed in Table 3.1.

Table 3.1 Societal clusters by country

Southern Asian country cluster	'Anglo' country cluster
India	England
Indonesia	Australia
Philippines	South Africa (white sample)
Malaysia	Canada
Thailand	New Zealand
Iran	Ireland
	USA

One purpose of grouping societies into clusters is to identify policies and practices which align with both cultural preferences and institutional arrangements present in that society. In these cases the Southern Asian cluster is associated with high degrees of loyalty to sub-societal groups such as work organisations and high PD, whereas the Anglo cluster is classed as individualistic (although, interestingly, people in that cluster often express a desire for more in-group collectivism). The GLOBE researchers suggest that participative leadership is, accordingly, likely to be more readily accepted and hence effective in the Anglo cluster of societies.

Clustering societies in this way does not preclude the identification of practices which could work in different clusters. For example, in these two cases charismatic leadership is valued highly in both Southern Asian and Anglo cultures.

INDIVIDUAL ACTIVITY 3.1

Choose any one country from each of the two clusters in Table 3.1 and identify any three ways in which you might expect relationships between managers and subordinates to differ in workplace settings in the two countries. Why would you expect these differences to be present?

● After completing your list, refer to the work of Hofstede (set out later in the chapter; see also **www.geert-hofstede.com** for a quick guide) to see whether your analysis is borne out by the findings of probably the most influential academic in this field.

Project GLOBE provides a good example of the existence of enduring themes underpinning the study of cross-cultural differences at organisational level, namely:

● the classification of societies according to dimensions of culture
● a theoretical framework which stresses individual socialisation as an important factor in maintaining differences between cultures
● the grouping of named societies into clusters which share specific features according to individual models of culture. These are often – but not always – located in a particular geographical region.

3.3 GEERT HOFSTEDE'S PIVOTAL CONTRIBUTION

Hofstede's work has been alluded to both in this and previous chapters, and it is now time to devote a section of this book to an outline and brief evaluation of his work. Hofstede is an absolutely key figure in the whole area of cross-cultural studies applied to work and the business area more generally. Koen (2005, p63) is among many commentators holding this view, claiming that, 'Comparative cross-cultural research at the societal or national level gathered significant impetus through the well-known work of the Dutch scholar Geert Hofstede.' Brooks (2009, p292) notes that, 'In many ways Geert Hofstede is seen as the major writer on cross-cultural analysis because the model he developed has survived the test of time, is relatively easy to use and is comprehensive.' Although not immune from criticism, as we shall see, Hofstede's contribution to the area can undoubtedly be viewed as pivotal.

The genesis of Hofstede's work dates back to the 1960s when he led two major surveys on cross-cultural differences in different centres of the computing company IBM. The surveys were carried out between 1968 and 1973, although Hofstede continues to publish in the twenty-first century. As we shall see, his work was further developed in the mid-1980s when, with Canadian academic Michael Bond, at that time working in Hong Kong, Hofstede identified an additional cultural dimension, Confucian dynamism – subsequently renamed 'long-term orientation' – which expanded the scope of the original work to encompass countries in East Asia. However, the essential approach adopted by Hofstede dates back to his original work in IBM when he devised surveys in which IBM employees were asked to complete questionnaires which required them to indicate the importance of specific items, thereby revealing their own preferences in these areas. The following questions are taken from Hofstede's IBM attitude survey as an illustration of his methodological approach:

● How important is it for you to have considerable freedom to adopt your own approach to the job? (1–5 scale)
● How satisfied are you with the freedom you have to adopt your own approach to the job?

- How often would you say your immediate manager insists that rules and procedures are followed?
- Respond to the statement that, by and large, companies change their policies and practices much too often (strongly agree through to strongly disagree).

Hofstede's very extensive IBM database drawn from his questionnaire responses included 116,000 participants from (eventually) 72 countries. Additional data has been collected from other populations unrelated to IBM.

Hofstede's theories can be grouped into two areas: the notion of collective programming, in which he sought to explain how culture was made up and maintained, and the 4+1 dimensions which sought to conceptualise differences between cultures.

In collective programming, Hofstede posited that individuals held 'portable' mental programmes which were first developed in early childhood via the influence of 'significant others' such as parents or other guardians. These mental programmes were subsequently reinforced in schools or other influential institutions (eg the media), and ultimately acted out through the values held by individuals from the relevant culture. In his own words (2001, p3), 'It is at the middle collective level that most of our mental programming is learned, which is shown by the fact that we share it with people who have gone through the same learning processes but do not have the same genetic makeup. The existence of the American people as a phenomenon is one of the clearest illustrations of the force of learning: With a multitude of genetic variations, it shows a collective mental programming that is striking to the non-American.' Critically, Hofstede's model then sets out a framework for understanding characteristic patterns of workplace behaviour. We have already considered this underlying approach to understanding culture in Chapter 2.

Hofstede initially put forward four dimensions of culture:

- *Power distance* – the degree of inequality that members of a culture both expect and accept (see earlier discussion of Project GLOBE).
- *Uncertainty avoidance* – the extent to which members welcome uncertainty and change as opposed to desiring structured situations (again the earlier discussion of GLOBE refers).
- *Individualism/collectivism* – individualism indicates the extent to which people in a culture learn to act as individuals and stress their own (or their immediate family's) interests; in contrast, a low index score on individualism (now referred to as collectivism) signals interdependence with wider groups and an associated desire to foster and maintain group harmony.
- *Masculinity/femininity* – the degree to which a culture emphasises so-called masculine values such as competitiveness and performance, or assumed feminine values such as relationships and a concern for the quality of life.

Immediately open to accusations of using outdated and stereotypical perceptions of gender-linked behaviour, it appears that this dimension when applied to countries does expose differences in consumer behaviour. For example, it can be argued that masculine cultures put a stress on car engine power whereas feminine cultures have more coffee-filter-makers per capita! Interestingly, the Project GLOBE researchers did not discard this dimension, but rather refined it in two sub-categories: gender egalitarianism and assertiveness.

3.4 THE CHINESE VALUE SURVEY AND THE FIFTH DIMENSION

Hofstede in his later work located some countries along a fifth (long-term orientation, or LTO) dimension, including all the societies listed in Table 3.2. In the previous section we noted the contribution of Bond, who, together with Chinese academics, first compiled the Chinese Value Survey (CVS), building on a list of values suggested by Eastern scholars. The survey was initially carried out with students living in selected countries. As a result, a new dimension emerged, linked to but separate from the previous four, which was related back to aspects of Confucianism. Hofstede added a fifth *time dimension* as a result (see Hofstede and Bond 1988), which has become synonymous with the term 'Confucian dynamism'. Many cultures scoring high on Confucian dynamism and therefore classified as long-term-oriented were at the time enjoying substantial economic growth, so considerable attention was paid to the possible cultural factors leading to their success. We should, of course, also consider whether such factors have played a role in explaining subsequent leaner economic periods; for example, the Asian recession following financial crises in 1997 (see Chen 2004).

Table 3.2 Hofstede's five dimensions of culture in respect of selected countries

	Power distance	Individualism/ collectivism	Masculinity/ femininity	Uncertainty avoidance	Long-term orientation
Australia	36	90	61	51	31
Brazil	69	38	49	76	65
China	80	20	66	30	118
Czech Republic	57	58	57	74	13
Germany	35	67	66	65	31
India	77	48	56	40	61
Singapore	74	20	48	8	48
Sweden	31	71	5	29	33
Thailand	64	20	34	64	56
UK	35	89	66	35	25

Table 3.2 shows Hofstede's five dimensions of culture applied to selected countries. Scores for the full range of countries can be found in Hofstede (2001), Hofstede et al (2010) and at **www.geerthofstede.com**

In some ways it is possible to argue that the fifth (LTO) dimension reflects differences in thinking on issues beyond uncertainty avoidance, PD and the other dimensions identified by Hofstede – and indeed beyond the specific business implications of taking a short- or long-term perspective. Rather, this additional dimension refers to generic differences between the tradition of analytical thinking in Western societies and the more holistic thinking predominant in East Asia. In East Asia, for example, a new supplier might not necessarily be chosen instead of an old supplier even though the new supplier's price is more competitive. The decision could depend on many other factors beyond price and ability to supply the product, such as historical relations with the old company, third-party references for the new company, and personal relations with executives in the new company.

Such considerations are of course not unique to Asian business – the issue of trust is a very important factor in inter-organisational relations in any society. However, the widely divergent scores apparent in Table 3.2 point to a greater preponderance of the combination of factors making up the long-term orientation in particular societies. As an increasingly major player in global business, China's score of 118 along this dimension is especially worthy of note.

3.5 HOFSTEDE'S LATER WORK

In 2010 a new edition of Hofstede's seminal work *Culture's Consequences* was published. Co-authored with his son, Gert-Jan Hofstede, and the Bulgarian academic Minkov, this edition included a new sixth dimension of culture: indulgence versus restraint. As a new contribution to the culture literature I have included this dimension, along with two others developed by Minkov, in Chapter 4; however, I will also summarise the new dimension at this point to round off our overview of Hofstede's work. A country scoring high on indulgence allows 'relatively free gratification of basic and natural human desires related to enjoying life and having fun' (Hofstede 2011, p15). In contrast, high levels of restraint are found in societies with stricter norms. In restrained societies (amongst other things) there are fewer 'very happy' people, one finds proscribed attitudes to sex, there is less importance attached to leisure and one finds a higher number of police officers per head of the population.

This sixth dimension of culture was included from 2010 as it dealt with aspects of culture not previously covered in Hofstede's model and also to reflect a growing 'happiness literature' both in psychology generally and in people management in particular. In common with the other five dimensions, country clusters were 'mapped'. In this case indulgent societies can be found in South and North America, Western Europe (eg the UK) and parts of sub-Saharan Africa. Restraint characterises Eastern Europe, Asia and the Muslim world (Hofstede 2011).

Two further dimensions of culture identified by Minkov (2007), but not added to the Hofstede framework, are set out in Chapter 4.

3.6 UTILISING HOFSTEDE'S MODEL OF CULTURE

When considered with caution, Hofstede and Bond's model (including its later variants) provides the user with an ability to make qualified assumptions about a culture's values. It is certainly the case that researchers continue to apply the models to individual and comparative settings, while training programmes for international managers also frequently utilise the models as a basis for activities.

Todeva (1999) provides just one example of a plethora of continuing academic research, based on what have now become well-established theories. In her research based on a sample of Polish students, Todeva (p621) concluded that, 'According to students' perception of what is typical for Polish culture, it is medium PD, low uncertainty avoidance, high individualism and medium masculinity. The medium PD means that they believe in equality and shared democratic values. The low UA could be interpreted as a strong support for entrepreneurial activities. The belief in high individualism means that people are prepared to take responsibilities themselves, and the medium masculinity response suggests an attitude of balance and harmony between the personal and the societal sphere.'

Although it is interesting to record Todeva's view that respondents can express different values in response to different research tools, suggesting that specific models and their application can predetermine results, she nonetheless provides one of many seemingly successful applications of Hofstede's model. Almost 50 years after the commencement of his work, it is realistic to claim that Hofstede's dimensions of culture and underlying theoretical stance have now entered the everyday vernacular of cross-cultural business studies.

There is no apparent sign of any waning of interest in Hofstede's research. Instead, we find continuing evidence of the durability of his work. Even so, there is a growing body of criticism highlighting the limitation of his paradigm, which ranges from an identification of perceived anomalies in his data to the fundamental questioning of the models' explanatory usefulness and efficacy. Notwithstanding these reservations Hofstede's work continues, as we have seen with the addition of new dimensions. For example, in the run-up to a significant expansion of the European Union, he was involved in a research programme (Kolman et al 2003) which measured his cultural dimensions in four acceding countries: Poland, the Czech Republic, Slovakia and Hungary. Once more the findings of this study were significant, unravelling both consistencies in the values displayed in these Central European countries and differences between them. The Czech Republic, for example, is distinctive in that it emerges from the research as the most individualist of these four countries, whereas Slovakia (with which it was previously conjoined as Czechoslovakia) is shown as the most collectivist. One can only speculate as to the next wave of societal comparisons which will employ Hofstede's classic dimensions. Meanwhile, new work emerges on an ongoing basis, locating cultural differences between countries and explaining behaviour in terms of central tendencies in values. Research data continues to be extracted from factor and correlation analysis from survey data based on constructed dimensions of culture; see Minkov (2007), whose work we will examine in detail in Chapter 4.

GROUP ACTIVITY 3.2

Look at the corporate websites of two companies, one whose ownership places it in a 'high LTO' society and one originating from a country whose score is low in this regard.

1   Is there any appreciable difference in the statements made on the two companies' websites which could be linked to

Hofstede and Bond's theories? Account also for any similarities between the rhetoric employed by the two companies.

2   How useful in practice do you think Hofstede and Bond's model is in explaining such differences?

3.7 CRITICISMS OF HOFSTEDE'S WORK

McSweeney (2002) devotes an entire paper to a critique of Hofstede's work. Including in the title of his critique the phrases 'A triumph of faith – a failure of analysis', McSweeney identifies four main areas of criticism:

- It is questionable whether Hofstede's IBM employee sample is nationally representative – did the IBM average response reflect the national average?
- Has Hofstede demonstrated that societal-level cultural factors affected the mental programming of his respondents to the exclusion of organisational, occupational and other influences?
- Has Hofstede's questionnaire method captured – or even, could it capture – the dominant dimensions of culture, as was claimed?
- In that the data was restricted to the workplace, it is limited in application and by definition excludes the non-employed from the analysis which followed.

Hofstede (2002) responds directly to McSweeney's criticisms of his work. He states that the IBM data was intended to bring out differences between cultures, and that by using well-matched data, ie from a company with a strong corporate culture and which allowed the inclusion of a large number of countries, such comparisons became meaningful. Hofstede concludes that McSweeney's critique of his research methodology essentially missed the point of what he (Hofstede) was attempting to achieve. Furthermore, and importantly, Hofstede claims that his findings have been validated by other studies, noting 400 significant correlations obtained via a variety of methods, not merely surveys. Readers are encouraged to read the exchange between Hofstede (2002) and McSweeney (2002) to assess the validity of arguments on both sides.

Methodological criticisms of Hofstede's work continue. Venaik and Brewer (2013) conclude that both Hofstede's and the GLOBE culture dimensions, scales and scores are unreliable and invalid. As such, Venailk and Brewer propose that methodological flaws inhibit the usefulness of the data for both management theorists and practitioners. Once again the arguments are intricate and best followed up with a detailed reading; for example, on the question of whether items used to intercorrelate culture dimensions are low and even negative at the level of individuals. Clegg et al (2011, p241) also questioned the validity of Hofstede's methodology in that it resulted in average scores taken from national sample data. The results, according to these writers, are 'similar to saying that the average Dutch person is taller than the average Chinese person – the statement accepts that the average is a summary device. The average tells you nothing about what any Dutch or Chinese person's height may be any more than it informs you about the values he or she holds. An average of values, although it is economical, is about as meaningful as an average of height.'

It is undoubtedly the case that Hofstede's comparative focus, which is shared by most of the researchers who relate societal cultural variables to the workplace, results in a large-scale approach thereby including a very wide range of cultures. In using such an approach he does not attempt to take an ethnographic qualitative stance which focuses on the subjective experience of being a member of that culture. For Hofstede, the value of using dimensions of culture lies in systematically differentiating cultures from each other. Similarly, the criticisms relating to his sampling could plausibly be seen as missing the target in that what was important in Hofstede's results was the extent to which groups differed in a meaningful and consistent way from those in other cultures.

We have already indicated that there is danger in the cross-cultural field of basing models on culturally derived assumptions. This in fairness may be unavoidable, but it should be explicitly acknowledged – which, while it may detract from the perceived universal applicability of the approach, would in practice enhance its relevance. This criticism can be laid at Hofstede's door. For example, his interpretation of masculine and feminine attributes could be seen as strictly derived from a particular time and place, despite his recognition (2001, p279) that 'duality of the sexes is a fundamental fact with which different societies cope in different ways'. Linstead et al (2009) also characterise Hofstede's model as being static and conservative. These authors propose that Hofstede's view of socialisation as occurring through family, school and workplace underestimates the extent to which young people have access to more social networks than ever before via new technologies such as the Internet and mobile phones, thereby enabling them to adopt shifting multiple identities.

It is also possible to criticise Hofstede's tendency to oversimplify complex social phenomena in two ways. Firstly, doubts persist over whether responses to values questions provided in surveys do in fact correspond to the operative values of managers, and even if they do, whether the values held are actually converted into behavioural outcomes. Secondly, the bipolarised approach in itself does not cope well with the diversity, complexity and dynamism of different cultures or give credence to the possible impact of other variables such as institutional frameworks, competitive environment, corporate cultures and sector/industry imperatives. Lu (2012) notes, for example, that Hofstede's work does not incorporate ethnicity and multiculturalism (a critique already put forward in more general terms in Chapters 1 and 2). Lu addresses these concerns squarely at Hofstede's work, giving the example of how Chinese culture is conceptualised. Lu indicates that Chinese culture is often viewed as the culture of the Han people, which does not reflect a multicultural society such as the People's Republic of China (PRC). Research findings which do not incorporate ethnicity and multiculturalism could paint an incomplete and inaccurate picture of the society in question.

Ultimately, there is no better way to gauge the value of Hofstede's work than to read his original books and articles with their wealth of data and insights. His research is the most extensive within the field and his model of culture typically takes a very prominent place in analyses of cultural differences as manifested at work. Buelens et al (2006, p606) in fact go further in stating that, 'The tremendous impact his research had on the contemporary thinking is reflected by the fact that Hofstede is currently the world's most cited author in the entire area of the social sciences.'

3.8 AT THE CORE OF CROSS-CULTURAL STUDIES: KLUCKHOHN AND STRODTBECK'S WORK

We have seen that Hofstede's model of culture points to classifications of societies – usually, but not only, countries – along dimensions which ultimately link back to *values* held by members of a group. His work has gained considerable attention, in part due to his concern with work-related values at a time when cross-cultural aspects of business became highly topical. However, our reverse chronological or 'time-tunnel' approach, which began with a look at a very recent contribution, Project GLOBE, and which was then traced back to Hofstede's work, now leads us even further back in time to the pioneering studies of two anthropologists, Florence Kluckhohn and Fred Strodtbeck (1961), who did not focus on the realm of work. These writers were influential in identifying core elements of culture more generally, which they considered arose from responses and, ultimately, solutions to eternal and universal problems faced by all societies.

Brief summaries of their work can be found in a number of cross-cultural management books, including Tayeb (2003). Hills (2002) examines their model in greater detail and takes a perspective grounded in the discipline of psychology. Kluckhohn and Strodtbeck put forward six value orientations based on how societies typically dealt with the following core issues:

- relationship with nature
- attitudes to time
- views of human nature
- activity
- relationships between people
- space.

Kluckhohn and Strodtbeck's model was formulated as a result of research conducted among five cultural groups including Navaho Native American Indians, Mexican-Americans and members of the Church of Jesus Christ of Latter-day Saints (Mormons), all of whom were at that time to be found in the south-west of the USA. The six generic problem areas set out above are of such a profound nature that they are faced by all social groups and consequently form the basis for a group's values. Nonetheless, it should be recognised that the sixth problem – how to relate to space – was not fully incorporated into their findings.

These anthropologists also concluded that the solutions to these problems could be conceptualised within a range of possible choices. For example, the problem of how to relate to time ultimately comes down to a choice of past, present or future orientations. The problem of how to relate to others is resolved according to either a preference for hierarchical relations, by which people will tend to defer to those they perceive to be in authority, or collateral relations in which the emphasis is on consensus among people who are seen as largely equal – although there is finally a third alternative: an individualistic orientation in which the emphasis is on individuals who make decisions independently of others.

The dimension relating to how we regard nature is worthy of particular consideration at this time. Where groups respond to problems of nature by exercising mastery, they go beyond both being submissive in the face of natural and/or supernatural forces and merely existing in harmony with the forces of nature, to attempting to exert control over nature. The attempt to conquer space resulting in the moon landings achieved by US astronauts has often been cited as an example of the assertive attitude to nature displayed in

American culture. The sharp angles of the Bank of China building in Hong Kong were contrastingly said to have violated principles of *feng shui*, and there have been documented fears that the building's shape will attract ill fortune, thus providing an illustration of the need for harmony with nature expressed in Chinese culture.

However, this dimension can also be related to sub-groups within a single society – as was Kluckhohn and Strodtbeck's original intention. Consider, for example, the following extract from an article from the *Boston Globe* newspaper (18 September 2005), commenting on the devastating floods in New Orleans following Hurricane Katrina, and in so doing drawing attention to the 'Southernness' of the disaster: 'You see a distinct sense of fatalism in the resignation both in advance of and after Katrina in terms of seeing these things as more a matter of God's will than anything under man's control. This interacts with a stronger attachment than most other Americans have to a particular place to produce a willingness to risk death and disaster in a familiar setting.'

If Kluckhohn and Strodtbeck's work continues to find echoes in contemporary world events, their legacy is more in the specific area of cross-cultural organisational studies. In a recent historical review Fink et al (2005, p6) state that, 'The fundamental approach of Kluckhohn and Strodtbeck provided the basic principles for all further research in the area of cross-cultural research aiming at quantitative measures of cultural values. Since the effective research was limited by scope and scale, further research based on Kluckhohn/Strodtbeck offers variation by sample, context and the set of values/dimensions used to describe cultures.' Put another way, their work can be seen as the building blocks on which contemporary models of cross-cultural differences at work have been constructed. No overview of cross-cultural aspects of business can be complete without a thorough appreciation of their groundbreaking work.

3.9 FONS TROMPENAARS' 7-D MODEL: PRACTICAL STEPS FOR DOING BUSINESS

Fons Trompenaars' work on culture – part of which was carried out in collaboration with Charles Hampden-Turner – draws on the central premises of Kluckhohn and Strodtbeck's theories, expanding their dimensions of culture to create seven, which we now come on to review. Before considering Trompenaars' contribution to this area it is also important to recognise his background as a business consultant with an expressed aim to provide practical guidance for managers engaged in cross-cultural business activity. His data is drawn from quantitative questionnaires supported with cluster and correlation analysis. As a result, Trompenaars has created an impressive body of evidence to support his theoretical stance. His work spans 30 years, and is ongoing, resulting in a database with over 50,000 participants, that includes over 50 countries, and has been derived from and reinforced by over 1,000 cross-cultural training programmes.

Trompenaars and Hampden-Turner (1997 and 2004) claim that their work can help managers construct a mental picture of culture which identifies the core assumptions or basic foundations of culture. They note (1997, p8) that 'every culture distinguishes itself from others by the specific solutions it chooses to certain problems which reveal themselves as dilemmas. It is convenient to look at these problems under three headings: those which arise from our relationships with other people; those which come from the passage of time; and those which relate to the environment.' These three areas underpin the seven dimensions of culture in their model.

An important aspect of Trompenaars' work is his questioning of managers on 'extreme scenario' situations – ie how people think they would respond if *x* or *y* occurred. As we will see, one part of his model examines the extent to which members of cultures adhere to rules which apply in all situations. The other end of this bipolar dimension identifies cultures where relationships are particularly important, even at the expense of rules. In Chapter 2 we confronted one of Trompenaars' extreme scenarios, namely, when a respondent faces an imagined situation in which they are a passenger in a car driven by a close friend which hits a pedestrian. The dilemma faced by the passenger is whether or not to lie about the accident if the friend asked him or her to. In a further complication, the driver was exceeding the speed limit and requests that the passenger make a false statement about the car's speed on impact. Trompenaars is clearly fond of this specific scenario, since it supplies the title of a 2002 work, *Did the Pedestrian Die?* The point of this additional question is to illustrate the strength of the relationship dimension where the propensity to lie – and by so doing support the friend – is positively related to the severity of the pedestrian's condition. It also has the effect of bringing home the importance of relationship cultures to those at the other, rule-bound, end of this spectrum, who may (wrongly) have assumed that the passenger would only lie if the pedestrian had emerged from the accident relatively unscathed!

The use of the extreme scenario method is certainly evocative in its illumination of the practical ways in which cultural differences might manifest themselves, and it also, importantly, brings into focus the *ethical dimension* of the subject matter (see also Chapter 9). It is furthermore inherent to the underpinning view of culture as deriving from group responses to dilemmas: here the core premise of the concept is mirrored within the methodologies employed in the research.

Trompenaars and Hampden-Turner located societies along each of the following seven dimensions:

- *Universalism v particularism* – Deals with the relative perceived importance of rules which would be applied in all cases (universally) as opposed to those where rules are applied more flexibly and where relationships assume particular importance – as illustrated by the 'pedestrian' story. The USA scores highly on universalism in contrast to China, which is classified as particularist.
- *Neutral v affective* – Cultures contrast those where emotion is 'masked' (neutral), with others in which emotion is displayed openly (affective), in particular within business settings. For example, Trompenaars' research revealed differences in the percentage of his national samples who would not be comfortable with expressing a strong emotion such as distress at work. This figure varied considerably: 74% of the Japanese sample indicating that they would not want to express this emotion in that context, whereas only 19% of the Spanish group agreed with the same statement. There are a number of countries where scores effectively divide the individual populations; for example, the percentage who would not show distress at work in the Indian sample was 51, whereas scores for both Australia and Singapore were 48. These findings, although realistic, pose their own dilemmas for managers who deal with nationals from these countries! Trompenaars goes on to refine this dimension by adding another sub-question: should emotion be separated from reasoning? Does the first vitiate the second? Thus according to Trompenaars and Hampden-Turner (1997, p73), 'Americans tend to exhibit emotion yet separate it from "objective" and "rational" decisions. Italians and south European nations in general tend to exhibit and not separate. Dutch and Swedes tend not to exhibit and to separate.'
- *Individualism v communitarianism* – Examines the extent to which individuals act independently as opposed to expressing high degrees of loyalty within tightly bonded groups. People form into groups in all societies; this dimension contrasts the degree to which people hold a strong shared sense of a greater public or group identification. The dimension is very close to that set out by Hofstede, although Trompenaars makes more frequent reference to managerial implications (1997, p52): 'Practices such as promotion for recognised achievements and pay-for-performance, for example, assume that individuals want to be distinguished within the group and that their colleagues approve of this happening. They also rest on the assumption that the contribution of any one individual to a common task is easily distinguishable and that no problems arise from singling him or her out for praise. None of this may, in fact, be true in more

communitarian countries.' We will look again at the implications of Trompenaars' work for the motivation of employees and human resource management more generally in Chapters 8 and 11.

- *Specific v diffuse* – Cultures contrast in that in specific cultures people compartmentalise their lives. For example, managers and subordinates in specific societies such as Finland and Switzerland may be on informal terms outside the workplace. One of the scenario questions posed to draw out this dimension was 'Would you paint your boss's house?' – assuming that the individual concerned is not a painter by trade. In a diffuse society such as China a higher proportion of employees (68%) would at least consider this unusual request, as opposed to only 9% in Sweden. Another key implication from this dimension is the need to prevent workers in diffuse societies from 'losing face': the casual phrase 'It's nothing personal' is meaningless in the diffuse society context, where everything is linked to everything else and an individual cannot easily separate out the personal from the work domain.

- *Achievement v ascription* – Cultures differ in that in the first status (eg Norway) is denoted by achievement whereas in an ascription culture status (eg South Korea) is more ascribed to a person due to inherent factors such as his or her age or education or social connections. Trompenaars, in common with other academics, recognises that cultural differences emanate from a number of aspects of a society's cultural environment. In this case religious traditions are important, as Trompenaars alerts readers to the presence of the Catholic, Buddhist and Hindu faiths in ascriptive societies as contrasted with the more Protestant background of the achievement cultures.

- *Inner- v outer-directed* – Societies also differ; note that in Trompenaars' more recent work this dimension is renamed as 'internal v external control'. The fundamental question in this case is whether people can control their own environment or merely have to work with it. The origins of this dimension lie very clearly in Kluckhohn and Strodtbeck's work. Trompenaars noted that although no country appeared to believe that it was totally worthwhile to control natural forces (Romania had the highest score, with 68%) there were still significant differences as expressed by his respondents (for example, 42% of his Canadian sample as against only 9% of the Egyptian group). There were also differences in the extent to which people felt that what happened to them was of their own making. Selected scores (on whether people agreed with this proposition) were: Israel 88, Ireland 77, Indonesia 70, Germany 66, Kuwait 55, and China 39.

- *Sequential v synchronic* – Cultures deal with time in different ways. A sequential orientation sees time as linear, comprising a series of discrete events, whereas synchronic perceptions of time are circular, seeing interrelationships between the past, present and future. It is therefore possible to identify societies with a greater overall focus on the past, present or future. In a sequential, time-oriented culture, activities are undertaken one at a time, punctuality is valued, there is a stress on rational planning, and time is measurable – a finite resource to be used effectively. Synchronic cultures are perceived as taking an opposing standpoint on each of these categories.

3.10 EVALUATING TROMPENAARS' WORK

The strength of Trompenaars' contribution lies in its applied focus whereby existing or future international managers are presented with a clearly defined framework within which to consider their own actual or anticipated work experiences. The use of the extreme scenario method results in some richly evocative examples which can be modified to fit more mundane and yet important situations. Trompenaars and Hampden-Turner certainly expected that an awareness of their approach would bear fruit in practical terms, believing that they could help managers structure their real-life experiences and give them insight into frequently experienced difficulties that might occur when dealing with people from diverse cultures.

Most importantly, these writers advocate that managers operating across cultural boundaries should *reconcile* the differences they would inevitably encounter. This is a new departure since without this steer such managers might otherwise polarise or, more commonly, compromise their own beliefs and actions, resulting in a diluted indeterminate cross-cultural management style which is largely ineffective and which satisfies none of the parties concerned. Recognising difference, being reconciled to it and retaining one's own cultural style would be more likely to result in success in the cross-cultural field. The strengths of individual societies' values could in fact be a source of competitive advantage.

In academic terms, Trompenaars and Hampden-Turner are realistic about the role of culture in business. Their country or society scores on individual dimensions are frequently 'middling', which may not propel the managers on their training courses along particular courses of action but do reflect the complex reality of their findings. They also express a guarded view on the role of societal culture at the organisational level, believing (1997, p151) that corporate culture 'is shaped not only by technologies and markets, but by the cultural preferences of leaders and employees', therefore acknowledging that societal culture is only one of a range of explanatory factors to be taken into account in understanding organisations.

There is, finally, an attempt to examine the role of gender in cross-cultural research, after which they conclude that there are some differences in scores which can be attributed to gender, although societal-level cultural influences remained paramount. Nonetheless, there are interesting findings. As Trompenaars and Hampden-Turner (1997, p223) note: 'There is some evidence that the French want their women to be different, while Americans want their women to be the same. The American female manager is more individualist than the male, the French female significantly less individualist.' We are aware that there are some assumptions in this statement which may need unpicking; however, the very recognition of a role for gender in this subject area is welcomed.

Criticisms have also been levelled against Trompenaars' work. Fontaine and Richardson (2003), in a preface to their own research carried out in Malaysia, summarise several critical comments made by Hofstede (1996) and (1997), who has claimed that Trompenaars' dimensions are based on literature emanating from the USA in the 1950s. In other words, the charge is that his dimensions are themselves rooted in a particular cultural context, which casts doubt on their applicability in a worldwide model. Hofstede (2011) has also questioned whether the seven dimensions identified by Trompenaars are self-standing or whether, alternatively, they are essentially sub-sets of one dimension (individualism v communitarianism). The final criticism levelled by Hofstede was that, in contrast to his own work, Trompenaars did not establish a correlation between findings at the individual, organisational and country-wide levels.

Broeways and Price (2011, p106) comment on Hofstede's critique of Trompenaars' work. They note that Trompenaars and Hampden-Turner have acknowledged the influence of Hofstede on their model and record the latter authors' view that their own view of culture sees it as, 'dancing from one end of a dimension to another when encountering various dilemmas'. Broeways and Price conclude that Trompenaars' work therefore contrasts with Hofstede's depiction of culture as linear, with individual countries being positioned either high or low or in the middle of dimensions. They claim that Trompeneaars and Hampden-Turner's contribution is 'a model to learn with' (as opposed to what they see as Hofstede's search for a perfect model).

Notwithstanding the validity of Hofstede's reservations, it is apparent that both he and Trompenaars and Hampden-Turner have worked within the same methodological paradigm, so the comments can be viewed as akin to a theological debate within a religion – the basic tenets are not questioned.

Koen (2005), in comparing the work of Trompenaars with both that of Hofstede and Schwartz (whom we consider next), submits the conclusion that the work of the first-named is overall less academically rigorous. The final comment we will make in this context concerns the extent to which Trompenaars' sample is representative. In that it largely comprises international managers – by definition, comparatively well-educated and travelled – one can certainly level an accusation that the data underlying the model was drawn from a narrow segment of society. Ultimately, much as was the case with Hofstede's data, the key point is that Trompenaars was comparing 'like with like' in an attempt to isolate the impact of culture on attitudes and behaviour so that this one variable would not be confounded by other socio-economic factors.

3.11 SHALOM SCHWARTZ'S UNIVERSAL VALUES MODEL

Schwartz's relatively recent contribution to this area – his work was first published in 1992 and continues to be refined and adapted in current studies – is widely regarded as a significant step forward in cross-cultural understanding. His work offers the promise of particular insights into work values and motivation, and as such is analysed further in Chapter 8. Here, we summarise the work of Schwartz and his colleagues, recognising that their strand of thinking on this subject is likely to be developed further in the future. Dahl (2004) provides a cogent summary of Schwartz's theories on values as they affect culture, and his work is recommended as an alternative source of understanding of a model which has not always been clearly elucidated in the cross-cultural management literature.

The first element within Schwartz's conception of values is his notion of *value types*. He defined values as desired goals which we can envisage as akin to a compass which guides the direction of people's lives. Schwartz identified ten value types, as listed below:

- power
- achievement
- hedonism
- stimulation
- self-direction
- universalism
- benevolence
- tradition
- conformity
- security.

It should be noted that discrete values contain a variety of associated 'sub-principles' which coalesce into a wider combination of values. Dahl concludes that self-direction (to take one example) will be linked to a desire for autonomy, creativity and independence. Such value combinations will characterise an individual over a long-term period, since in his original article in 1992 Schwartz proposed that values would typically be enduring. We could take this further by claiming that within this framework values are 'portable' in that we retain them in the course of our daily lives, leading to the possibility that a particular situation will result in the value's being activated. For example, someone about to leave home for a beauty therapy session, thereby attending to hedonistic concerns, might see an underweight hedgehog in their garden. If their underlying value priority was for benevolence, they would feel compelled to abandon their intended journey and instead take the hedgehog to an animal shelter. Although Schwartz saw the value types as generic to all of us, and indeed overlapping, he also indicated that we place the values in order of the importance they have for us, thereby allowing for very diverse ranking of values.

The second element of Schwartz's work, which is highly relevant for our purposes, concerns the relationships between values. In claiming that some values were less compatible with each other (for example, security and stimulation), he then moved on to the issue of value dimensions.

The two core bipolar dimensions initially identified were:

● *Self-transcendence and self-enhancement* – Where there is self-transcendence we accept others on their merits and may express concern for others' well-being. Self-enhancement, contrastingly, involves the pursuit of self-interest and potentially the exercise of dominance over others.
● *Conservatism and openness to change* – These could again be regarded as bipolar dimensions, the first stressing security, conformity and even submissiveness, and the second stimulation, independence and action.

There is clearly scope to expand this analysis to incorporate cross-cultural comparisons. Sagiv and Schwartz (2000) provide a model which locates a large number of countries along what by this stage had become three classification indices. These are set out in Figure 3.1.

● *Hierarchy v egalitarianism* – A culture veering towards hierarchy (eg Zimbabwe) places emphasis on social power and authority, whereas one closer to the egalitarian extreme (eg Spain) exhibits values of social justice and shared responsibility.
● *Embeddedness v autonomy* – In embedded societies, values include group identification and respect for social order. Derived from the conservatism/conservation index, there is here a desire to prevent fragmentation of groups or the established social order. In autonomous societies there is a preoccupation with self-expression, whether in the intellectual (int) sphere or affective (aff) area; for example, the enjoyment of a challenging and varied life outside work.
● *Mastery v harmony* – Mastery represents a greater effort to control and change the natural and social environment. As can be seen, this applies to Japan in this model. The harmony value when manifested in societies represents a desire to understand and protect the environment.

Figure 3.1 Countries located on Sagiv and Schwartz's three cross-cultural dimensions

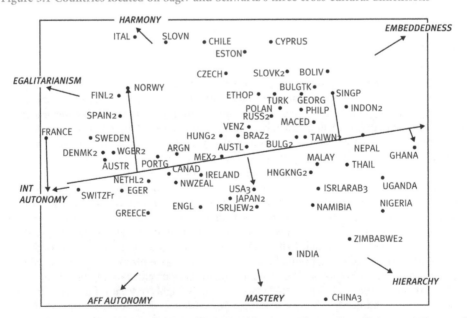

Note: Information in this figure is pre-1990, as, for example, in the references to East and West Germany.

To plot an individual country along any of the bipolar dimensions in Figure 3.1, identify the middle point of the particular line that links the two extreme positions, eg between hierarchy and egalitarianism (see above for further description of the dimensions). The same exercise should be completed for all three dimensions, and a country's position on all three can then be identified.

Having extended the model from the individual to the societal level, it was only a relatively short step to move the analysis back to the national workplace level. Schwartz (1999) has, as a further development of his work, developed data based on the extent of work centrality within a society, postulating that where there is emphasis on mastery and hierarchy, as in Hong Kong and the USA, work itself is more likely to be regarded and experienced as central to life than in those societies plotted towards the relevant opposing dimensions. As indicated earlier, there is scope to apply this finding within the field of managing people. In Chapter 8 we describe the implications of worker motivation.

To take just one example at this point, Fisher and Yuan (1998) report that notions of job enrichment and redesign were perceived to be more important to American workers than to their Chinese counterparts, although it was recognised that this could change with the anticipated economic developments in China.

3.12 A POTENTIALLY VALUABLE DEPARTURE

Although Schwartz's work can be located within a well-established tradition of bipolar constructions of culture based on embedded individual values, his approach is distinctive in several important ways. Respondents were asked to assess 56 values in terms of how they regarded them as deeply held life principles. No scenario or dilemma was indicated as a stimulus for action, so one can anticipate that the respondents were not influenced by the demands of a particular situation. In other words, their values should not have been compromised; save, of course, for the ever-present 'Hawthorne effect' whereby merely being part of a research effort could possibly distort responses. Schwartz also clearly demarcated the individual and cultural levels, by separating out his samples by occupation: chiefly, teacher and student. However, it is possible to argue that the idealised nature of Schwartz's research in itself could have led to unrealistic responses, and we are also – typically in research undertaken on values or attitudes – faced with the difficulty of separating out the cognitive (beliefs), affective (emotional) and behavioural (acting-out) components of the values.

Patel (2014) makes a renewed case for Schwartz's framework as a useful tool for analysing cultures. She concludes that Schwartz's cultural dimensions are linked and integrated so we can conceive of seemingly conflicting values coexisting within any one society. This might accurately reflect the picture of modern diverse societies; more so than the models of other influential writers. Patel also sees potential for explaining behaviour in Schwartz's notion that values are influenced and activated by specific situations and circumstances. This, she suggests, offers scope for understanding how values can play out in action – as opposed to an implicit view of values as pre-determined and therefore unchanging. In summary, Schwartz's work, while offering a classification scheme for understanding cultural difference (a classic etic formulation), also points towards a view of culture, based on values, which is dynamic and open to change.

GROUP ACTIVITY 3.3

It is likely that among your class, or your university/college more generally, there are students of different nationalities. Ask up to six of your fellow students to rank Schwartz's ten value types in terms of their guiding life principles. Include within your sample at least two students from countries different both from you and from each other.

Can you identify any responses which may be influenced by national culture? (Ask your fellow students whether they think this too.) Or are their responses more the result of individual personality differences?

Share your findings with your tutor as part of a discussion of Schwartz's work.

3.13 CULTURAL DIFFERENCES IN COMMUNICATION STYLE

In Chapter 2 we suggested that communication and culture were interlinked in several important respects. Firstly, cultural values are communicated to individual members either implicitly (enculturation) or explicitly. It is also realistic to claim that cultures are sustained through communication between members. Guirdham (2011) took this idea to its logical conclusion by suggesting that cultures would ultimately disappear if the levels of intra-culture communication dropped in inverse relation to frequency of communication with people outside the cultural group.

More generally, whereas the majority of explanations of cultural difference stress the importance of values held by group members – this of course having been one of the main themes of this chapter – an alternative perspective on the topic views cultural difference primarily in terms of differences in the ways people communicate. Particularly relevant in this school of thought is Edward Hall, some of whose work was co-authored with his wife, Mildred.

It is important to recognise at the outset that this approach to the topic raises the possibility of a 'deep' model of culture in which we may not be entirely self-aware of our cultural influences. The role of subconscious forces is integral to the study of, for example, non-verbal communication (NVC). Social psychologists, eg Argyle (1967), hold the view that some NVC (eg gestures or body movements) are in part vestigial examples of early childhood behaviour. For instance, children may hold their hands over their ears when they listen to an unpleasant message. This would be deemed inappropriate behaviour for adults in most social settings. But touching the ear can be understood as a substitute for that childlike response. Importantly, we may not be consciously aware of even making the gesture, let alone appreciating its significance. Hall (1976, p69) applies the same notion to cross-cultural study: 'Frequently we don't even know what we know. We pick expectations and assumptions up in the cradle. We unconsciously learn what to notice and what not to notice, how to divide time and space, how to walk and talk and use our bodies, how to behave as men or women...This applies to all people.'

Hall's entire conceptualisation of culture was as a series of *languages*; for example, the language of time, the language of space and the language of agreements. To pick one part of his framework – the language of time – uncovers some very different assumptions concerning time found across the world. In monochronic cultures such as the USA, UK and Germany, time is regarded as a resource (to be spent); limited and sequential. One practical consequence of adopting this viewpoint on time involves clearing delineated timeslots for particular activities, which is regarded as good business practice within this overall perspective. In contrast, polychronic cultures view time as malleable: it should accommodate events rather than be determined by task achievement, and it is deemed more acceptable to undertake simultaneous tasks. Hall located Latin cultures (both in the European and American continents) as exhibiting polychronic features. Hall also identified differences in attitudes towards time in terms of relative perceived importance of past, present and future. Trompenaars and Hampden-Turner's later work also encompassed time as a dimension of culture, as we have seen.

In respect of a 'language of space', it is widely recognised that cultures vary in terms of acceptable physical distance between people in specific situations (this field is referred to as proxemics). For an American we are told that personal space, when with friends, varies between 18 inches and four feet (45 centimetres and 1.2 metres). Acceptable intimate space is perceived as anything less than 18 inches, while social space (measured against strangers) begins at four feet and extends to 12 feet (3.66 metres). There are two important points arising from this measurement exercise: firstly, that space may be regarded differently across societies (we examine this area again in Chapter 6), and secondly, that such perceptions may not be fully present at the conscious level, thus pointing again to deeper manifestations of cultural difference.

Hall's best-known contribution to the study of culture involved the organisation of his languages of culture into an explanatory model which contrasted high- and low-context societies. We have already referred briefly to this categorisation in Chapter 2. According to Hall (1990, p6), 'Context is the information that surrounds an event; it is inextricably bound up with the meaning of the event. In a high-context society, the context of communication can be equally as important as the content.'

One example of context in communication is the relative power and status of the communicating parties. Guides to business practice in high-context societies often stress the importance of establishing good social relations based on trust and respect. The China ASEAN Business Net in its online business guide to Vietnam outlines a series of steps relating to the exchange of business cards when on a business trip to that country, noting that this behaviour replaces verbal introductions at the start of a first meeting, thus becoming in effect a form of non-verbal communication. The ritual described in this guide – there are clear norms on who to present one's card to first and on the extent to which cards should be read – is clearly intended to establish and reinforce part of the context of the encounter, namely, the communication of status.

Hall characterised high-status societies as having the following features:

- implicit shared understandings among the cultural group
- little coded (ie spoken or written) information transmitted in communication
- indirect communication styles, including great use of non-verbal communication
- relationships regarded as of great importance: an example can be found in the Chinese term *guanxi*, or network of reciprocal relationships.

Additionally, Hall considered that high-context societies regarded time in a distinctive way. There was great emphasis on the importance of the past, and business transactions could take a relatively long time and depend on the build-up of strong relationships.

Low-context societies unsurprisingly contrast on all of these points:

- much information is coded (put into words) in communication
- direct communication style; essentially verbal or written, and including detailed precise information
- low importance attached to the past and an emphasis on concluding business quickly
- significant value placed on performance and expertise.

Although Hall provides a distinctive starting point for his analysis (ie identifying communication as the underlying factor in explaining culture and cultural difference), it is evident that his work has produced some findings similar to those of other writers. For example, the emphasis on relationships and understanding 'the whole person' in his high-context category and the contrasting compartmentalisation of people's lives in the low-context type is similar to Trompenaars' diffuse and specific society model (respectively). Indeed, the underlying issues dealt with in Hall's work could be seen to have their antecedents in Kluckhohn and Strodtbeck's fundamental problems (eg of how to conceptualise time and how to deal with others).

The other commonality which emerges from Hall's contribution lies in his clustering of countries into types, thereby both linking the societies within a group and distinguishing them from those in other categories. It is important to realise, however, that Hall accepted that there are incidences of both high- and low-context communication in *all* societies. For example, within a family or other close social grouping, a great deal of information and emotion can be expressed without the use of words even in a low-context society, while an employment tribunal held in a high-context country will proceed in a low-context fashion, ie by establishing facts.

The following societies are selected from Hall's categories. As is apparent, these can be linked to some extent by geographical region.

- High-context: China, Korea, Japan, African and Latin American countries.
- Medium-context: France, Spain, Greece and Middle Eastern countries.
- Low-context: USA, UK, Germany and Scandinavian countries.

Hall's work provides another reminder for us that because a very high proportion of theory regarding management and business has emanated from one cultural cluster – in this case, the low-context group – and in the light of the fundamental nature of the differences he uncovered, we must question the worldwide applicability of much of the business studies canon.

Many of the generic criticisms of cross-cultural work in this area can be seen to apply to Hall, including the scientific status of his work in terms of obtaining the original data and some measure of over-generalisation in both his findings and consequent clusters: accepted personal space, for example, is different in the UK and USA, which are, however, clustered together in Hall's work.

3.14 REVIEWING HALL'S WORK: RECENT DEVELOPMENTS

There has been renewed interest in Hall's work from 2011, with contrasting views put forward on the value of his specific work and overall approach to understanding culture and cultural difference. Kittler et al (2011) reviewed literature relating to Hall's high- and low-context model. These authors found that research based on Hall's model, identifying societies falling within the high-/low-context classification, was based on weak and unsubstantiated findings. They concluded that there is no comprehensive list of countries within each category. Research based on Hall's original dichotomy had a USA/Asian bias with Arab and African countries 'blind spots' in the data. Kittler et al also identify a number of countries which have been classified as both high- *and* low-context societies, including the USA and India. Other research did, however, support Hall's original classification. Kittler et al (p78) conclude, however, that, 'virtually all studies that utilized HC/LC country classifications are based on less-than-adequate evidence and stem from dated, unsubstantiated claims, which can even be traced back to Hall's own anecdotal-evidence based classification'. A critique of methodology (as we saw when evaluating Hofstede's work) should be taken seriously, although it is possible that even if we accept the critique, Hall's work may contain underlying truths and serve as a useful starting point for ordering our thoughts on culture and how to connect with other people.

Warner-Soderholm (2013) also draws attention to limitations in Hall's work. She identifies ambiguity in Hall's concepts which makes them difficult to apply via quantitative research. A further problem is that Hall offered no ranking to show where individual countries are positioned along the high-/low-context continuum. Warner-Soderholm develops a new scale in order to 'resurrect and quantitatively measure Hall's cross-cultural dimension' (p34). The scale was derived from Likert-type responses; in this case along a seven-point range from 'completely agree' to 'completely disagree'. One statement used for this purpose was, 'In our region we like to say it as it is.' Warner-Soderholm carried out her research in Norway, receiving 714 questionnaires electronically from Norwegian individuals working in Norwegian private sector companies. This contribution is interesting both in its validation of Hall's classification – in this case pointing to difference between regions in Norway – and also the scope it offers for a more quantitative treatment of what hitherto has been a topic studied via subjective methods and even relying on anecdote.

APPLYING THEORY TO PRACTICE 3.1

In 2002 the Hong Kong and Shanghai Banking Corporation (HSBC) introduced a worldwide advertising campaign which defined this banking group as 'the world's local bank'. This highly successful campaign included advertisements run on British television, which showed how cultures differed via a series of cultural misunderstanding scenarios. One such advert depicted a Western businessman in an unspecified Asian location who is taken out for a meal by his hosts. He considers it polite to finish eating the food offered to him, while his hosts interpret him clearing his plate as a sign that he is still hungry. The upshot is that he is presented with more and more unusual dishes which he does not want to eat, but continues to do so.

HSBC wish to portray the world as a rich and diverse place in which local cultures need to be recognised and respected. The advertisements stress the importance of communication in cross-cultural encounters. It is possible to see echoes of Hall's characterisation of high- and low-context cultures in the scenario depicted in the HSBC televison advert. Consider also the relevance of Trompenaars' classification of culture to this situation, for example his distinction between neutral and affective cultures.

3.15 CONCLUSION

The emergence of cross-cultural management as a topic area is a relatively recent development which was given huge impetus with the publication of Hofstede's seminal work, *Culture's Consequences*, in 1980. Hofstede's contribution, together with much subsequent work, can be characterised within an etic perspective, involving the identification of differences between cultures, or more accurately, between clusters of cultures, on the basis of core dimensions – for example a society's degree of individualism as opposed to collectivism. Soderberg and Holden (2002, p107) characterise this notion of culture as, 'a relatively stable, homogenous, internally consistent system of assumptions, values and norms transmitted by socialisation to the next generation'. The etic approach provides a useful framework for managers to consider the nature of culture, cultural difference and the key importance of cross-cultural awareness.

The etic approach to some extent inevitably precludes in-depth analysis of individual cultures, and also neglects the forces accounting for change, while it has been argued that an etic perspective solidifies cultural differences by highlighting them while offering only limited guidance on how to make cross-cultural teams work effectively. All of these points will be addressed more fully in Chapter 4 when we turn to analyse alternative approaches to cross-cultural management that have emerged in the early twenty-first century.

One final interesting point to note when evaluating etic models of culture involves questioning whether there are, paradoxically, ethnocentric assumptions underpinning the models; for instance, concerning the choice of dimensions which form the building-blocks for comparing cultures. It would be interesting, to take one example, if a Chinese professor in the late 1970s had formulated a model based on bipolar dimensions. One could reasonably anticipate that the categories selected would have been fundamentally different from those addressed by the writers considered in this chapter. Furthermore, it is arguable whether such a hypothetical model could have adequately explained Western management and work organisations, based as it would have been on Chinese cultural assumptions.

CASE STUDY 3.1

NORWEGIAN VALUES IN THE AIR AND ON THE GROUND

Norwegian, part of the Norwegian Group, is an airline which in 2014 was the second largest carrier in Scandinavia and the third largest low-cost airline in Europe. Its corporate website (**www.norwegian.com/uk/about-norwegian/our-company**) contained a section on 'Vision', which in turn included a brief summary of some of its core values. The website also had a section on 'Human Worth'. The following paragraphs are extracts from these parts of the company website:

'Norwegian values are simplicity, directness and relevance. Everyone has a joint responsibility to create a good working environment and develop a sound corporate culture marked by openness and tolerance.

'Norwegian supports the international human rights as outlined by The UN Declaration and Conventions. No one shall in any way cause or contribute to the violation or circumvention of human rights. We place great importance on ensuring compliance with employees' basic human rights as outlined by the International Labour Organization's core conventions.

'Equality must be guaranteed between men and women in terms of employment, working conditions and remuneration.'

Read the case study above, and respond to the following questions. In answering keep in mind Norwegian's status as an airline, which grew up and is headquartered in Norway.

Questions

1   Locate Norway within Hofstede's model of culture. Account for the preceding statements from Norwegian's corporate website with reference to Norway's position and scores on Hofstede's dimensions of culture.

2   With reference to material from Chapters 2 and 3, state how accurate you would expect Hofstede's analysis of Norwegian culture to be and identify three criticisms of his work.

3   Identify some non-cultural factors that could have influenced Norwegian's organisational culture, and in particular, the values set out in the above statements.

4   Which of the factors identified in your responses to Questions 1 and 2 do you think are the most significant in shaping Norwegian's expressed values? Give reasons for your answer.

REVIEW QUESTIONS

1   What do you understand by the etic approach to cross-cultural management? Provide two examples from academic sources to illustrate your answer.

2   What are the distinctive features of Hall's model of culture and cultural difference? Show how his model can be applied to work situations.

3   Indicate how people from different cultures may exhibit differences in preferred communication styles. Refer to both academic sources and your own experience when answering.

FURTHER READING

HOFSTEDE, G. (2001) *Culture's consequences.* 2nd ed. Thousand Oaks, CA: Sage. There is no substitute for the original! Read what is widely acknowledged as the seminal work on the subject.

KOEN, C. (2005) *Comparative international management.* Maidenhead: McGraw Hill. In Chapter 2 the author provides a scholarly analysis of major models of culture which includes an in-depth discussion of methodological issues.

MINKOV, M. (2007) *What makes us different and similar: a new interpretation of the World Values Survey and other cross-cultural data.* Sofia: Bulgaria: Klasika i Stil Publishing House. This book will be useful as further reading covering Chapters 2, 3 and 4 of this textbook as it provides both a new model of cultural similarity and difference and an alternative review of previous research in this area.

Visit this book's companion website (**www.cipd.co.uk/olr**) to find further exercises including self-assessment questions and also weblinks to media and academic journal articles.